Biological and Computer Vision

Imagine a world where machines can see and understand the world the way humans do. Rapid progress in artificial intelligence has led to smartphones that recognize faces, cars that detect pedestrians, and algorithms that suggest diagnoses from clinical images, among many other applications. The success of computer vision is founded on a deep understanding of the neural circuits in the brain responsible for visual processing. This book introduces the neuroscientific study of neuronal computations in the visual cortex alongside of the psychological understanding of visual cognition and the burgeoning field of biologically inspired artificial intelligence. Topics include the neurophysiological investigation of the visual cortex, visual illusions, visual disorders, deep convolutional neural networks, machine learning, and generative adversarial networks, among others. It is an ideal resource for students and researchers looking to build bridges across different approaches to studying and developing visual systems.

Gabriel Kreiman is a professor at the Center for Brains, Minds, and Machines and the Children's Hospital at Harvard Medical School. He is the recipient of the New Innovator Award from the National Institute of Health (NIH), National Science Foundation (NSF) Career Award, Pisart Award for Vision Research, and the McKnight Foundation Research Award.

Biological and Computer Vision

GABRIEL KREIMAN

Harvard University

CAMBRIDGE
UNIVERSITY PRESS

University Printing House, Cambridge CB2 8BS, United Kingdom

One Liberty Plaza, 20th Floor, New York, NY 10006, USA

477 Williamstown Road, Port Melbourne, VIC 3207, Australia

314–321, 3rd Floor, Plot 3, Splendor Forum, Jasola District Centre, New Delhi – 110025, India

79 Anson Road, #06–04/06, Singapore 079906

Cambridge University Press is part of the University of Cambridge.

It furthers the University's mission by disseminating knowledge in the pursuit of education, learning, and research at the highest international levels of excellence.

www.cambridge.org
Information on this title: www.cambridge.org/9781108483438
DOI: 10.1017/9781108649995

First published 2021

A catalogue record for this publication is available from the British Library.

ISBN 978-1-108-48343-8 Hardback
ISBN 978-1-108-70500-4 Paperback

To all my teachers – current, past, and future

Contents

Figures

Preface

I have enjoyed the privilege of teaching a class on biological and computer vision for undergraduate and graduate students for almost a decade now. The class consists of 10 lectures and a vigorous discussion of seminal or state-of-the-art literature in the field. During this time, a large cadre of extraordinary students took the class; juggled academic, social, and athletic commitments; won fellowships, broke up with their boyfriends and girlfriends or married their sweethearts; joined laboratories for research; pursued internships in computer vision industries; got their first academic rejections; published their first papers, and eventually graduated. After graduation, many of the students continued carrying the torch of research in vision; others became philosophers; some created start-up companies; some became stars in the field; some decided to go after other career options.

Throughout the years, interacting with the students invigorated me, got me thinking, made me revisit some of my preconceptions, and encouraged me to explain things in different ways. This book is a consequence of all of those interactions, all of those iterations, and all of those discussions. It is a story that I write carrying the voices, hopes, puzzles, and questions of all those students.

I had a broad audience in mind while writing these pages. Students have joined our class from a wide spectrum of majors (called concentrations in our jargon). The two modes of the distribution are neurobiology and computer science. However, we also had philosophers, physicists, mathematicians, molecular biologists, psychologists, economists, historians, electrical engineers, and statisticians. We also had a student from public health and a talented film concentrator, either because they were lost the first day of classes or perhaps on purpose. It is my hope that computer scientists, mathematicians, and physicists will be excited to learn about advances in our understanding of visual brains and behavior. It is also my hope that neuroscientists, biologists, and psychologists will be excited to learn about how to train computers to interpret the visual world.

The purpose of this book is not to provide an exhaustive discussion of every possible aspect of vision. The number of scholarly publications on vision is enormous. There have already been more vision studies reported during the last two decades than the total cumulative number in the previous two millennia. The goal of this book is to whet the student's appetite for research in vision.

I am afraid that I cannot do justice to all the exciting work in the field of vision. Each of the topics covered here could well deserve a book of its own. Indeed, there are entire books devoted to the topics in Chapter 2, like John Dowling's *The Retina*. Entire books discuss the visual behavior topics in Chapter 3, such as Dale Purves's *Why We See What We Do*. Even a single one of the visual deficit conditions introduced in Chapter 4 has been expanded into a whole book (Martha Farah's *Visual Agnosia*). Tomaso Poggio teaches an excellent class covering the topics in Chapter 8. I could go on listing other great specialized books that expand on the material of the other chapters as well.

Instead of discussing the different approaches to vision in isolation, my objective in this book is to build bridges, to connect the exquisite recent advances in the study of the neural circuits underlying vision, and the fast-paced developments in computer vision.

The last decade has seen the beginning of a revolution in the field of vision. We now have tools that allow us to examine brains at unprecedented resolution. We can begin to build detailed connectomes describing at high resolution who talks to whom in neuronal hardware. We can simultaneously listen to the activity of hundreds or even thousands of individual neurons. We can turn specific circuits on and off in a reversible manner through impressive new techniques introduced by Ed Boyden and Karl Deisseroth. At the same time, for the first time in the short but exciting history of computer vision, we have algorithms that work quite well in a variety of pattern-recognition tasks. Computational models of vision are rapidly becoming a standard tool for experimentalists. Furthermore, the neurobiological insights capture the imagination of many computational experts to build ever more sophisticated models that provide a reasonable initial approximation to visual behavior and visual neurophysiology.

As a consequence of the vast literature and my modest didactic goal of making links across different areas of vision, many important and exciting topics are left out of this book. I apologize in advance for the major omissions. One enormous topic that is mostly ignored here is vision across the animal kingdom. I have focused on work in rodents, cats, and especially in monkeys and humans at the expense of elegant work in many other species such as flies, salamanders, and locusts. There is a bewildering and fascinating complexity in the diversity of visual systems, and I barely scratched the surface of this richness in Chapter 3. I am convinced that we must study many different species to understand how neural circuits for visual processing work, and we have much to learn from those other species.

Another topic that occupies a substantial literature that has been left out involves noninvasive studies of the human brain: this body of work is so vast that one could probably write entire books about those studies. However, the techniques are evolving so rapidly that I suspect that my notes would be obsolete pretty soon, and new and better measurements will replace the old ones in the near future. Another aspect of human vision omitted here is the clinical practice in ophthalmology. When I tell laypeople that I study vision, they immediately think about the eyes, corrective lenses, cataracts, and glaucoma. Yet another branch of human vision deals with aesthetics and art. My amazing colleague, Margaret Livingstone, has written a delightful book connecting what we know about visual cortex (here discussed in Chapters 5 and 6) to the depiction and interpretation of art (*Vision and Art: The Biology of Seeing*). I would like to encourage readers to venture into all of those other aspects of vision. The work described here provides a foundation to dig deeper into more specialized work in the field.

I have deliberately tried to establish as many links between the different chapters as possible. I am particularly excited about connecting biological and computational circuits. Biological vision is the product of millions of years of evolution. There is no reason to reinvent the wheel when developing computational models. We can learn from how biology solves vision problems and use the solutions as inspiration to build better algorithms. The converse is also true. Ingenious developments in computer vision can help guide us toward what to look for in neural circuits and how to model the complex interactions between neurons.

The sequence of chapters follows the trajectory that I have led students through in my class. This narrative starts with a discussion of the primary constraints in vision, and a definition of the types of problems that the visual system needs to solve (Chapters 1–3), moving onto how neurobiology tackles these challenges (Chapters 2–6), and finally putting it all together through computational models (Chapters 7–9). Although I find this order to be didactically effective, readers and teachers may prefer to create their own curriculum and follow alternative routes.

I conclude the book with a chapter that attempts to connect biology, computer science, and philosophy, discussing a particularly mysterious aspect of vision: conscious experience. I inherited the passion for this problem from my Ph.D. mentor, Christof Koch. Readers interested in consciousness are encouraged to study Prof. Koch's multiple treatises on the topic, particularly *The Quest for Consciousness* and *Confessions of a Romantic Reductionist*.

Another consequence of the rich literature in the field is that one could easily fill out the pages with a long list of references. I struggled with deciding whether to include citations for every statement or not. As a scientist, I am accustomed to justifying every assertion, either by showing data or citing the relevant sources. As a teacher, I was concerned that the references would disrupt the flow in the text and scare students away. While I have not studied this phenomenon carefully, it is my impression that the number of cited works that readers consult is inversely proportional to the number of references. Therefore, I have strictly cut the list of references to only five per chapter. These five references are not meant to represent an exhaustive discussion of work in the field by any means. I tried to mix in historic seminal papers with other interesting and relevant recent work. In the web material accompanying this book, I provide a more extensive list of references for each chapter: (http://klab.tch.harvard.edu/publications/Books/BiologicalAndComputerVision/TableOfContents.html). Even though the web provides a more extensive reference list, it is also by no means intended to be comprehensive in any way. Instead, the references are intended as an invitation to dig deeper into the topics presented in each chapter.

The web material also includes links to relevant video material for each chapter. There are many cases where videos can convey material in ways that are not possible on the printed page. Furthermore, the younger generations are particularly fond of learning from videos. If readers find any educational material that is relevant to the content of this book, or have other comments about the book, I would appreciate receiving feedback to add it potentially. I cannot guarantee that I will add all the material, in part, because of the purported inverse relationship between the number of links and whether people follow through or not. However, I can certainly guarantee that I will take the suggestions very seriously. In this way, these pages open the doors to a discussion on vision, an invitation to commence a dialogue with the readers.

In this dialogue, I did not shy away from discussing controversial topics in the field or outlining speculative ideas about topics that are far from settled. Science is not merely a collection of theorems and facts. It took extensive back and forth between theories and experiments to understand the nature of light in physics. Similarly, research in vision is undoubtedly full of themes that remain the topic of intense debate. I find it useful to engage students and readers in how experiments were designed, what the key ideas and hypotheses were, and how scientists can be wrong and correct their thinking based on the empirical results. I hope that including such interpretation of the findings can help convey the dynamic and vibrant nature of discussions in the field, as opposed to merely pouring a list of facts.

In opening up a dialogue with the readers, highlighting the process of discovery, what is known and what is not known, I would be particularly happy if this book inspires new generations of scholars to take up the challenge and help us figure out how vision works. I would be happy if these pages inspire courageous young scholars to prove that some of the speculations in here are wrong. I hope that these pages will motivate others to figure out how to solve the many open questions in the field.

The ability to bridge neurobiological investigations of the underlying neural circuits and computational models is still in its infancy. Despite recent claims in prominent newspapers, the problem of vision is not solved yet. There has been exhilarating progress in computer vision lately, and we now have machines that can solve certain visual recognition problems at the same level as humans and, in some cases, even algorithms that surpass human performance. However, we are still quite far from solving vision. There is no impediment, no fundamental limit in the laws of physics imposing that we cannot build machines that see and interpret the visual world. I am convinced that we *will* solve vision. The best is yet to come.

Acknowledgments

Some movies depict a scientist as a lonely creature, often evil and with white hair, locked in a faraway room for decades until the apple falls from the tree, which is when she suddenly realizes how everything works. My life as a scientist has little to do with this Hollywood style of rendering the practice of research. Science is particularly appealing to me because of its objective and rigorous endeavor to discover Truth, with capital T. Science does not occur in a vacuum, but, instead, it is part of a social construct, and I have yet to experience an apple hitting me in the head. I am incredibly indebted to a great number of people who have helped in one way or another put these pages together. This book would not have been possible without the insights and help from a very large number of individuals.

First, I would like to thank all the students in the biological and computer vision class. Their perennial curiosity, their seemingly naïve yet astute ways to make me rethink what I was trying to explain, and their constant questioning of our assumptions and statements have kept me on my toes and propelled this work forward. I cannot quite do justice to all of them, but I would like to mention a few students who have stood out – including Kristen Fang, Grigori Guitchounts, Katherine Harrison, Javier Masis, Olivia McGinnis, Daniel Rothchild, Sean Sullivan, Kenneth Shinozuka, Duncan Stothers, Annabelle Tao, Saloni Vishwakarm, and Will Xiao.

The teaching assistants in the class – Joseph Olson, Will Xiao, and Yuchen Xiao – have also played an essential role in this work. We split each class into a lecture and a discussion of primary literature in the field. The teaching assistants always bring provocative questions, new ways of thinking critically about the literature, and they engage the students in exciting discussions about the why and how of a particular study.

Several colleagues have also given guest lectures in this class, and their way of presenting the material was also extremely influential. I would like to thank Frederico Azevedo, Andrei Barbu, Xavier Boix, David Cox, Camille Gomez-Laberge, Till Hartmann, Leyla Isik, Kohitij Kar, Jiye Kim, Bill Lotter, Diego Mendoza-Halliday, Ken Nakayama, Carlos Ponce, Sarit Szpiro, Hanlin Tang, Kasper Vinken, and Will Xiao.

Another constant source of inspiration has been the students and postdocs in my lab. I especially want to mention Yigal Agam, Arjun Bansal, Xavier Boix, Calin Buia, Kendra Burbank, Stephen Casper, Prabaha Gangpadhyay, Camille Gomez-Laberge, Stephan Grzekowski, Shashi Gupta, Walter Hardesty, Eleonora Iaselli, Leyla Isik, Jiye Kim, Phil Kuhnke, Garrett Lam, Daniel Lopez Martinez, Bill Lotter, Radhika

Madhavan, Thomas Miconi, Pranav Misra, Charlotte Moermann, Candace Ross, Martin Schrimpf, Nimrod Shaham, Jedediah Singer, Hanlin Tang, Ben Tsuda, Kasper Vinken, Jerry Wang, Farahnaz Wick, Eric and Kevin Wu, Will Xiao, Ege Yumusak, and Mengmi Zhang. Many of them have provided useful comments and criticism to the pages here. They have also made outstanding scientific contributions that are reflected in the work discussed here.

In the ever more demanding modern days, I see my colleagues continually rushing to meet deadlines and juggling their myriad contributions to the scientific enterprise. I am therefore extremely honored and certainly in debt to many of my friends and colleagues who have been kind enough to read these pages, correct my mistakes, suggest additional material, and provide critical comments. The following people have been particularly kind: Arash Afraz, Katarina Bendtz, Xavier Boix, Alfonso Caramazza, Stephen Casper, Wenqiang Chen, Michael Do, John Dowling, Kohitij Kar, Talia Konkle, Bill Lotter, Richard Masland, David Mazumder, Liad Mudrik, Carlos Ponce, Nao Tsuchiya, Will Xiao, Yaoda Xu, and Mengmi Zhang. I am especially indebted to Ellen Hildreth. She has made major contributions to computer vision herself and she leads the education initiatives at the Center for Brains, Minds and Machines. She has read the entire book and has helped make it better through her detailed corrections, astute questions, and encouraging comments.

Finally, I am eternally thankful to the Center for Brains, Minds and Machines (CBMM), a center sponsored by the National Science Foundation. CBMM has provided an inspiring and influential home to brainstorm about new ideas and synergistically push the frontiers of neuroscience and artificial intelligence research by bringing together a large cadre of talented scholars from multiple fields.

Thank you all!

Abbreviations

We defined all abbreviations in the text. Here are a few that are used throughout.

AI   artificial intelligence (Chapters 1 and 9)

Alexnet   prominent deep convolutional neural network for visual recognition (Krizhevsky et al. 2012); other deep convolutional neural network architectures like VGG, ResNet, and Inception are also mentioned in Chapters 8 and 9

CLEVR   compositional language and elementary visual reasoning dataset (Johnson et al. 2016, Chapter 9)

DCNN   deep convolutional neural network (Chapter 8)

DeepDream   a technique to visualize the type of images that lead to high activation for units in a neural network (Chapter 9)

GAN   generative adversarial network (Goodfellow et al. 2014, Chapter 9)

HMAX   computational model of visual recognition (Riesenhuber and Poggio 1999, Chapter 8)

ImageNet   large dataset of images used to train and test computer vision algorithms (Russakovsky et al. 2014, Chapters 8 and 9)

IOR   inhibition-of-return mechanism to prevent eye movements from always landing on the most salient part of the image (illustrated in Figure 8.9)

ITC   inferior temporal cortex (Chapters 4 and 6)

IVSN   Invariant Visual Search Network (Chapter 8, Figure 8.9)

L2 norm   Euclidian distance between two vectors, typically used to define the error in machine learning (as opposed to the L1 norm, which is the sum of the absolute values of each component of the distance vector) (Chapter 8)

LGN   lateral geniculate nucleus, part of the thalamus that receives input from the retina and projects to primary visual cortex (Chapter 2)

LSTM   Long Short-Term Memory recurrent neural network (Horchreiter and Schmidhuber 1997, Chapter 8)

MNIST   database consisting of images of handwritten digits (Chapter 8)

MSCOCO   segmented object dataset (Lin et al. 2015, Chapter 9)

Neocognitron   computational model of visual recognition (Fukushima 1980, Chapter 8)

PredNet	predictive coding deep convolutional neural network (Lotter et al. 2017, Chapter 8)
QR code	quick response code, matrix barcode that can easily be read by smartphones (Chapter 9)
ReLU	rectifying linear unit (Chapter 7)
ResNet	deep convolutional neural network architecture (He et al. 2015, Chapter 8)
RGC	retinal ganglion cells, output neurons of the retina (Chapter 2)
ROC	receiver operating characteristic curve (Green and Swets 1966, Chapter 9)
Softmax	a function that converts a vector of input numbers into a probability distribution that adds up to 1, where each output value is proportional to the exponential of the input numbers (Chapter 8)
SVM	Support Vector Machine (Chapter 6)
tSNE	t-distributed stochastic network embedding (van der Maaten and Hinton 2008, Chapter 8)
UCF101	large dataset of videos used to train and test action recognition algorithms (Soomro et al. 2012, Chapter 9)
V1	primary visual cortex; other visual areas are defined, including V2, V3, V4, and V5, also known as area MT (Chapters 4 and 5)
WTA	winner-take-all mechanism (for example, the one used in Figure 8.9)
XDream	eXtending DeepDream with real-time evolution for activation maximization, algorithm to probe neuronal tuning in an unbiased manner (Ponce et al. 2019, Chapter 8)

1   Introduction to the World of Vision

Supplementary content at http://bit.ly/2TqTDt5

Understanding how the brain works constitutes the greatest scientific challenge of our times, arguably the greatest challenge of all times. We have sent spaceships to peek outside of our solar system, and we study galaxies far away to build theories about the origin of the universe. We have built powerful accelerators to scrutinize the secrets of subatomic particles. We have uncovered the secrets to heredity hidden in the billions of base pairs in DNA. But we still have to figure out how the three pounds of brain tissue inside our skulls work to enable us to do physics, biology, music, literature, and politics.

The conversations and maneuvers of about a hundred billion neurons in our brains are responsible for our ability to interpret sensory information, to navigate, to communicate, to feel and to love, to make decisions and plans for the future, to learn. Understanding how neural circuits give rise to cognitive functions will transform our lives: it will help us alleviate the ubiquitous mental health conditions that afflict hundreds of millions, it will lead to building true artificial intelligence machines that are as smart as or smarter than we are, and it will open the doors to finally understanding who we are.

As a paradigmatic example of brain function, we will focus on one of the most exquisite pieces of neural machinery ever evolved: the visual system. In a small fraction of a second, we can get a glimpse of an image and capture a substantial amount of information. For example, we can take a look at Figure 1.1 and answer an infinite series of questions about it: *who is there, what is there, where is this place, what is the weather like, how many people are there, and what are they doing?* We can even make educated guesses about a potential narrative, including describing *the relationship between people in the picture,* what *happened before,* or *what will happen next.* At the heart of these questions is our capacity for visual cognition and intelligent inference based on visual inputs.

Our remarkable ability to interpret complex spatiotemporal input sequences, which we can loosely ascribe to part of "common sense," does not require us to sit down and solve complex differential equations. In fact, a four-year-old can answer most of the questions outlined before quite accurately, younger kids can answer most of them, and many non-human animal species can also be trained to correctly describe many aspects of a visual scene. Furthermore, it takes only a few hundred milliseconds to deduce such profound information from an image. Even though we have computers that excel at

Figure 1.1 We can visually interpret an image at a glance. Who is there? What is there? Where is it? What are they doing? What will happen next? These are just examples among the infinite number of questions that we can answer after a few hundred milliseconds of exposure to a novel image.

tasks such as solving complex differential equations, computers still fall short of human performance at answering common-sense questions about an image.

1.1   Evolution of the Visual System

Vision is essential for most everyday tasks, including navigation, reading, and socialization. Reading this text involves identifying shape patterns. Walking home involves detecting pedestrians, cars, and routes. Vision is critical to recognize our friends and decipher their emotions. It is, therefore, not much of a strain to conceive that the expansion of the visual cortex has played a significant role in the evolution of mammals in general and primates in particular. It is likely that the evolution of enhanced algorithms for recognizing patterns based on visual inputs yielded an increase in adaptive value through improvements in navigation, discrimination of friend versus foe, differentiation between food and poison, and through the savoir faire of deciphering social interactions. In contrast to tactile and gustatory inputs and, to some extent, even auditory inputs, visual signals bring knowledge from vast and faraway areas. While olfactory signals can also diffuse through long distances, the speed of propagation and information content is lower than that of photons.

The ability of biological organisms to capture light is ancient. For example, many bacteria use light to perform photosynthesis, a precursor to a similar process that captures energy in plants. What is particularly astounding about vision is the possibility of using light to capture *information* about the world. The selective advantage conveyed by visual processing is so impactful that it has led the zoologist Andrew Parker to propose the so-called light switch theory to explain the rapid expansion in number and diversity of life on Earth.

About five hundred million years ago, during the early Cambrian period, there was an extraordinary outburst in the number of different species. It is also at around the same time where fossil evidence suggests the emergence of the first species with eyes, the trilobites (Figure 1.2). Trilobites are extinct arthropods (distant relatives of insects and spiders) that conquered the world and expanded throughout approximately three hundred million years. The light switch theory posits that the emergence of eyes and the explosion in animal diversity is not a mere coincidence. Several investigators have argued that eyes emerged right before the Cambrian explosion. Eyes enabled some lucky early trilobite, or its great grandfather, to capture information from farther away, detecting the presence of prey or predator, endowing it with a selective advantage over other creatures without eyes, who had to rely on slower and coarser information for survival. Using these new toys, the eyes, an evolutionary arms race commenced between prey and predators to make inferences about the world around them and to hide from those scrutinizing and powerful new sensors. All of a sudden, body shapes, textures, and colors became fascinating, powerful, and dangerous. It seems likely that

Figure 1.2 Fossil record of a trilobite, circa 500 million years ago. Trilobites such as the one shown in this picture had compound eyes, probably not too different from those found in modern invertebrate species like flies. Trilobites proliferated and diversified throughout the world for about 300 million years. By Dwergenpaartje, CC BY-SA 3.0

body shapes and colors began to change to avoid detection through the initial versions of camouflage – in turn, leading to keener and better eyes to be more sensitive to motion and to subtle changes through the ability to better discriminate shapes. Let there be light, and let light be used to convey information.

1.2   The Future of Vision

Fast-forward several hundred million years, the fundamental role of vision in human evolution is hard to underestimate. Well before the advent of language as it is known today, vision played a critical role in communication, interpreting emotions and intentions, and facilitating social interactions. The ability to visually identify patterns in the position of the moon, the sun, and the stars led to understanding and predicting seasonal changes, which eventually gave rise to agriculture, transforming nomadic societies into sedentary ones, begetting the precursors of future towns. Art, symbols, and eventually the development of written language also fundamentally relied on visual pattern-recognition capabilities.

The evolution of the visual system is only poorly understood and remains an interesting topic for further investigation. The future of the visual system will be equally fascinating. While speculating about the biological changes in vision in animals over evolutionary time scales is rather challenging, it is easier to imagine what might be accomplished in the near future over shorter time scales, via machines with suitable cameras and computational algorithms for image processing. We will come back to the future of vision in Chapter 9; as a teaser, let us briefly consider machines that can achieve, and perhaps surpass, human-level capabilities in visual tasks. Such machines may combine high-speed and high-resolution video sensors that convey information to computers implementing sophisticated simulations that approximate the functions of the visual brain in real time.

Machines may soon excel in face-recognition tasks to a level where an ATM will greet you by your name without the need for a password, where you may not need a key to enter your home or car, where your face may become your credit card and your passport. Self-driving vehicles propelled by machine vision algorithms have escaped the science fiction pages and entered our streets. Computers may also be able to analyze images intelligently to search the web by image or video content (as opposed to keywords and text descriptors). Doctors may rely more and more on artificial vision systems to analyze X-rays, MRIs, and other images, to a point where image-based diagnosis becomes the domain of computer science entirely. Future generations may be intrigued by the notion that we once let fallible humans make diagnostic decisions. The classification of distant galaxies, or the discovery of different plant and animal species, might be led by machine vision systems rather than astronomers or biologists.

Adventuring further into the domain of science fiction, one could conceive of brain–machine interfaces that might be implanted in the human brain to augment visual capabilities for people with visual impairment or blind people. While we are at it, why not also use such interfaces to augment visual function in normally sighted people to endow humans with the capability to see in 360 degrees, to detect infrared or ultraviolet wavelengths, to see through opaque objects such as walls, or even directly witness remote events?

When debates arose about the possibility that computers could one day play competitive chess against humans, most people were skeptical. Simple computers today can beat even sophisticated chess aficionados, and good computers can beat world champions. Recently, computers have also excelled in the ancient and complex game of Go. Despite the obvious fact that most people can recognize objects much better than they can play chess or Go, visual cognition is actually more challenging than these games from a computational perspective. However, we may not be too far from building accurate computational approximations to visual systems, where we will be able to trust computers' eyes as much as, or even more than, our own eyes. Instead of "seeing is believing," the future moto may become "computing is believing."

1.3   Why Is Vision Difficult?

The notion that seeing is computationally more complicated than playing Go may be counterintuitive. After all, a two-year-old child can open her eyes and rapidly recognize and interpret her environment to navigate the room and grab her favorite teddy bear, which may be half-covered behind other toys. She does not know how to play Go. She certainly has not gone through the millions of hours of training via reinforcement learning that neural network machines had to go through to play Go. She has had approximately ten thousand hours of visual experience. These ten thousand hours are mostly unsupervised; there were adults nearby most of the time, but, by and large, those adults were not providing continuous information about object labels or continuous reward and punishment signals (there certainly were labels and rewards, but they probably constituted a small fraction of her visual learning).

Why is it so difficult for computers to perform pattern-recognition tasks that appear to be so simple to us? The primate visual system excels at recognizing patterns even when those patterns change radically from one instantiation to another. Consider the simple line schematics in Figure 1.3. It is straightforward to recognize those handwritten symbols even though, at the pixel level, they show considerable variation within each row. These drawings only have a few traces. The problem is far more complicated with real scenes and objects. Imagine the myriad of possible variations of pictures taken at Piazza San Marco in Venice (Figure 1.1) and how the visual system can interpret them with ease. Any object can cast an *infinite* number of projections onto the eyes. These variations include changes in scale, position, viewpoint, and illumination, among other transformations. In a seemingly effortless fashion, our visual systems can map all of those images onto a particular object.

Identifying specific objects is but one of the important functions that the visual system must solve. The visual system can estimate distances to objects, predict where objects are heading, infer the identity of objects that are heavily occluded or camouflaged, determine which objects are in front of which other objects, and make educated

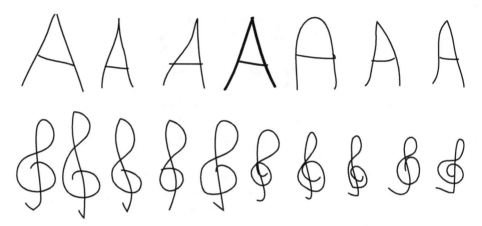

Figure 1.3 Any object can cast an infinite number of projections onto the eyes. Even though we can easily recognize these patterns, there is considerable variability among different renderings of each shape at the pixel level.

guesses as to the composition and weight of objects. The visual system can even infer intentions in the case of living agents. In all of these tasks, vision is an ill-posed problem, in the sense that multiple possible solutions are consistent with a given pattern of inputs onto the eyes.

1.4   Four Key Features of Visual Recognition

In order to explain how the visual system tackles the identification of patterns, we need to account for four key features of visual recognition: *selectivity, tolerance, speed*, and *capacity*.

Selectivity involves the ability to discriminate among shapes that are very similar at the pixel level. Examples of the exquisite selectivity of the visual system include face identification and reading. In both cases, the visual system can distinguish between inputs that are very close if we compare them side by side at the pixel level. A trivial and useless way of implementing *Selectivity* in a computational algorithm is to memorize all the pixels in the image (Figure 1.4A). Upon encountering the same pixels, the computer would be able to "recognize" the image. The computer would be very selective because it would not respond to any other possible image. The problem with this implementation is that it lacks *tolerance*.

Tolerance refers to the ability to recognize an object despite multiple transformations of the object's image. For example, we can recognize objects even if they are presented in a different position, scale, viewpoint, contrast, illumination, or color. We can even recognize objects where the image undergoes nonrigid transformations, such as the changes a face goes through upon smiling. A straightforward but useless way of implementing tolerance is to build a model that will output a flat response no matter the input. While the model would show tolerance to image transformations, it would not

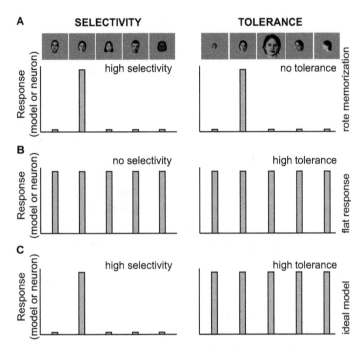

Figure 1.4 A naïve (and not very useful) approach to model visual recognition. Two simple models that are easy to implement, easy to understand, and not very useful. A rote memorization model (**A**) can have exquisite selectivity but does not generalize. In contrast, a flat response model (**B**) can generalize but lacks any selectivity. (**C**) An ideal model should combine selectivity and tolerance.

show any selectivity to different shapes (Figure 1.4B). Combining *selectivity* and *tolerance* (Figure 1.4C) is arguably the key challenge in developing computer vision algorithms for recognition tasks. To consider a real-world example, a self-driving car needs to selectively distinguish pedestrians from many other types of objects, no matter how tall those pedestrians are, what they are wearing, what they are doing, or what they are holding.

Given the combinatorial explosion in the number of images that map onto the same "object," one could imagine that visual recognition requires many years of learning at school. Of course, this is far from the case. Well before a first grader starts to learn the basics of addition and subtraction (rather trivial problems for computers), she is already quite proficient at visual recognition, a task that she can accomplish in a glimpse. Objects can be readily recognized in a stream of other objects presented at a rate of 100 milliseconds per image. Subjects can make an eye movement to indicate the presence of an object in a two-alternative forced-choice task about 200 milliseconds after showing the visual stimulus. Furthermore, both scalp and invasive recordings from the human brain reveal signals that can discriminate among complex objects as early as ~150 milliseconds after stimulus onset. The *speed* of visual recognition constrains the number of computational steps that any theory of recognition can use to account for recognition performance. To be sure, vision does not stop at 150 milliseconds. Many aspects of visual cognition emerge over hundreds of milliseconds, and recognition performance under challenging tasks improves with longer presentation times. However, a basic understanding of an image or the main objects within the image can be accomplished in ~150 milliseconds. We denote this regime as *rapid visual recognition.*

One way of making progress toward combining selectivity, tolerance, and speed has been to focus on object-specific or category-specific algorithms. An example of this approach would be the development of algorithms for detecting cars in natural scenes by taking advantage of the idiosyncrasies of cars and the scenes in which they typically appear. Another example would be face recognition. Some of these category- and context-specific heuristics are useful, and the brain may learn to take advantage of them. For example, if most of the image is blue, suggesting that the image background may represent the sky, then the prior probabilities for seeing a car would be low (cars typically do not fly), and the prior probabilities for seeing a bird would be high (birds are often seen against a blue sky). We will discuss the regularities in the visual world and the statistics of natural images in Chapter 2. Despite these correlations, in the more general scenario, the visual recognition machinery is capable of combining selectivity, tolerance, and speed for an enormous range of objects and images. For example, the Chinese language has more than three thousand characters. Estimations of the *capacity* of the human visual recognition system vary substantially across studies. Several studies cite numbers that are considerably more than ten thousand items.

In sum, a theory of visual recognition must be able to account for the high selectivity, tolerance, speed, and capacity of the visual system. Despite the apparent immediacy of seeing, combining these four key features is by no means a simple task.

1.5   The Travels and Adventures of a Photon

The challenge of solving the ill-posed problem of selecting among infinite possible interpretations of a scene in a transformation-tolerant manner within 150 milliseconds of processing seems daunting. How does the brain accomplish this feat? We start by providing a global overview of the transformations of visual information in the brain.

Light arrives at the retina after being reflected by objects in the environment. The patterns of light impinging on our eyes are far from random, and the natural image statistics of those patterns play an important role in the development and evolution of the visual system (Chapter 2). In the retina, light is transduced into an electrical signal by specialized photoreceptor cells. Information is processed in the retina through a cascade of computations before it passes on to a structure called the thalamus and, from there, on to the cortical sheet. The cortex directs the sequence of visual computation steps, converting photons into percepts. Several visual recognition models treat the retina as analogous to the pixel-by-pixel representation in a digital camera. A digital camera is an oversimplified description of the computational power in the retina, yet it has permeated into the general jargon as introduced by manufacturers who boast of a "retina display" for monitors.

It is not unusual for commercially available monitors these days to display several million pixels. Commercially available digital cameras also boast tens of millions of pixels. The number of pixels in such devices approximates or even surpasses the number of primary sensors in some biological retinas; for example, the human retina contains ~6.4 million so-called cone sensors and ~110 million so-called rod sensors (we will discuss those sensors in Chapter 2). Despite these technological feats, electronic cameras still lag behind biological eyes in essential properties such as luminance adaptation, motion detection, focusing, energy efficiency, and speed.

The output of the retina is conveyed to multiple areas, including the superior colliculus, the suprachiasmatic nucleus, and the thalamus. The superficial layers of the superior colliculus can be thought of as an ancient visual brain. Indeed, for many species that do not have a cortex, the superior colliculus (referred to as optic tectum in these species) is where the main visual elaborations of the input take place. The suprachiasmatic nucleus plays a central role in regulating the circadian rhythm. Humans have an internal daily clock that runs slightly longer than the usual 24-hour day, and light inputs via the suprachiasmatic nucleus help modulate and adjust this cycle.

The main visual pathway carries information from the retina to a part of the thalamus called the lateral geniculate nucleus (LGN). The LGN projects to the primary visual cortex, located in the back of our brains. Without the primary visual cortex, humans are mostly blind, highlighting the critical importance of the pathway conveying information into the cortex for most visual functions. Investigators refer to the processing steps in the retina, LGN, and primary visual cortex as "early vision" (Chapter 5). The primary visual cortex is only the first stage in the processing of visual information in the cortex. Researchers have discovered tens of areas responsible for different aspects of vision (the actual number is still a matter of debate and depends on what is meant by "area"). An influential way of depicting these multiple areas and their interconnections is the diagram proposed by Felleman and Van Essen, shown in Figure 1.5. To the untrained eye, this diagram appears to depict a bewildering complexity, not unlike the circuit diagrams typically employed by electrical engineers. We will delve into this diagram in more detail in Chapters 5 and 6 and discuss the areas and connections that play a crucial role in visual cognition.

Despite the apparent complexity of the neural circuitry in Figure 1.5, this scheme is an oversimplification of the actual wiring diagram. First, each of the boxes in this diagram contains millions of neurons. There are many different types of neurons. The arrangement of neurons within each box can be described in terms of six main layers of the cortex (some of which have different sublayers) and the topographical arrangement of neurons within and across layers. Second, we are still far from characterizing *all* the connections in the visual system. One of the exciting advances of the last decade is the development of techniques to scrutinize the connectivity of neural circuitry at high resolution and in a high-throughput manner.

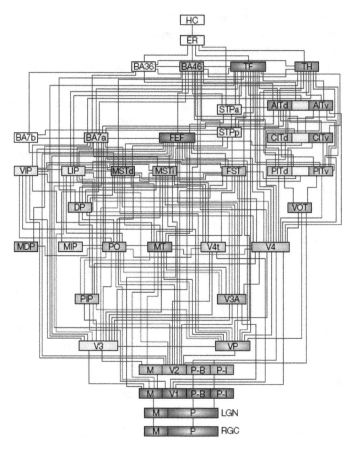

Figure 1.5 The adventures of a photon. Schematic diagram of the connectivity in the primate visual system. Adapted from Felleman and Van Essen 1991

For a small animal like a one-millimeter worm with the fancy name of *Caenorhabditis elegans*, we have known for a few decades the detailed connectivity pattern of each one of its 302 neurons, thanks to the work of Sydney Brenner (1927–2019). However, the cortex is an entirely different beast, with a neuronal density of tens of thousands of neurons per square millimeter. Heroic efforts in the burgeoning field of "connectomics" are now providing the first glimpses of which neurons are friends with which other neurons in the cortex. Major surprises in neuroanatomy will likely come from the use of novel tools that take advantage of the high specificity of molecular biology.

Finally, even if we did know the connectivity of every single neuron in the visual cortex, this knowledge would not immediately reveal the computational functions (but knowing the connectivity would still be immensely helpful). In contrast to electrical circuits where we understand each element and the overall function can be appreciated by careful inspection of the wiring diagram, many neurobiological factors make the map from structure to function a nontrivial one.

1.6   Tampering with the Visual System

One way of finding out how something works is by taking it apart, removing different parts, and reevaluating its function. For example, if we remove the speakers from a car, the car will still function pretty well, but we will not be able to listen to music. If we take out the battery, the car will not start. Removing parts is an important way of studying the visual system as well. For this purpose, investigators typically consider the behavioral deficits that are apparent when parts of the brain are lesioned through studies in nonhuman animals.

In addition to the work in animals, there are various unfortunate circumstances where humans suffer from brain lesions that can also provide insightful clues as to the function of different parts of the visual pathway (as well as other aspects of cognition). Indeed, the fundamental role of the primary visual cortex in vision was discovered through the study of lesions. Ascending through the visual system beyond the primary visual cortex, lesions may yield specific behavioral deficits. For example, subjects who suffer from a rare but well known condition called *prosopagnosia* typically show a significant impairment in the ability to recognize faces (Chapter 4).

One of the challenges in interpreting the consequences of lesions in the human brain is that these lesions often encompass large brain areas and are not restricted to neuroanatomically- or neurophysiologically-defined loci. Several more controlled studies have been performed in animal models – including rodents, cats, and monkeys – to examine the behavioral deficits that arise after lesioning specific parts of the visual cortex. Are the lesion effects specific to one sensory modality, or are they multimodal? How selective are the visual impairments? Can learning effects be dissociated from representation effects? What is the neuroanatomical code? We will come back to these questions in Chapter 4.

Another important path to study brain function is to examine the consequences of externally activating specific brain circuits. One of the prominent ways to do so is by injecting currents via electrical stimulation. Coarse methods of electrically stimulating parts of the cortex often disrupt processing and mimic the effects of a circumscribed lesion. One advantage of electrical stimulation is that the effects can be rapidly reversed, and it is possible, therefore, to study the same animal performing the same task under the influence of electrical stimulation in a specific circuit or not. Intriguingly, in some cases, more refined forms of electrical stimulation can lead not to disrupted processing but instead to enhanced processing of specific types of information. For example, there is a part of the brain referred to as the MT (middle temporal cortex), which receives inputs from the primary visual cortex and is located near the center of the diagram in Figure 1.5. Neurons in this area play an important role in the ability to discriminate the direction of moving objects. Injecting localized electrical currents into area MT in macaque monkeys can bias the animal's perception of how things are moving in their visual world. In other words, it is possible to directly create visual motion thoughts by tickling subpopulations of neurons in area MT (Chapter 4). Combined with careful behavioral measurements, electrical stimulation can provide a glimpse at how influencing activity in a given cluster of neurons can affect perception.

There is also a long history of electrical stimulation studies in humans in subjects with epilepsy. Neurosurgeons need to decide on the possibility of resecting the epileptogenic tissue to treat seizures. Before the resection procedure, neurosurgeons use electrical stimulation to examine the function of the tissue that may undergo resection. The famous American-Canadian neurosurgeon Wilder Penfield (1891–1976) was among the pioneers in using this technique to map brain function. One of his famous discoveries is the "homunculus" map of the sensorimotor world: there is a topographical arrangement of regions where electrical stimulation leads to subjects moving or reporting tactile sensations in the toes, legs, fingers, torso, tongue, and face. Similarly, subjects report seeing localized flashes of light upon electrically stimulating the primary visual cortex.

How specific are the effects of electrical stimulation? Under what conditions is neuronal firing causally related to perception? How many neurons and what types of neurons are activated during electrical stimulation? How do stimulation effects depend on the timing, duration, and intensity of electrical stimulation? We will come back to these questions in Chapter 4.

1.7   Functions of Circuits in the Visual Cortex

The gold standard to examine function in brain circuits is to implant a microelectrode (or multiple microelectrodes) into the area of interest (Figure 1.6). A microelectrode is a thin piece of metal, typically with a diameter of about 50 μm, that can record voltage changes, often in the extracellular milieu. This technique was introduced by Edgar Adrian (1889–1977) in the early 1920s to examine the activity of single nerve fibers. These recordings required clever use of the electronics available at the time to be able to amplify the small voltage differences that characterize electrical communication within neurons. These extracellular recordings (as opposed to the much more challenging intracellular recordings) allow investigators to monitor the activity of one or a few neurons in the near vicinity of the electrode (~200 μm) at neuronal resolution and sub-millisecond temporal resolution.

Many noninvasive techniques aim to examine what happens in the brain only in a very indirect fashion by measuring signals that have a weak correlation with the aggregate activity of millions of different cells. These techniques probably include an indirect assessment of neuronal activity but also of the myriad of other cells present in the brain. To make matters even worse, some noninvasive techniques average activity over many seconds, several thousand times slower than the actual interactions taking place in the brain. As an analogy, imagine a sociologist interested in what people in Paris think about climate change; she can interview many individuals, which is laborious but quite precise (equivalent to invasive single neuron recordings), or else she can average the total amount of sound produced in the whole city over an entire week, which is much easier but not very informative (equivalent to noninvasive measurements).

Recording the activity of neurons has defined what types of visual stimuli are most exciting in different brain areas. One of the earliest discoveries was the receptive field of

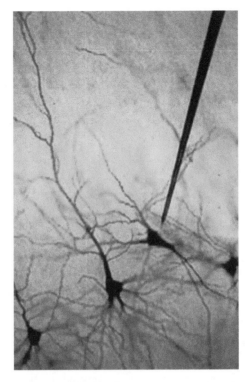

Figure 1.6 Listening to the activity of individual neurons with a microelectrode. Illustration of electrical recordings from microwire electrodes. Reproduced from Hubel 1995

neurons in the retina, LGN, and primary visual cortex. The receptive field is defined as the area within the visual field where a neuronal response can be elicited by visual stimulation (Figure 2.9, Chapter 2). Visual neurons are picky: they do not respond to changes in illumination at any part of the visual field. Each neuron is in charge of representing a circumscribed region of the visual space. Together, all the neurons in a given brain area form a map of the entire visual field – that is, a map of the accessible part of the visual field (e.g., humans do not have visual access to what is happening behind them). The size of these receptive fields typically increases from the retina all the way to those areas like the inferior temporal cortex situated near the top of the diagram in Figure 1.5.

Spatial and temporal changes in illumination within the receptive field of a neuron are necessary to activate visual neurons. However, not all light patterns are equal. Neurons are particularly excited in response to some visual stimuli, and they are oblivious to other stimuli. In a classical neurophysiology experiment, David Hubel (1926–2013) and Torsten Wiesel inserted a microelectrode to isolate single neuron responses in the primary visual cortex of a cat. After presenting different visual stimuli, they discovered that the neuron fired vigorously when a bar of a specific orientation was presented within the neuron's receptive field. The response was weaker when the bar showed a different orientation. This orientation preference constitutes a hallmark of a large fraction of the neurons in the primary visual cortex (Chapter 5).

Hubel and Wiesel's discovery inspired generations of visual scientists to insert electrodes throughout the visual cortex to study the stimulus preferences in different brain areas. Recording from other parts of the visual cortex, investigators have characterized neurons that show enhanced responses to stimuli moving in specific directions, neurons that prefer complex shapes such as fractal patterns or faces, and neurons that are particularly sensitive to color contrast.

How does selectivity to complex shapes arise, and what are the computational transformations that can convert the simpler receptive field structure at the level of the retina into more complex shapes? How robust are the visual responses in the visual cortex to stimulus transformations such as the ones shown in Figure 1.3? How fast do neurons along the visual cortex respond to new stimuli? What is the neural code – that is, what aspects of neuronal responses better reflect the input stimuli? What are the biological circuits and mechanisms to combine selectivity and invariance? Chapters 5 and 6 delve into the examination of the neurophysiological responses in the visual cortex.

There is much more to vision than filtering and processing images for recognition. Visual processing is particularly relevant because it interfaces with cognition; it connects the outside world with memories, current goals, and internal models of the world. A full interpretation of an image such as Figure 1.1 and the ability to answer an infinite number of questions on the image rely on the bridge between vision and cognition, which we will discuss in Chapter 6.

1.8   Toward the Neural Correlates of Visual Consciousness

The complex cascade of interconnected processes along the visual system must give rise to our rich and subjective perception of the objects and scenes around us. We do not quite know how to directly assess subjective perception from the outside. How do we know that what one person calls red is the same as someone else's perception of red? Some time ago, there were wild discussions in the media about the color of a dress; the photograph became viral, so much so, that it is now known as *the* dress (Figure 1.7). Some people swear that the dress is blue and black. To me, this is as mysterious as if they told me that those people have thirty fingers in their right hand. Why would any honest human being try to convince me that this evidently white and gold dress is actually black and blue? And yet, some people see the dress as white and gold, and others perceive it as distinctly black and blue.

Perception is in the eye of the beholder. To be more precise, perception is in the *brain* of the beholder. If we only worked at the perceptual level without communicating, we would have never figured out that people can see the same dress in such drastically different ways. To indirectly access subjective perception, we need to study behavior. The dress emphasizes that we should not let our introspection guide the scientific agenda. Our intuitions are fallible, as we will discuss again and again.

Figure 1.7 The viral photograph of the dress.

A whole field with the charming name of *psychophysics* deals with careful quantification of behavior as a way of assessing perception (Chapter 3). We will examine where, when, and how rapidly subjects perceive different shapes to construct their own subjective interpretation of the world surrounding them. We will also discuss why brains can be easily deceived by visual illusions. Behavioral measurements will constitute the central constraint toward building a theory of visual processing.

Visual perception is certainly not in the toes and not even in the heart, as some of our ancestors believed. Most scientists would agree that subjective feelings and percepts emerge from the activity of neuronal circuits in the brain. Much less agreement can be reached as to the mechanisms responsible for subjective sensations. The "where," "when," and particularly "how" of the so-called neuronal correlates of consciousness constitute an area of active research and passionate debates. Historically, many neuroscientists avoided research in the field of consciousness as a topic too convoluted or too far removed from what we understood to be worth a serious investment of time and effort. In recent years, however, the tide has begun to change. While still very far from a solution, systematic and rigorous approaches guided by neuroscience may one day unveil the answer to one of the greatest mysteries of our times – namely, the physical basis for conscious perception.

Due to several practical reasons, the underpinnings of subjective perception have been mainly (but not exclusively) studied in the domain of vision. There have been heroic efforts to study the neuronal correlates of visual perception using animal models. A prevalent experimental paradigm involves dissociating the visual input from perception. For example, in multistable percepts (e.g., Figure 1.8), the same input can lead to

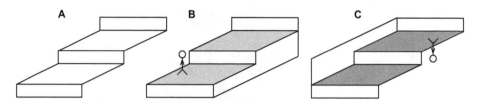

Figure 1.8 A bistable percept. (A) The image can be interpreted in two different ways. (B) In one version, the person is climbing up the stairs. (C) The other version involves an upside-down world.

two distinct percepts. Under these conditions, investigators ask which neuronal events correlate with the alternating subjective percepts.

It has become clear that the firing of neurons in many parts of the brain is *not* correlated with perception. In an arguably trivial example, activity in the retina is essential for seeing, but the perceptual experience does not arise until several synapses later when activity reaches higher stages within the visual cortex (Chapter 10). Neurophysiological, neuroanatomical, and theoretical considerations suggest that subjective perception correlates with activity occurring after the primary visual cortex. Similarly, investigators have suggested an upper bound in terms of where in the visual hierarchy the circuits involved in subjective perception could be. Although lesions restricted to the hippocampus and frontal cortex (thought to underlie memory and associations) yield severe cognitive impairments, these lesions leave visual perception largely intact. Thus, neurophysiology and lesion studies constrain the neural circuits involved in subjective visual perception to the multiple stages involved in processing visual information along the ventral cortex. Ascending through the ventral visual cortex, several neurophysiological studies show that there is an increase in the degree of correlation between neuronal activity and visual percepts.

How can visual consciousness be studied using scientific methods? Which brain areas, circuits, and mechanisms could be responsible for visual consciousness? What are the functions of visual consciousness? Which animals show consciousness? Can machines be conscious? Chapter 10 will provide initial glimpses into what is known (and what is not known) about these fascinating questions.

1.9   Toward a Theory of Visual Cognition

Richard Feynman (1918–1988), a Nobel-winning physicist from Caltech, famously claimed that understanding a device means that we should be able to build it. We aim to develop a theory of vision that can explain how humans and other animals perceive and interpret the world around them. In one of the seminal works on vision, David Marr (1945–1980) defined three levels of understanding, which we can loosely map onto (1) what is the function of the visual system?, (2) how does the visual system behave under different inputs and circumstances?, and (3) how does biological hardware instantiate those functions and behaviors?

A successful theory of vision should be amenable to computational implementation, in which case we can directly compare the output of the computational model against behavioral performance measures and neuronal recordings. A complete theory would include information from lesion studies, neurophysiological recordings, psychophysics, and electrical stimulation studies. Chapters 7 and 8 introduce state-of-the-art approaches to building computational models and theories of visual recognition.

In the absence of a complete understanding of the wiring circuitry, and with only sparse knowledge about neurophysiological responses, it is important to ponder whether it is worth even thinking about theoretical efforts. Not only is it useful to do so, but it is actually *essential* to develop theories and instantiate them through computational models to push the field forward. Computational models can integrate existing data across different laboratories, techniques, and experimental conditions, and help reconcile apparently disparate observations. Models can formalize knowledge and assumptions and provide a quantitative, systematic, and rigorous path toward examining computations in the visual cortex. A good model should be inspired by the empirical findings and should, in turn, produce nontrivial and experimentally testable predictions. These predictions can be empirically evaluated to validate, refute, or expand the models. Refuting models is not a bad thing. Showing that a model is wrong constitutes progress and helps us build better models.

How do we build and test computational models? How should we deal with the sparseness in knowledge and the vast number of parameters often required in models? What are the approximations and abstractions that can be made? If there is too much simplification, we may miss crucial aspects of the problem. With too little simplification, we may spend decades bogged down by nonessential details.

As a simple analogy, consider physicists in the pre-Newton era discussing how to characterize the motion of an object when a force is applied. In principle, one of these scientists may think of many variables that might affect the object's motion – including the object's shape, its temperature, the time of the day, the object's material, the surface where it stands, and the exact position where force is applied. We should perhaps be thankful for the lack of computers in the time of Newton: there was no possibility of running complex machine learning simulations that included all these nonessential variables to understand the beauty of the linear relationship between force and acceleration. At the other extreme, oversimplification (e.g., ignoring the object's mass in this case) would render the model useless. A central goal in computational neuroscience is to achieve the right level of abstraction for each problem, the Goldilocks resolution that is neither unnecessarily detailed nor too simplified. Albert Einstein (1879–1955) referred to models that are as simple as possible, but not any simpler.

A particularly exciting practical corollary of building theories of vision is the possibility of teaching computers how to see (Chapters 8 and 9). We continuously use vision to solve a wide variety of everyday problems. If we can teach some of the tricks of the vision trade to computers, then machines can help us solve those tasks, and they can probably solve many of those tasks faster and better than we can. The last decade has witnessed a spectacular explosion in the availability of computer vision algorithms to solve many pattern-recognition tasks. From a phone that can recognize faces to computers that can help doctors diagnose X-ray images, to cars that can detect pedestrians, to the classification of images of plants or galaxies, the list of exciting applications continues to proliferate.

Chapter 9 will provide an overview of the state-of-the-art of computer vision approaches to solve different problems in vision. Humans still outperform computers in many visual tasks, but the gap between humans and machines is closing rapidly. We trust machines to compute the square root of seven with as many decimals as we want, but we do not have yet the same level of rigor and efficacy in automatic pattern recognition. Many real-world applications may not require that type of precision, though. After all, humans make visual mistakes too. We may be content with an algorithm that makes fewer mistakes than humans for the same task. For instance, when automatically identifying faces in photographs, correctly labeling 99 percent of the faces might be pretty good. Blind people may be very excited to use devices to recognize where they are heading toward, even if their mobile device can only recognize a fraction of the buildings in a given location.

Alan Turing (1912–1954), a famous British mathematician who helped decipher the codes used by the Nazis to communicate, and who is considered to be one of the founding fathers of computer science, proposed a simple test to assess how smart a machine is. In the context of vision, imagine that we have two rooms with their doors closed. In one of the rooms, there is a human; in the other room, there is a machine that we want to test. We can pass any picture into the room, and we can ask any questions about the picture. The machine or the human return the answers in a typewritten piece of paper so that we cannot identify its voice or handwriting, and there is no other trick. Based on the questions and answers, we need to decide which room has the machine and which one has the human. If, for any picture and any question about the picture, we cannot identify which answers come from a machine and which answers come from the human, we say that the machine has passed the Turing test for vision.

It is tantalizing, exciting, and perhaps also a little bit scary, to think that well within our lifetimes, we may be able to build computers that pass at least some restricted forms of the Turing test for vision. Andrew Parker's theory proposed that animal life as we know it started with the light switch caused by the first eyes on Earth. We might be close to another momentous transformation, the machine visual switch. It is quite likely that life will change radically when machines can see the world the way we do. Perhaps a second Cambrian explosion is on the horizon – an explosion that might lead to the rapid appearance of new hybrid species with machine-augmented vision, where we may trust machine vision more than we trust our own eyes, and where machines can lead the way to discovery in the same way that our visual sense has guided us over the last millennia.

1.10   Summary

- The light switch theory posits that the appearance of eyes during the Cambrian explosion gave rise to the rapid growth in the number and diversity of animal species.

- A theory of visual recognition must account for four fundamental properties: selectivity, tolerance, speed, and large capacity.
- Brain lesions and electrical stimulation provide a window to causally intervene with vision and thus begin to uncover the functional architecture responsible for visual processing.
- Scrutinizing the activity of individual neurons in the visual system opens the door to elucidate the neural computations responsible for transforming pixels into percepts.
- Perception is in the brain of the beholder. Vision is a subjective construct.
- The search for the mechanisms of consciousness requires identifying neural correlates of subjective perception.
- Inspired and constrained by neurophysiological function, neuroanatomical circuits, and lesion studies, we can train computers to see and interpret the world the way humans do.

Further Reading

See http://bit.ly/2TqTDt5 for more references.
- Hubel, D. (1979). The brain. *Scientific American* 241: 45–53.
- Marr, D. (1982). *Vision*. San Francisco: Freeman Publishers.
- Parker, A. (2004). *In the blink of an eye: how vision sparked the big bang of evolution*. New York: Basic Books.
- Poggio, T.; and Anselmi, F. (2016). *Visual cortex and deep networks*. Cambridge, MA: MIT Press.
- Ullman, S. (1996). *High-level vision*. Cambridge, MA: MIT Press.

2 The Travels of a Photon
Natural Image Statistics and the Retina

Supplementary content at http://bit.ly/3aeW07Z

And there was light. Vision starts when photons reflected from objects in the world impinge on the retina. Although this may seem rather clear to us right now, it took humanity several centuries, if not more, to arrive at this conclusion. The compartmentalization of the study of optics as a branch of physics and visual perception as a branch of neuroscience is a recent development. Ideas about the nature of perception were interwoven with ideas about optics throughout antiquity and the middle ages. Giants of the caliber of Plato (~428–~348 BC) and Euclid (~300 BC) supported a *projection* theory according to which cones of light emanating from the eyes either reached the objects themselves or met halfway with other rays of light coming from the objects, giving rise to the sense of vision. The distinction between light and vision can be traced back to Aristotle (384–322 BC) but did not reach widespread acceptance until the investigations of properties of the eye by Johannes Kepler (1571–1630).

Light is transduced into electrical signals by photoreceptor cells, one of the astounding feats of evolution, rapidly allowing the organism to make inferences about distant objects and events in the environment. The function of the visual system is to rapidly extract information about what may be out there. Therefore, the structure of the environment plays a critical role in dictating the pattern of connections and physiological responses throughout the visual system and marks the beginning of our journey.

2.1   Natural Images Are Special

Let us consider a digital image of 100×100 pixels, and let us further restrict ourselves to a monochromatic world where each pixel can take 256 shades of gray ($0 = $ black, $255 = $ white). Such small, colorless image patches constitute a far cry from the complexity of real visual input. Nevertheless, even under these constraints, there is a vast number of possible images. There are 256 one-pixel images, 256^2 two-pixel images, etc. All in all, there are $256^{10,000}$ possible 100×100-pixel images. This number is bigger than a one followed by 24,000 zeros: there are more of these image patches than the current estimate for the total number of stars in the universe.

Now take a digital camera, a rather old one with a sensor comprising only 100×100 pixels, turn the settings to gray images with eight bits ($2^8 = 256$), and go around shooting random pictures (Figure 2.1). If you shoot one picture per second, and if

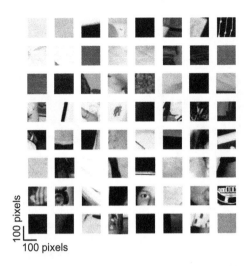

100 pixels

100 pixels

Figure 2.1 Natural images are special. Sixty-four example grayscale patches of 100 × 100 pixels extracted from photographs. Naturally occurring patches constitute a tiny subset of all possible random 100 × 100 image patches.

you spend an entire week collecting pictures without sleeping or pausing to eat, you will have accrued less than a million pictures, a very tiny fraction of all possible image patches. However, even with this tiny sample, you will start to notice rather curious regular patterns. The distribution of *natural* image patches that you collected tends to have peculiar properties that span an interesting subset of all possible image patches.

In principle, any of the $256^{10,000}$ grayscale patches could show up in the natural world. However, there are strong correlations and constraints in the way natural images look. A particularly striking pattern is that there tends to be a strong correlation between the grayscale intensities of any two adjacent pixels (Figure 2.2). In other words, grayscale intensities in natural images typically change smoothly and contain surfaces of approximately uniform intensity. Those surfaces are separated by edges that represent discontinuities, where such correlations between adjacent pixels break; these edges tend to be the exception rather than the rule. Edges play a significant role in vision (Chapter 5), yet they constitute a small fraction of the image.

One way of quantifying these spatial patterns is to compute the *autocorrelation function*. To simplify, consider an image in one dimension only. If $f(x)$ denotes the grayscale intensity at position x, then the autocorrelation function A measures the average correlation in the pixel intensities as a function of the separation Δ between two points:

$$A(\Delta) = \int f(x)f(x - \Delta)dx, \qquad (2.1)$$

where the integral goes over the entire image. This definition can be readily extended to images with more dimensions and colored images. The autocorrelation function of a natural image typically shows a peak at small pixel separations, followed by a gradual drop.

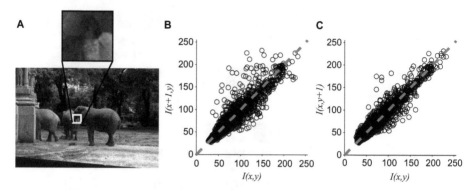

Figure 2.2 The world is rather smooth. For the small 100×100 pixel patch from the image in part **A** (white box, enlarged in the inset), the scatterplots show the grayscale intensity at position (x,y) versus the grayscale intensity at position $(x + 1,y)$ (**B**, horizontally adjacent pixel) or position $(x,y + 1)$ (**C**, vertically adjacent pixel). There is a strong correlation in the intensities of nearby pixels in natural images.

A related way of evaluating the spatial correlations in an image is to compute its power spectrum. Intuitively, one can convert correlations from the *pixel domain* into the *frequency domain*. Note that here when we say frequency, we are referring to *spatial* frequencies – that is, how fast things change in space. If there is much power at high frequencies, that implies substantial changes across small pixel distances, as one might observe when there is an edge. Conversely, much power at low frequencies implies more gradual changes and smoothness in the pixel domain. If P denotes power and f denotes the spatial frequency, natural images typically show that power decreases with f approximately as

$$P \sim 1/f^2. \tag{2.2}$$

There is significantly more power at low frequencies than at high frequencies in natural images. Such a function is called a power law. Power laws are pervasive throughout multiple natural phenomena: the sizes of craters on the moon, the frequency of word usage, the sizes of power outages, the number of criminal charges per convict, and the human judgments of stimulus intensities all follow power-law distributions. An important property of power laws is scale invariance. Specifically, if $P(f) = a \cdot 1/f^2$, where a is a constant, and if we multiply f by a scalar c, $f' = c\,f$, then $P(f') = a \cdot 1/(cf)^2 = a/c^2 \cdot 1/f^2 = a' \cdot 1/f^2$, with the new constant $a' = a/c^2$. If we change the scale of the image, its power spectrum will still have the same shape defined by the preceding equation.

2.2   Efficient Coding by Allocating More Resources Where They Are Needed

One of the reasons why we are interested in characterizing the properties of natural images is the conjecture that the brain is especially well adapted to represent the real world.

This idea, known in the field as the *efficient coding principle*, posits that the visual system is specialized to represent the type of variations that occur in nature. If only a fraction of the $256^{10,000}$ possible image patches is present in any typical image, it may be smart to use most of the neurons to represent this fraction of image space that is occupied. Evolution places a constraint on brain sizes, and it is tempting to assume that brains are not filled with neurons that encode characteristics of images that would never show up in the natural world. Additionally, brains are costly from an energetic viewpoint, and therefore, it makes sense to allocate more resources where they are needed.

By understanding the structure and properties of natural images, it is possible to generate testable hypotheses about the preferences of neurons representing visual information. We will come back to this topic when we delve into the neural circuitry involved in processing visual information (later in this chapter and also in Section 6.12). Such specialization to represent the properties of natural images could arise as a consequence of evolution (*nature*) and as a consequence of learning via visual exposure to the world (*nurture*). The question of nature versus nurture appears repeatedly throughout the study of virtually all aspects of brain function. As in other domains of the nature-versus-nurture dilemma, it seems quite likely that both are true.

Certain aspects of the visual system are hardwired, yet visual experience plays a central role in shaping neuronal tuning properties. For example, the type of light-sensitive molecules in photoreceptors are hardwired; we cannot start to see colors outside the visible spectrum, no matter how much exposure we have to such frequencies. On the other hand, altering the statistics of the visual regime can lead to changes in how neurons respond to visual stimuli. We will come back to the question of what aspects of the neural circuitry are hardwired and which ones are plastic when we discuss the visual cortex (Section 6.12). As an initial guideline, a reasonable conjecture is that plasticity increases as we move up the visual system from the basic sensory elements to the cortical responses. According to this conjecture, the initial processing of visual information discussed in this chapter is mostly hardwired.

2.3   The Visual World Is Slow

The visual properties of nearby locations in the natural world are similar. In addition to those *spatial* correlations, there are also strong *temporal* correlations in the natural world. Extending the collection of natural world photographs in Section 2.1, imagine that you go back to the same locations, and now collect short videos of two-second duration while keeping the camera still. Because the camera is not allowed to move, the only changes across frames in the video will be dictated by the movement of objects in the natural world. If you use a camera that captures 30 frames per second, in most cases, adjacent frames in those videos will look remarkably similar. With some exceptions, objects in the world move rather slowly. Consider a cheetah, or a car, moving at a rather impressive speed of 50 miles per hour. Assuming that we have a camera capturing a distance of about 40 yards in 2,000 pixels, the cheetah will move approximately 30 pixels from one frame to the next. Most objects move at slower speeds. Therefore, the *temporal* power spectrum of the natural world also shows a peak at low temporal frequencies, with large changes typically occurring over tens to hundreds of milliseconds. The visual world is slow and mostly continuous.

Several computational models have taken advantage of the continuity of the visual input under natural viewing conditions to develop algorithms that can learn about objects and their transformations, a theme that we will revisit when discussing computational accounts of learning in the visual system (Chapter 8). Because movement is rather slow and continuous, we can assume that a sequence of images that reach the eyes typically contains the same object, thus automatically generating multiple slightly transformed examples of the same object. These multiple examples can be used to achieve the type of tolerance to transformations highlighted in Chapter 1. The notion of using temporal continuity as a constraint for learning is often referred to as the "slowness" principle.

2.4   We Continuously Move Our Eyes

The assumption that the camera is perfectly still in the previous section is not quite right when considering real brains. To begin with, we can move our heads, therefore changing the information impinging on the eyes. However, head movements are also rather sparse and relatively slow. Even with our heads perfectly still, it turns out that humans and other primates move their eyes all the time. The observation that the eyes are in almost continuous motion might seem somewhat counterintuitive. Unless you have reflected on eye movements or spent time scrutinizing another person's eye movements, introspection might suggest that the visual world around us does not change at all in the absence of external movements or head movements. However, it is dangerous to accept concepts derived from introspection without questioning our assumptions and testing them via experimental measurements.

Nowadays, it is relatively straightforward to measure eye positions quite precisely and rapidly in a laboratory, but this was not always the case, and physicists built ingenious contraptions to capture these rapid eye movements. Figure 2.3 shows an example of a sequence of eye movements during the presentation of a static image. The eyes typically stay more or less in one location, and then rapidly jump to another location, exploring the new location, before adventuring yet again into a new target. These rapid jumps are called visual *saccades* and typically take a few tens of milliseconds to execute from initial position to final position. The approximately constant positions in between saccades are called *fixations*.

During scene perception, subjects typically make saccades of approximately four degrees of visual angle. Degrees of visual angle are the most relevant and standard unit to measure sizes and positions in the visual field and capture the fact that there are many combinations of object sizes and distances to the eye that subtend the same angle (Figure 2.4). One degree of visual angle approximately corresponds to the size of your thumb at arm's length. Under natural scene perception, subjects tend to make saccades approximately every 250–300 milliseconds.

Figure 2.3 Humans frequently move their eyes. Pattern of fixations while a subject observed the image for 12 seconds. This figure shows the eye positions averaged every 33 milliseconds (red circles), and the yellow lines join consecutive eye positions. The whole display was approximately 20 × 30 degrees of visual angle.

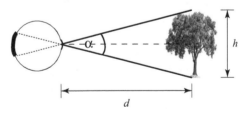

Figure 2.4 Sizes are measured in degrees of visual angle. The size of the tree is characterized by the angle α subtended in the eye. Different combinations of heights h and distances d give the same visual size in degrees of visual angle.

The intuition that our eyes are mostly still is simply wrong. Why is it that the world does not appear to be jumping from one fixation to the next several times per second? Watching a movie where the camera moves in a ballistic fashion three to four times a second can be quite irksome. The brain takes those retinal inputs that change a couple of times per second and creates the illusion of stability. Additionally, saccades are one of the fastest movements produced by the human body, reaching peak velocities of up to 900 degrees of visual angle per second. Considering a typical saccade spanning five inches in 20 milliseconds, this amounts to almost 15 miles per hour; peak velocities can be much greater than 100 miles per hour. During the few tens of milliseconds when the eyes are moving from one location to another, the sensory inputs change so fast that it is virtually impossible to see anything during a saccade. Every time we make a saccade, we are virtually blind to sensory inputs for a few tens of milliseconds. However, we are usually not aware of these saccades. Our brains have a saccade suppression mechanism so that we perceive a stable world. Even faster than saccades are blinks, which happen about 15 times a minute and typically last about 100–200 milliseconds. There is essentially no input to our eyes for more than 100 milliseconds, about 15 times a minute, and yet we are mostly oblivious to blinks unless we pay special attention to them. Saccadic suppression, blink suppression, and the stability of the visual world when the eyes are jumping from one place to another constitute persuasive examples that show that our subjective perception of the world is a construct. Perception constitutes an interpretation built by our brain based on the incoming sensory information, combined with expectations and with our general knowledge of the world. What we see is not a mere copy of what the eyes dictate.

The pattern of fixations depends on the image, temporal history, and current goals. The characteristics of the image influence eye movements: for example, high-contrast regions are more salient and tend to attract eye movements. The temporal history of previous fixations is also relevant: on average, subjects tend to avoid returning to a location they recently fixated on, a phenomenon known as *inhibition of return*. Current goals also play a critical role as well: if you are looking for your car in the parking lot, you will probably make more fixations on cars, and nearby objects of the same color as your car.

Zooming into Figure 2.3, in addition to the ballistic eye movements spanning several degrees of visual angle and occurring every 200–300 milliseconds (saccades), there are also many other smaller and faster eye movements. These eye movements are called *microsaccades* and typically span a fraction of a visual degree. Because these eye movements take place during the more or less stable fixations, they are referred to as fixational eye movements. Most saccades are involuntary (as noted before, we are typically not even aware that we are making saccades), but, of course, we can volitionally control our saccades. In contrast, microsaccades are involuntary. Together with other fixational eye movements, these small shifts in eye position may play a critical role in preventing adaptation. As we will see in Section 6.9, in the absence of any type of external movement, head movement, or eye movement, neurons quickly adapt to the inputs by reducing their activity. In fact, surprising experiments have shown that if the image on the retina is perfectly stabilized – through an apparatus that is capable of slightly moving the image to account for small eye movements – then the image quickly fades from perception. In other words, without constant eye movements, we would not be able to see anything except for transient changes due to moving objects or head movements.

2.5   The Retina Extracts Information from Light

The adventure of visual processing in the brain begins with the conversion of photons into electrical signals in the *retina* (diminutive form of the word *net*, in Latin). Due to its accessibility, the retina is the most studied part of the visual system. The conversion of

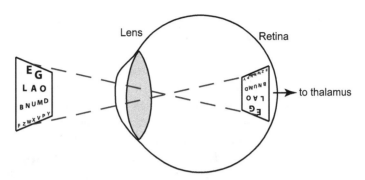

Figure 2.5 The eye lens inverts the image. As in many other types of lenses, the image is inverted when focused on the retina.

light into electrical signals, combined with the precise retinal circuitry, can well be considered one of the great achievements of evolution. The ability to convert light patterns into information and the structure of the eye made Charles Darwin (1809–1882) ponder whether such a feat could be achieved via natural selection. Elegant biochemical and electrophysiological work has characterized the signal transduction cascade responsible for capturing photons and using the photon's energy to trigger a set of chemical reactions that lead to voltage changes in photoreceptor cells.

Light information reaches the eye through a lens. When the light reaches the focal plane, the retina, the image is inverted (upside down and left/right, Figure 2.5). This basic fact of optics sometimes puzzles those who reflect about perception for the first time. Why don't we see everything upside down? This question has also tormented some of the brightest minds ever since the basic principles of optics were discovered. None other than the great Leonardo Da Vinci (1452–1519) erroneously assumed that we do not see upside down because of a second lens in the eye inverting the image again. Moreover, Johannes Kepler (1571–1630), who otherwise played a central role in advancing our thinking about visual perception, clearly described the inversion by the eye and left the problem of perception to be solved by natural philosophers (at the time, a mixture of what we would now call physicists and philosophers). Other philosophers assumed that newborn infants do see objects upside down and that this percept is eventually "corrected" by virtue of aligning visual inputs with the sense of touch. These philosophical ideas are another example of erroneous interpretations based on introspective models without an anchor on real experiments: there is no evidence that the sense of touch is needed to develop a visual system capable of interpreting what is up and down in the world.

We do not see objects upside down because perception constitutes our brain's construction of the outside world based on the pattern of activity from neurons in the retina. Since the day we are born, our brains learn that a specific pattern of activation in the retina is the way things are in the world. The brain does not know about what is right side up; it is all electrical signals. It is even possible to teach the brain to adapt to images with different rules, for example, by wearing glasses that invert the image. It is not easy to adapt to such glasses, and it takes dedication, but people can learn to ride a bicycle wearing glasses containing lenses that shift the world upside down or glasses that shift the image left and right. After adapting to these new rules, taking the glasses off becomes quite confusing, and subjects need to learn again to interpret the visual world without the inversions. Upon taking these nasty glasses off, relearning to adjust to the natural world is much faster than the initial brain training with the reversed world.

The network of neurons in the retina is a particularly beautiful structure that has mesmerized neuroscientists for more than a century. The history of retinal studies is intimately connected to the history of neuroscience and commences with the drawings of the famous Santiago Ramón y Cajal (1852–1934). Santiago Ramón y Cajal, considered to be the father of neuroscience, had a skillful hand for drawing and wanted to become an artist. However, his parents had other plans; Ramón y Cajal ended up following their advice and becoming a medical doctor. After obtaining his medical degree, he studied the techniques to stain neural tissue from the great Camillo Golgi (1843–1926), with whom he would engage in a ferocious scientific dispute about the fundamental structure of brain tissue, and with whom he shared the Nobel Prize in 1906.

The retina soon became a persistent passion for Ramón y Cajal. The retina is located at the back of the eyes; in humans, it has a thickness of approximately 250 μm and encompasses the surface area of about half a sphere of one-inch diameter. The retina is part of the central nervous system: it originates from the same embryonic structures that give rise to the rest of the brain, and it has a blood barrier similar to the one in the rest of the brain.

The schematic diagram of the retina in Figure 2.6 illustrates the stereotypical connectivity composed of three main cellular layers (photoreceptors, bipolar cells, and ganglion cells), interconnected through two additional intermediate layers (horizontal cells and amacrine cells). In vertebrate animals, light has to traverse through all the other cell types to get to the photoreceptors, shown at the top in Figure 2.6. Photoreceptors come in two main varieties: rods and cones. There are about 10^8 rods; these cells are very sensitive to light, and they are specialized for capturing photons under low-light conditions. Night vision depends on rods. Because the cones have different spectral sensitivities that enable interpretation of colors, and because cones are much less sensitive than rods to low illumination, we barely see colors at night. Rods are so sensitive that they can capture and transmit a single photon, which constitutes about 10^{-19} joules of energy in the visible portion of the spectrum. Meticulous experiments suggest that sometimes humans can detect single photons above chance.

In addition to the rods, there are about 10^7 cones specialized for vision under bright-light conditions. Most people have three types of cones: long-wavelength sensitive peaking at ~560 nanometers, medium-wavelength sensitive peaking at ~530 nanometers, and short-wavelength sensitive peaking at ~420 nanometers. Color vision relies on the activity of cones. Some humans show variations of color blindness – in most cases, due to deficiencies or even absence of one of these types of cones; in rare cases, there is an absence of more than one type of cone. Even with only two types of cones, people can still see different hues. For example, if people are missing the short-wavelength cones, they can still distinguish light of 400 nanometers versus 500 nanometers wavelength because of the differential responses triggered in the long- and

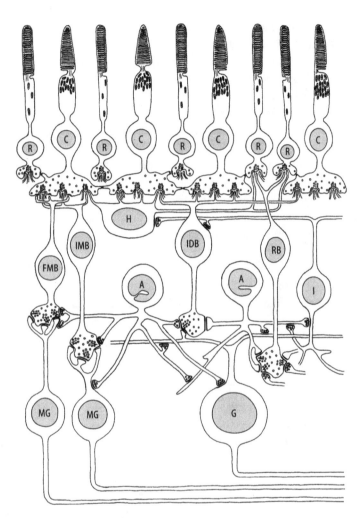

Figure 2.6 Schematic diagram of the cell types and connectivity in the primate retina. In this diagram, light comes from the bottom and goes through all the layers to reach the photoreceptors. R = rod photoreceptors; C = cone photoreceptors; FMB = flat midget bipolar cells; IMB = invaginating midget bipolar cells; H = horizontal cells; IDB invaginating diffuse bipolar cells; RB = rod bipolar cells; I = inner plexiform cell; A = amacrine cells; G = ganglion cells; MG = midget ganglion cells. Reproduced with permission from Dowling 2012

medium-wavelength sensitive cones. Color *blindness* is, therefore, a misnomer and should be reserved only for people who see in grayscale – that is, people who are only sensitive to intensity without any color sensation. A condition known as *achromatopsia* – caused by damage in the brain, not in the eye – can lead to complete color blindness, as related brilliantly by the famous British neurologist and author Oliver Sacks (1933–2015) in one of his books (Section 4.8).

People missing one type of cone have specific confusion points – that is, certain combinations of wavelengths that they cannot distinguish. To be able to demonstrate these colors that they cannot differentiate, it is critical to equalize light intensity. Under natural conditions, colors are often correlated with different intensities, and, therefore, people with cone deficiencies may use those intensity cues to circumvent their reduced resolution in the color spectrum. The *Ishihara* test is a common way of assessing color deficiencies, and there are plenty of such tests available online. Many people are surprised when they take these tests and find out that they cannot distinguish certain color combinations. Color vision deficiency is actually quite common in males (about one in 12!), with a much lower prevalence in women (about one in 200). A politically incorrect joke states that women know hundreds of colors and men only know five. This joke is not entirely wrong for some men (though strictly speaking, even with only two cones, it is possible to distinguish lots of different colors).

Rods and cones are not uniformly distributed throughout the retina. In particular, there is a part of the retina, called the *fovea*, which is specialized for high acuity. This ~300 μm region contains no rods and a high density of cones, with an astonishing 17,500 cones. This high density leads to a fine sampling of the visual field, thereby providing subjects with higher resolution at the point of fixation. For example, our ability to read depends strictly on the fovea: try fixating on the letter "R" on the second line in Figure 2.7. Next, try to read a word that is five words away and two lines below the "R," *without moving your eyes*. Cellular density and the degree of convergence from cones to downstream neurons decreases with eccentricity – that is, with distance from the fovea. In addition, the optics of the eye lens has enhanced contrast modulation transfer at the fovea. Because of the optics of the eye and the nonuniform sampling, we only see in high resolution in the fovea (Figure 2.8B). Therefore, saccadic eye movements bring the center of fixation into sharp focus to obtain detailed information. People with *macular degeneration* show progressively more damage in the foveal area, leading to a deterioration of the quality of high-resolution information, eventually perceiving noise or a blurry version of the image (Figure 2.8C).

Even though locations that are far from the fovea have coarser sampling, we have the illusion of perceiving approximately equal resolution throughout the visual field. Eye movements are partly responsible for this illusion: every time we move our eyes, we

Reading depends strictly on foveal resolution. Try to fixate on the letter "**R**" shown here in large bold font. Make sure that you do not move your eyes away from the R. If you do, then your high resolution area rapidly shifts to whatever location you are fixating on. Once you are fixating, try to read a word that is four lines below the letter "R". This task is basically impossible for us because the resolution drops sharply outside of the fovea. The notion that we can capture the entire visual scene at high resolution is merely an illusion created by our rapid eye movements and the fact that whenever we land on a particular location, it appears in high resolution!

Figure 2.7 We can only read in the foveal region. Fixate on the large bolded R on the second line and try to read words on another line without moving your eyes.

A  B  C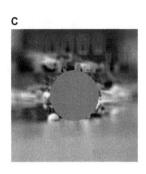

Figure 2.8 Only the area around fixation is seen in high resolution. (**A**) Original photograph. If you were at this place, fixating on the location indicated by the + sign, you would have the illusion that the entire field is full of details. (**B**) However, the image conveyed to the brain by the retina is closer to the one in **B**, with high resolution at the fixation location and increasingly more blurring toward the periphery. Our perception seems to be closer to **A** than to **B**, because we constantly move our eyes, sampling new locations at high resolution. (**C**) People with macular degeneration see noise or a blurry image in the center, in addition to the regular blurriness of the periphery.

fixate on a new location, which appears in high resolution. We naturally assume that the whole visual field has the same resolution. Additionally, there is probably information stored about previous fixations. When we move our eyes to a new location, the old fixation location now appears in the periphery, with lower resolution. However, the low-resolution version could be combined with a version stored in working memory based on the previous high-resolution fixation.

There is a region in the back of each eye that contains no photoreceptors. This region is where the axons of the retinal output cells, the retinal ganglion cells (RGCs), exit the eye. People cannot detect light that is focused on precisely this region, which is thus denominated the *blind spot*. The easiest way to detect the blind spot is to close one eye, fixate on a given distant spot, and slowly move your index finger from the center to the periphery until part of the finger disappears from view (but not in its entirety, which would imply that you moved your finger entirely outside of your visual field). There are many demos online to help detect the blind spot. Legend has it that King Charles II of England was fascinated with the blind spot and used to entertain himself by placing the head of a prisoner in his blind spot to imagine him headless before the actual decapitation.

Under normal circumstances, we are not aware of the blind spot – i.e., we have the subjective feeling that we can see the entire field in front of us (even with one eye closed). Given that we do not normally perceive the blind spot, one may surmise that it is actually rather small. However, you can fit the projection of nine full moons in the sky into the blind spot. How is it possible to be so utterly oblivious to such a large and empty region of the visual field? We are generally not aware of the blind spot because the brain fills in and compensates for the lack of receptors in the blind spot. This filling-in process emphasizes again the notion that our visual percepts are not a literal reflection of reality but rather a reconstruction concocted by our brains. We will return to the notion of vision as a subjective construction when we discuss visual illusions (Section 3.1) and visual consciousness (Chapter 10).

Information from the photoreceptors is conveyed to a second cellular layer consisting of horizontal cells, bipolar cells and amacrine cells, and finally to retinal ganglion cells (RGCs). The human retina contains approximately 6.4 million cones, about 110 million rods, and about one million retinal ganglion cells. Thus, on average, there is a convergence of about 100 photoreceptors to one ganglion cell, but these numbers vary depending on the location in the retina. As noted before, convergence is minimal in the fovea and more extensive in the distant periphery. In the fovea, one cone is upstream of one RGC, and in the periphery, there are about 15 cones per RGC and hundreds of rods per RGC.

Figure 2.6 shows a simplified schematic of the connectivity in the retina from photoreceptors to horizontal and bipolar cells, then onto amacrine cells and ganglion cells. Molecular and anatomical markers have helped define different types of horizontal and bipolar cells and even more types of amacrine cells and ganglion cells, each of which is involved in specific computations to capture different aspects of the incoming images. Furthermore, serial electron microscopy is beginning to elucidate the *retinal connectome* – that is, the precise pattern of synaptic connections in the retina. In the not-too-distant future, it is conceivable that we may have access to a rather complete anatomical map of the retina.

2.6   It Takes Time for Information to Reach the Optic Nerve

At first glance, vision may seem to be instantaneous. We open our eyes, and the world emerges rapidly in all its glory. However, there is no such thing as instantaneous signal propagation. It takes time for the cascade of processes that converts incoming photons into the spiking activity of retinal ganglion cells. The latency of retinal ganglion cell responses to a stimulus flash depends on multiple factors – including the previous history of visual stimulation, the intensity of the stimulus flash, its size, and its color, among others.

The axons from the retinal ganglion cells that convey information to the rest of the brain are collectively known as the optic nerve. On average, it takes 30–50 milliseconds from the onset of a stimulus flash for spikes to emerge from the optic nerve and propagate down to the rest of the brain. This latency is further combined with the computational time required to interpret the information in the brain, to be elaborated upon in Section 5.12. Because of these delays, what we see reflects what transpired in the world in the recent past. The delays are sufficiently short to trick our perception and allow us to get a rapid assessment of what happens in the world.

2.7   Visual Neurons Respond to a Specific Region within the Visual Field

Like most neurons throughout the brain, retinal ganglion cells (RGCs) convey information by emitting action potentials, also known as spikes. Cells before RGCs in the

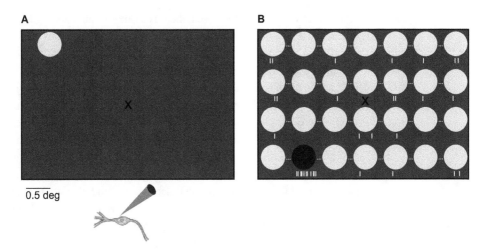

Figure 2.9 Neurons have localized receptive fields. (**A**) A light stimulus (white circle) is flashed in a circumscribed location while recording the activity of a neuron in a fixating animal ("X" denotes the fixation location). (**B**) The procedure is repeated in multiple different locations. The small vertical ticks denote neuronal activity. The location of maximum activity (black circle) denotes the neuron's receptive field. The stimulus size is also changed to map the boundaries of the receptive field. The neuron also shows a low spontaneous rate at other locations.

retina constitute the exception to this rule and communicate using graded voltage signals without emitting spikes. To understand how RGCs represent visual information, we need to examine how different inputs map onto spiking responses. The functional properties of RGCs have been extensively examined by electrophysiological recordings that go back to the prominent work of Haldan Hartline (1903–1983), Horace Barlow (1921–2020), and Stephen Kuffler (1913–1980). RGCs (as well as most neurons in the visual cortex) respond most strongly to a circumscribed region of the visual field called the *receptive field* (Figure 2.9). The receptive field can be mapped by flashing a stimulus at different locations and different sizes to locate the areas that trigger neuronal activation. Neurons tend to also fire spontaneously so that there are small neuronal responses even when the retina is in complete darkness or when the stimulus is very far from the receptive field. In other words, neuronal firing rates are not necessarily zero in the absence of visual stimulation inside the receptive field. It should be emphasized that the location of the receptive field is always specified with respect to the fixation point, not with respect to a fixed location in space. If subjects move their eyes, the location of the receptive field in the environment changes, but the position with respect to the fixation point does not.

These receptive fields tile the entire visual field. Without moving your eyes, any location in the visual field where you can see anything implies that there is an RGC with a receptive field that encompasses that location. The receptive fields of RGCs are topographically organized – that is, nearby RGCs in the retina represent nearby locations in the visual field. This topography is preserved in the projections from RGCs onto the thalamus, and from there onto the cortex as well. The nonuniform distribution of neurons from the fovea to the periphery means that there is a consistent eccentricity dependence in the size of the receptive fields. In the fovea, there is a one-to-one mapping between cones and RGCs. Receptive fields near the fovea are smallest, and receptive field sizes grow approximately linearly with eccentricity. The large receptive fields in the periphery are one of the main reasons why we have less resolution outside of the fovea.

The RGC schematically illustrated in Figure 2.9 increases its firing rate with increased luminance inside the receptive field. This type of cell is referred to as an *on-center* cell. There are also other RGCs, *off-center* cells, which increase their firing rate when there is a decrease in luminance in the center of their receptive fields.

RGC activity does not directly reflect the pattern of photons arriving at the retina due to the distortions introduced by the eye lens, due to the temporal delays and intermediate processing introduced by the previous cellular layers, and due to the eccentricity-dependent variations in convergence from photoreceptors onto RGCs. However, it is still possible to make an educated guess about incoming visual stimuli by examining RGC responses. We do not have the tools to record the activity of every RGC. Current technologies only allow simultaneously registering the activity of a few hundred RGCs. Even with such a small population, it is possible to reconstruct a rather accurate version of the light patterns reaching the retina.

2.8   The Difference-of-Gaussians Operator Extracts Salient Information and Discards Uniform Surfaces

Even when the center of an on-center cell is bombarded with a high-luminance flash, its response will be modulated by what is outside of the receptive field center. In particular, for most RGCs, a perfectly uniform high-luminance white wall will *not* trigger high activation. Consider the following experiment: a small uniform white circle is shown in the center of the receptive field, and the neuron fires above baseline levels (Figure 2.9). Next, the circle is slightly enlarged, and the neuron shows a higher firing rate. If we keep increasing the size of the circle, at some point, the firing rate reaches its peak value. Making the circle any larger leads to a *reduction* in firing rate; this phenomenon is known as *surround inhibition*. Surround inhibition is observed not only for RGCs; it is also prevalent throughout the entire visual system. On-center neurons are particularly interested in spatial changes – i.e., increased luminance within the receptive field combined with decreased luminance outside the receptive field. The converse is true for off-center neurons.

This form of spatial context-dependent response pattern is known as center-surround receptive fields and is typically modeled as a difference of two Gaussian curves (Figure 2.10). Considering an on-center cell, and assuming that the center of the receptive field is at location $x = 0$, $y = 0$, the neuronal activity in response to illumination at a new position x, y will be driven by an excitatory component proportional to $(1/2\pi\sigma_{cen}^2)e^{-(x^2+y^2)/2\sigma_{cen}^2}$, where σ_{cen} reflects the spatial extent of the excitatory driving force (dashed line in Figure 2.10). This excitation is counterbalanced by a surround inhibitory component given by $(1/2\pi\sigma_{sur}^2)e^{-(x^2+y^2)/2\sigma_{sur}^2}$, where σ_{sur} reflects the spatial extent of the inhibitory driving force (dotted line in Figure 2.10). The difference-of-Gaussians operator is used to describe the receptive field structure of RGCs:

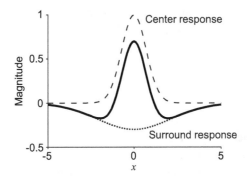

Figure 2.10 Mexican-hat receptive field. The receptive field in retinal ganglion cells is often characterized as a difference between a center response (dashed line) and a broader and weaker surround response (dotted line), resulting in a "Mexican-hat" shape (solid line).

$$D(x, y) = \pm \left(\frac{1}{2\pi\sigma_{cen}^2} e^{-\frac{x^2+y^2}{2\sigma_{cen}^2}} - \frac{B}{2\pi\sigma_{sur}^2} e^{-\frac{x^2+y^2}{2\sigma_{sur}^2}} \right), \tag{2.3}$$

where the scaling factor $B < 1$ controls the relative strength of excitation and inhibition, where $\sigma_{sur} > \sigma_{cen}$, and where the $\pm$ corresponds to on-center and off-center cells, respectively. The difference between the two terms yields a "Mexican-hat" structure with a peak in the center and an inhibitory dip in the surround. Biology is full of surprises and exceptions. The responses of some RGCs cannot be accounted for by Equation (2.3).

2.9   Visual Neurons Show Transient Responses

In the same way that a large spatially uniform stimulus does not elicit strong activation because neurons are tuned to detect spatial changes, temporal changes are critical too. A constant stimulus generally does not lead to sustained neuronal responses. Some RGCs respond at the onset of the stimulus, others respond at the offset, and others respond at the onset and offset. In all these cases, the responses tend to rapidly adapt when the stimulus remains constant and in the absence of any other external changes (in the absence of eye or head movements). Some neurons maintain a constant response above baseline during the duration of the stimulus after the initial transient. In contrast, the firing rate in other neurons decreases to baseline levels after the initial transient. RGCs are, therefore, sensitive not only to spatial context but also to temporal context.

The incorporation of contextual information allows neurons to efficiently encode spatial changes and temporal changes without spending abundant and energetically expensive spikes to indicate that the stimulus is constant in space or time. The regularities in the structure of the visual stimulus described in Sections 2.1 and 2.2 are thus reflected in the firing properties of RGCs.

Equation (2.3) can be expanded to provide a quantitative description of the *dynamic* responses of retinal ganglion cells when presented with a stimulus that begins at $t = 0$ and stays constant:

$$D(x, y, t) = \pm \left(\frac{D_{cen}(t)}{2\pi\sigma_{cen}^2} e^{-\frac{x^2+y^2}{2\sigma_{cen}^2}} - \frac{BD_{sur}(t)}{2\pi\sigma_{sur}^2} e^{-\frac{x^2+y^2}{2\sigma_{sur}^2}} \right), \tag{2.4}$$

where $D_{cen}(t) = \alpha_{cen}^2 t e^{-\alpha_{cen}t} - \beta_{cen}^2 t e^{-\beta_{cen}t}$ describes the dynamics of the center excitatory function and $D_{sur}(t) = \alpha_{sur}^2 t e^{-\alpha_{sur}t} - \beta_{sur}^2 t e^{-\beta_{sur}t}$ describes the dynamics of the surround inhibitory function.

Equation (2.4) describes the internal dynamics of an RGC upon presentation of a stimulus that remains constant. In addition to these types of responses, some RGCs are also strongly activated by a stimulus that moves within the receptive field. One such type of cell is the *on–off direction-selective RGC*, which shows enhanced responses when a stimulus within the receptive field is moving in a specific direction. Such direction-selective responses are also modulated by the surrounding context: neurons respond most vigorously when there is a *difference* in the direction of motion between the receptive field and the surround. An entire visual field moving in the same direction constitutes a weak stimulus for this type of neuron. This contextual subtraction helps the neurons distinguish the movement of external objects from self-motion. In addition, locations of depth boundaries also lead to motion discontinuities during self-motion relative to a static scene. Motion-sensitive RGCs tend to have large dendritic arbors and are particularly abundant in the periphery. Because of this, detecting an object in the periphery is easier when it moves, an observation that you can readily test by fixating on any given letter here, extending your hand in the periphery, and comparing your perception of the hand when it is static versus when it is moving.

The conduction velocities of RGCs have been used to separate between *magnocellular cells* (M-type RGCs) and *parvocellular* cells (P-type RGCs, also called midget cells). M-type cells have large dendritic arbors, have fast conduction velocity, respond to low-contrast stimuli, show transient responses, and have little sensitivity for colors. In contrast, P-type cells show small dendritic arbors, have color sensitivity, and tend to exhibit more sustained responses and low conduction velocities.

There continues to be exciting research geared toward elucidating all the different types of functional and structural specializations of RGCs; current estimates suggest that there are at least tens of distinct ganglion cell types, depending on how exactly a "type" is defined. Except for the fovea, different ganglion cell types are approximately distributed throughout so that the same external stimulus features can be captured throughout the visual field.

2.10   On to the Rest of the Brain

The principal destination of the output of retinal ganglion cells is a part of the thalamus called the lateral geniculate nucleus (LGN). The retina also projects to the suprachiasmatic nucleus and the superior colliculus, among many of other regions (anatomical studies have mapped more than 40 brain regions that receive inputs from the retina). The suprachiasmatic nucleus plays a vital role in regulating circadian rhythms, while the superior colliculus constitutes the main visual processing center for many species before the expansion of the cerebral cortex. Primates can recognize objects after lesions to the superior colliculus, but not after lesions to visual cortical regions. Therefore, the key pathway for visual perception involves the one going from RGCs to the LGN to the cortex.

As we will discuss in Sections 5.17 and 6.11, there are massive *back projections* throughout the visual system (Figure 1.5). If area A projects to area B, then in most cases area B also projects back to area A. One of the few exceptions to this rule is the connection from the retina to the LGN. There are no connections from the LGN back to the retina. Therefore, the pathways from photoreceptors to RGCs to LGN can be thought of as mostly feedforward.

The thalamus has often been succinctly called the gateway to the cortex, modulating what type of sensory information reaches the cortex. The receptive fields of LGN cells also display the center-surround structure depicted in Figure 2.10 and can be approximated by Equations (2.3) and (2.4). Thalamic cells are often referred to – in a rather unfair fashion – as *relay cells*, advocating the idea that the thalamus merely copies and pastes the output of RGCs and conveys this output to the cortex.

One obvious distinction between RGC and LGN cells is the pattern of connectivity. While we often think of the LGN predominantly in terms of the input from RGCs, there is a large number of back-projections from diverse cortical areas, predominantly from the primary visual cortex, onto the LGN. Precisely how these feedback connections modulate the response to visual stimuli in the LGN is not well understood.

Like the vast majority of brain structures, there are two copies of the LGN, one in each hemisphere. The right LGN receives input from both eyes, but only from the left hemifield (mostly the part of the visual field to the left of the fixation point) while the converse holds for the left LGN. The right eye receives information from both hemifields and sends right hemifield information to the LGN in the left hemisphere and left hemifield information to the LGN in the right hemisphere.

Six layers can be distinguished in the LGN. Layers 2, 3, and 5 receive *ipsilateral* input (i.e., information from the eye on the same side). Layers 1, 4, and 6 receive *contralateral* input (i.e., information from the eye on the opposite side). A single point in space is therefore represented in six different maps at the level of the LGN. Information from the right and left eyes does not merge in the LGN. Layers 1 and 2 are called magnocellular layers and receive input from M-type RGCs. Layers 3–6 are called parvocellular layers and receive input from P-type RGCs. There are about 1.5 million cells in the human LGN. Thus, the overall density of LGN neurons allocated to different parts of the visual field is comparable to that in RGCs, whereas there is a large expansion in the number of neurons as we move on to the cortex.

Because the LGN, and the thalamus in general, is connected to multiple cortical areas, it sits in a rather unique position to integrate sensory inputs with different forms of processed information throughout the cortex. The description of the LGN as a relay structure is only a major oversimplification, and the picture of the LGN will change dramatically as we understand more about the neuronal circuits and computations in the LGN.

2.11 Digital Cameras versus the Eye

In Chapters 7–9, we will examine computational models of visual processing. By and large, state-of-the-art computer models start with the output of a regular digital camera that has captured a picture and represents it as a two-dimensional matrix of pixels, each one of which is coded in a three-dimensional color world (such as red, green, and blue intensities). However, the sophisticated series of computations by the retina is still not quite matched by even the best digital cameras out there.

The angle of view of a digital camera depends on the focal length of the lens. For a focal length of 17 mm (approximate distance from the optical center of the eye lens to the retina), the field of view is approximately 90 degrees, whereas the field of view for humans spans almost 180 degrees. The resolution of the human eye has been estimated to be on the order of 500 megapixels, still much more than some of the fanciest commercially available digital cameras out there.

Another difference is that digital cameras are approximately uniform in their sensitivity to light. In contrast, the retina allocates more resources than the best current cameras to process conditions with low illumination. If you have ever tried to take pictures at night, you probably have noticed that it is not easy to take digital pictures under low-light conditions. To circumvent these challenges, photographers may use contraptions such as tripods to stabilize the camera and leave the camera shutter open for many seconds, if not minutes or more. In contrast, the eye can convey accurate information and help us navigate in the forest even under starlight only. We would not want to have to wait for many seconds or minutes before we can see anything at night. One of the tricks to achieve this is that the retina can adapt to low-light conditions and change its gain to achieve higher sensitivity. The eye has to work under conditions of strong sunlight all the way to moonless nights, a difference of about nine orders of magnitude in light intensity. This adaptation takes time, as can be appreciated when going from a dark place out into the sunlight or vice versa.

In addition to this adaptation to the average illumination, the light intensity can vary over three log units within a scene. The retina can accommodate this because of adaptation mechanisms spanning different spatial and temporal scales. In contrast, taking digital pictures in a scene with such significant variations in illumination is tricky: either one part of the image is completely dark or another part of the image is completely overexposed.

Digital cameras typically lack many of the sophisticated motion detection and contextual correction mechanisms described in this chapter for RGCs. Images are rarely blurry for us, whereas digital cameras need to implement a lot of additional correction mechanisms to yield crisp images. Another striking difference is the way that we compensate for the spectral composition of the illuminant: we do not see those orangey photos that digital cameras give us. However, the most striking difference between biological vision and digital cameras is the presence of an exquisitely sophisticated computational device to process the output of RGCs, the cortex, which we begin to examine next.

2.12   Summary

- Natural images are special: they are spatially smooth and change slowly in time.
- The efficient coding hypothesis posits that neuronal resources are allocated optimally to represent the statistics of environmental inputs.
- Positions and sizes in the visual field are measured in degrees of visual angle. One degree corresponds approximately to the size of your thumb at arm's length.
- Humans and other primates make frequent eye movements denominated *saccades,* spanning multiple degrees of visual angle, and occurring three to four times a second.
- Two types of photoreceptors convert light into electrical signals for visual perception: *rods* and *cones*. Rods are primarily responsible for night vision and cones for color vision.
- Retinal ganglion cells communicate the output of the retina to the rest of the brain.
- Retinal ganglion cells respond to a localized region of the visual field denominated the *receptive field.*
- The center of focus is projected onto the *fovea*, an area populated by cones, with higher cellular density and smaller receptive field sizes, providing high resolution.
- On-center retinal ganglion cells are excited by light within their receptive field and inhibited by light in the surrounding region. Their responses can be described by a difference-of-Gaussians function.
- Information from retinal ganglion cells is conveyed to the lateral geniculate nucleus in the thalamus.
- As a coarse approximation, the eye can be considered to be a specialized digital camera, though eyes are capable of many sophisticated tricks that current digital cameras cannot perform.
- Perception is a construct, an interpretation made by the brain, inspired by sensory formation, but not a literal reflection of the outside world.

Further Reading

See http://bit.ly/3aeW07Z for more references.
- Barlow, H. (1972). Single units and sensation: a neuron doctrine for perception. *Perception* 1, 371–394.

- Helmstaedter, M.; Briggman, K. L.; Turaga, S. C.; Jain, V.; Seung, H. S.; and Denk, W. (2013). Connectomic reconstruction of the inner plexiform layer in the mouse retina. *Nature* 500, 168–174.
- Kuffler, S. (1953). Discharge patterns and functional organization of mammalian retina. *Journal of Neurophysiology* 16, 37–68.
- Simoncelli, E.; and Olshausen, B. (2001). Natural image statistics and neural representation. *Annual Review of Neuroscience* 24, 193–216.
- Yarbus, A. (1967). *Eye movements and vision*. New York: Plenum Press.

3 The Phenomenology of Seeing

Supplementary content at http://bit.ly/38buAhB
We want to understand the neural mechanisms responsible for visual cognition, and we want to instantiate these mechanisms into computational algorithms that resemble and perhaps even surpass human performance. In order to build such biologically inspired visually intelligent machines, we first need to define visual cognition capabilities at the behavioral level. What types of shapes can be recognized, and when and how? Under what conditions do people make mistakes during visual processing? How much experience and what type of experience with the world is required to learn to see? To answer these questions, we need to quantify human performance under well-controlled visual tasks. A discipline with the picturesque and attractive name of *psychophysics* aims to rigorously characterize, quantify, and understand behavior during cognitive tasks.

3.1   What You Get Ain't What You See

As already introduced in Section 2.5, it is clear that what we end up perceiving is a significantly transformed version of the pattern of photons impinging on the retina. Our brains filter and process visual inputs to understand the physical world around us by constructing an interpretation that is consistent with our experiences. The notion that our brains make up stuff may seem counterintuitive at first: our perception is a sufficiently reasonable representation of the outside world to allow us to navigate, to grasp objects, to predict where things are going, and to discern whether a friend is happy or not. It is extremely tempting to assume that our visual system actually captures a perfect literal rendering of the outside world.

Visual illusions constitute convincing examples of the dissociation between what is in the real world and what we end up perceiving. Chapter 2 presented several examples of the dissociation between inputs and percepts: the blind spot (Section 2.5), the complete elimination of inputs during blinks and during the ultra-rapid input changes accompanying saccadic eye movements (Section 2.4). In all of these cases, our brains fill in the missing information.

Visual illusions are not the exception to the rule; they illustrate the fundamental principle that our perception is a construct, a confabulation, inspired by the visual inputs. There is substantial information in the world that we just do not see. For example, we cannot perceive with our eyes information in the ultraviolet portion of

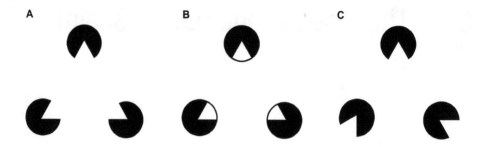

Figure 3.1 Our brains make up stuff. (A) The brain creates a white triangle from the incomplete information provided by the Pacman in the figure. The illusion is broken by closing the circles (B) or rotating the Pacman (C).

the light spectrum (but other animals, like mice, do). As another example, our visual acuity has a limit: there are small things like bacteria that we cannot see with our eyes.

There are things out there that we cannot see, and there are things that do not exist but we do see. For example, when we watch a movie, the screen depicts a sequence of frames in rapid succession, typically presented at a rate of 30 frames per second. Our brains do not perceive this sequence of frames. Instead, the brain interprets the presence of objects that are moving on the screen. As another example, consider the triangle illustrated in Figure 3.1, known as the Kanizsa triangle. We perceive a white triangle in the center of the image, and we can trace each of the sides of said triangle. However, those edges are composed of *illusory contours*: in between the edge of one Pacman and the edge of the adjacent Pacman, there is no white edge. The triangle is purely in our brains.

3.2   Perception Depends on Adequately Grouping Parts of an Image through Specific Rules

Our brains are confabulators, pretty useful confabulators that follow systematic rules to create our perceptual worlds. One of the early and founding attempts at establishing basic principles of visual perception originated from the German philosophers and experimental psychologists in the late nineteenth century. The so-called *gestalt* laws (in German, "gestalt" means shape) provide elementary constraints about how patterns of light are integrated into perceptual sensations. These rules arose from attempts to understand the basic principles that lead to interpreting objects as wholes rather than the constituent isolated lines or elements that give rise to them. These grouping laws are usually summarized by pointing out that the forms are more than the mere sum of the parts.

■   *Figure–ground segregation.* We readily separate the figure from the background based on the relative contrast, size, color, and other properties (Figure 3.2). The famous artist M. C. Escher (1898–1972) capitalized on this aspect of cognition to render ambiguous images where the figure and background merge back and forth in different regions. Evolution probably discovered the importance of separating figure from ground when detecting a prey – leading to the phenomenon of camouflage, whereby the figure blends into the background, making it difficult to spot.

■ *Closure*. We complete lines and extrapolate to complete known patterns or regular figures. We tend to put together different parts of the image to make a single, recognizable shape. For example, our brain creates a triangle in the middle of the Kanizsa image from incomplete information (Figure 3.1).

■ *Similarity*. We tend to group similar objects together. Similarity can be defined by shape, color, size, brightness, and other properties (Figure 3.3).

■ *Proximity*. We tend to group objects based on their relative distances (Figure 3.4). Proximity is a potent cue that can often trump some of the other grouping criteria.

■ *Symmetry*. We tend to group symmetrical images.

■ *Continuity*. We tend to continue regular patterns (Figure 3.5).

Figure 3.2 Figure–ground segregation. We tend to separate figure – here, a person running – from the background – here, uniform black.

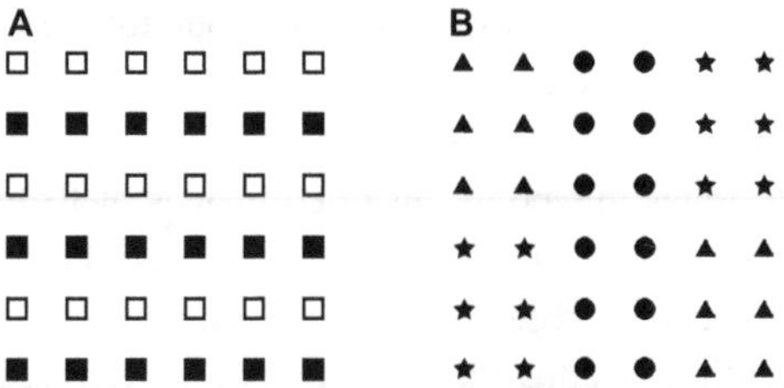

Figure 3.3 Grouping by similarity. We tend to group objects that share common properties. (**A**) We perceive horizontal lines composed of black squares interleaved with horizontal lines composed of white squares, grouping the items by their color. (**B**) We perceive five distinct groups based on grouping shapes.

Figure 3.4 Grouping by proximity. We perceive this figure as vertical lines.

Figure 3.5 Grouping by continuity. We tend to assume that the dark gray circles form a continuous line.

■   *Common fate*. Elements with the same moving direction tend to be grouped together. Movement is one of the strongest and most reliable cues for grouping and segmentation of an image, superseding the other criteria. Because of this, an animal that wants to camouflage with the background should stay very still.

3.3   The Whole Can Be More than the Sum of Its Parts

The gestalt grouping rules dictate the organization of elements in an image into higher-order structures, new interpretable combinations of simple elements. A demonstration of the combination of elements beyond what can be discerned from the individual components is referred to as *holistic processing*. A particularly extensively studied form of holistic processing is the interpretation of faces.

Three main observations have been put forward to document the holism of face processing. First, the *inversion effect* describes how difficult it is to distinguish local changes in a face when it is turned upside down. An illusion known as the "Thatcher effect" illustrates this point: distorted images of Britain's prime minister can be easily distinguished from the original when they are right side up but not when they are upside down. The second observation suggesting holistic processing is the *composite face illusion*: putting together the upper part of a given face A and the bottom part of another face B creates a novel face that appears to be perceptually distinct everywhere from the two original ones. The third argument for holistic processing is the *parts and wholes effect*: changing a local aspect of a face distorts the overall perception of the entire face. The observation that the whole can be more than the sum of its parts is not restricted to faces; expertise in other domains, including fingerprint identification or recognition of novel arbitrary shapes, also leads to similar holistic effects.

3.4   The Visual System Tolerates Large Image Transformations

The observation that the interpretation of the whole object is not merely a list of components makes it challenging to build models of object recognition that are based on a checklist of specific object parts. Another serious challenge to this type of checklist model of recognition is that often several of the parts may not be visible or may be severely distorted. A hallmark of visual recognition is the ability to identify and categorize objects despite large transformations in the image. An object can cast an *infinite* number of projections onto the retina due to changes in position, scale, rotation, illumination, color, and other variables. This tolerance to image transformations is critical to recognition, it constitutes one of the fundamental challenges in vision (Chapter 1), and it is, therefore, one of the key goals for computational models (Sections 8.1 and 8.2). Visual recognition capabilities would be quite useless without the ability to abstract away image changes.

To further illustrate the critical role of tolerance to image transformations in visual recognition, consider a straightforward algorithm that we will refer to as "the rote memorization machine" (Figure 1.4). This algorithm receives inputs from a digital camera and perfectly remembers every single pixel. It can remember the Van Gogh sunflowers; it can remember a selfie taken two weeks ago on Monday at 2:30 p.m.; it can remember precisely what your car looked like three years ago on a Saturday at 5:01 p.m. While such extraordinary pixel-based memory might seem quite remarkable at first, it turns out that this would constitute a brittle approach to recognition. This algorithm would not be able to recognize your car in the parking lot today, because you may see it under different illumination, a different angle, and with different amounts of dust than in any of the memorized photographs. The problem with the rote memorization machine is beautifully illustrated in a short story by Argentinian fiction writer Jorge Luis Borges, titled "Funes the Memorious." The story relates the misadventures of a character called Funes, who acquires infinite memory due to a brain accident. Funes's initial enthusiasm with his extraordinary memory soon fades when he cannot achieve visual invariance as manifested, for example, by failing to understand that a dog at 3 p.m. is the same dog at 3:01 p.m. when seen from a slightly different angle. Borges concludes: "To think is to forget differences, generalize, make abstractions."

Our visual system can abstract away many image transformations to recognize objects (Figure 3.6), demonstrating a degree of robustness to changes in several image properties, including the following ones:

- Tolerance to scale changes, i.e., recognizing an object at different sizes. In vision, object sizes are typically measured in degrees of visual angle (Figure 2.4). Now consider again the sketch of a person running in Figure 3.2. If you are holding the page approximately at arm's length, the person will subtend approximately two

Figure 3.6 Tolerance in visual recognition. The lighthouse can be readily recognized despite large changes in the appearance of the image.

degrees of visual angle. Moving the page closer and closer will lead to a multiple-fold increase in its size, mostly without affecting recognition. There are limits to recognition imposed by visual acuity (if the page is moved too far away), and there are also limits to visual recognition at the other end, if the image becomes too large (if the page touches your nose). However, there is a broad range of scales over which we can recognize objects.

- Position with respect to fixation – i.e., recognizing an object placed at different distances from the fixation point. For example, fixate on a given point, say your right thumb. Make sure not to move your eyes or your thumb. Then move the running man in Figure 3.2 to different positions. You can still recognize the image at different locations with respect to the fixation point. As discussed in Section 2.5, acuity decreases sharply as we move away from the fixation point. Therefore, if you keep moving the page away from fixation (and then you stop, because motion is easily detected in the periphery), eventually, the image of the running man will become unrecognizable. However, there is a wide range of positions where recognition still works.

- Two-dimensional rotation, i.e., recognizing an object that is rotated in the same plane (Figure 3.6G). You can recognize the running man even if you rotate the page, or if you tilt your head. Recognition performance is not completely invariant to two-dimensional rotation, as mentioned earlier in the case of the Thatcher illusion.
- Three-dimensional rotation, i.e., recognizing an object from different viewpoints. Recognition shows some degree of tolerance to three-dimensional rotation of an object, but it is not quite completely invariant to viewpoint changes. Rotation in the three-dimensional world is a particularly challenging transformation because the types of features revealed about the object can depend quite strongly on the viewpoint. In particular, some objects are much easier to recognize from certain canonical viewpoints rather than from other viewing angles.
- Color. In many cases, objects can be readily recognized in a photograph – whether it is in color, sepia, or grayscale (Figure 3.6E). Color can certainly add valuable information and can enhance recognition, yet recognition abilities are quite robust to color changes.
- Illumination. In most cases, objects can be readily identified regardless of whether they are illuminated from the left, right, top, or bottom. Also, perception is largely robust to changes in intensity or spectral composition of the illuminant.
- New transformations. To some extent, we can also identify objects under novel transformations that we have not experienced before. Perhaps we have never seen a lighthouse depicted as in Figure 3.6F or K. The ability to extrapolate to such new conditions is particularly remarkable and a formidable challenge for computational models of visual recognition.

These are but a few of the myriad transformations an object can go through with minimal impact on recognition; many other examples are illustrated in Figure 3.6. The visual system can also tolerate many types of nonrigid transformations – such as recognizing faces even with changes in expression, aging, makeup, or shaving. The examples in Figure 3.6 all depend on identifying the lighthouse based on its sharp contrast edges, but objects can be readily identified even without such edges. For example, motion cues can be used to define an object's shape.

An intriguing example of tolerance is given by the capability to recognize caricatures and line drawings (Figure 3.7). At the pixel level, these images bear little resemblance to the actual objects, and yet we can recognize them quite efficiently, sometimes even better than the real images. It is likely that the ability to interpret line drawings like the ones in Figure 3.7 depends on specifically learning to identify symbols and certain conventions about how to sketch those objects more than on visual shape similarity with the objects represented by those drawings. In the case of face caricatures, artists capture essential recognizable features of the person, as opposed to the symbols and conventions in other simple line drawings, therefore highlighting a strong degree of invariance for image transformations.

In all of these cases, recognition is robust to image changes, but it is not perfectly invariant to those changes. It is possible to break recognition by changing the image. Thus, although many investigators refer to *invariant* visual recognition, a better term is

Figure 3.7 Recognition of line drawings. We can identify the objects in these line drawings despite the extreme simplicity in the traces and the minimal degree of resemblance to the actual objects.

probably *transformation-tolerant* visual recognition, to emphasize that we do not expect complete invariance to any amount of image change.

3.5   Pattern Completion: Inferring the Whole from Visible Parts

A particularly challenging form of tolerance that is rather ubiquitous during natural vision is the recognition of occluded objects. Looking at the objects around us, oftentimes, we only have direct access to partial information due to poor illumination or because another object is in front. Deciphering what an object is when only parts of it are visible requires extrapolating to complete patterns. A crude example of occlusion is shown in Figure 3.6A. It is easy to identify the lighthouse even though less than half of its pixels are visible. The visual system has a remarkable ability to make inferences from incomplete information. This ability is not exclusive to vision, but, rather, it is apparent in many other modalities, including understanding speech corrupted by noise, or even in higher domains of cognition such as imagining a story from a few words printed on a page or deciphering social interactions from sparse information.

Vision is an ill-posed problem because the solution is not unique. In general, there could be infinite interpretations of the world that are consistent with a given retinal image. The infinity of solutions is easy to appreciate in the case of occlusion. There are infinitely many ways to complete contours from partial information. For example, in Figure 3.6A, the lighthouse might have a large hole in it, or there could well be an elephant hidden behind the black box. However, this is not how we would usually interpret the image. Despite these infinite possible solutions, the visual system typically lands on a single interpretation of the image – which is, in most cases, the correct one. Investigators refer to amodal completion when there is an explicit occluder (e.g., Figure 3.8A) and modal completion when illusory contours are created to complete the object without an occluder (e.g., Figure 3.1A). The presence of an occluder leads to inferring depth between the occluder shape and the occluded object. Such inferences about depth help create a surface-based representation of the scene. The occluder helps

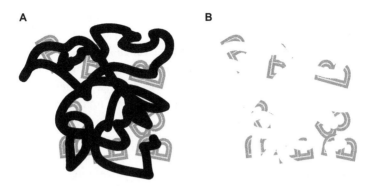

Figure 3.8 Pattern completion. (**A**) It is possible to recognize the rotated B letters despite partial information. (**B**) It is easier to recognize the objects when an explicit occluder is present (**A**) compared to the same object parts when the occluder is absent (**B**).

interpret the occluded object, as demonstrated in the famous illusion by Bregman with rotated B letters (compare Figure 3.8A versus B).

The visual system can work with tiny amounts of information. It is possible to occlude up to 80 percent of the pixels of an object with only a small deterioration in recognition performance. Recognition depends on which specific object features are occluded. Certain parts of an object are more diagnostic than others. One approach to investigating which object parts are diagnostic is to present objects through *bubbles* randomly positioned in the image, controlling which parts of the object are visible and which ones are not. Averaging performance over multiple recognition experiments, it is possible to estimate which object features lead to enhanced recognition and which object features provide less useful information. Instead of presenting an image through an occluder, or revealing features through bubbles, another approach to studying pattern completion is to reduce an image by cropping or blurring until it becomes unrecognizable. Using this approach, investigators have described *minimal images* that can be readily recognized but which are rendered unrecognizable upon further reduction in size.

3.6   Visual Recognition Is Very Fast

To recap, what we perceive is a subjective construct created by our brains following a series of phenomenological rules to group elements in the image. Our brains make inferences to arrive at a unique solution for an ill-posed problem, giving rise to a representation that allows us to interpret a scene and identify objects and their inter-actions. Given the complexity of this process, one might imagine that it would take an enormous amount of computational time to see anything. On the contrary, vision *seems* almost instantaneous.

The German physicist and physician Hermann von Helmholtz (1821–1894) demonstrated that conduction of signals in nerve tissue had a finite and measurable speed, which was a rather revolutionary concept at the time. As we discussed in Section 2.6, there is no such thing as instantaneous vision: even the conversion of incoming light signals into the output of the retinal ganglion cells takes time, on the order of 40 milliseconds. Subsequent processing of the image by the rest of the brain also takes additional time. What is quite remarkable is that all the processing of sensory inputs, tolerance to transformations, and inferences from incomplete information can be accomplished in a small fraction of a second. This speed is quite critical: vision would be far less useful if it took many seconds to arrive at an answer (Chapter 1).

Reaction time measurements have been used to study the mechanisms of perception since the very beginnings of psychophysics. Measuring reaction times provided investigators with an objective measurement as opposed to introspective evaluations. For example, these measurements allowed psychophysicists to quantify the notion of a trade-off between speed and accuracy, evident throughout visual and other tasks and forming the basis of models of decision making.

One of the original studies to document the speed of vision consisted of showing images in a rapid sequence (known in the field as rapid serial visual presentation tasks). Subjects could interpret each of the individual images even when objects were presented at rates of eight per second. Nowadays, it is relatively easy to present stimuli on a screen for short periods spanning tens of milliseconds or even shorter time scales. In earlier days, investigators had to go through ingenious maneuvers to ensure that stimuli were presented only briefly. A device invented in 1859 to accomplish rapid exposure to light signals, called a *tachistoscope*, uses a projector and a shutter similar to the ones in single-lens reflex photo cameras. This device was subsequently used during World War II to train pilots to rapidly discriminate silhouettes of aircraft. Complex objects can be recognized when presented tachistoscopically for <50 milliseconds, even in the absence of any prior expectation or other knowledge.

Reaction times measured in response to visual stimuli take much longer than 50 milliseconds. Emitting any type of response (pressing a button, uttering a verbal response, or moving the eyes) requires several steps beyond visual processing, including decision making and the neural steps to prepare and execute the behavior. In an attempt to constrain the amount of time required for visual recognition, Simon Thorpe and colleagues recorded evoked response potentials from scalp electroencephalographic (EEG) signals while subjects performed a go/no-go animal categorization task. Subjects were shown a photograph that either contained an animal or not and were instructed to press a key whenever they detected an animal. What exactly these EEG signals measure remains unclear. However, it is possible to measure minute voltages, on the order of a few microvolts at the scalp level, and detect changes that are evoked by the presentation of visual stimuli. The investigators found that EEG revealed a signal at about 150 milliseconds after stimulus onset that was different between trials when an animal was shown versus those trials when no animal was present. It is not known whether this EEG measurement constitutes a visual signal, a decision signal, a motor signal, or some combination of all of these types of processes. Regardless of the exact interpretation of these measurements, the results impose an upper bound for this specific recognition task; the investigators argued that visual discrimination of animals versus non-animals embedded in natural scenes should happen *before* 150 milliseconds. Similar behavioral and physiological reports have been observed in macaque monkeys. Consistent with this temporal bound, in another study, subjects had to make a saccade as soon as possible to one of two alternative locations to discriminate the presence of a face versus non-face stimulus. Saccades are appealing to measure behavioral reaction times because they are faster than pressing buttons or verbally producing a response. It took subjects, on average, 140 milliseconds from stimulus onset to initiate an eye movement in this task. These observations place a strong constraint on the computational mechanisms that underlie visual processing (see Section 8.2).

Such speed in object recognition also suggests that the mechanisms that integrate information in time must occur rather rapidly. Under normal viewing conditions, all parts of an object reach the eye more or less simultaneously (in the absence of occlusion and object movement). By disrupting such synchronous access to the parts of an object, it is possible to probe the speed of temporal integration in vision. In a behavioral experiment to quantify the speed of integration, investigators presented different parts of an object asynchronously (Figure 3.9), like breaking Humpty Dumpty and trying to put the pieces back together again. In between the presentation of object parts, subjects were presented with noise for a given amount of time known as the stimulus onset asynchrony (SOA). The researchers conjectured that if there were a long interval between the presentation of different objects' parts (long SOA), subjects would be unable to interpret what the object was. Conversely, if the parts were presented in close temporal proximity, the brain would be able to integrate the parts back to a unified perception of the object. The results showed that subjects could integrate information up to asynchronies of about 30 milliseconds.

Another striking example of rapid temporal integration is the phenomenon known as *anorthoscopic perception*, defined as the interpretation of a whole object in cases where only a part of it is seen at a given time. In classical experiments, an image is shown through a slit. The image moves rapidly, allowing the viewer to catch only a small part of the whole at any given time. The brain integrates all the snapshots and puts them together to create a perception of a whole object moving. The perception of motion from snapshots in this and related experiments eventually inspired the development of movies, where a sequence of slightly displaced frames presented at a sufficient rate is integrated by the brain to give rise to a continuous visual experience.

The power of temporal integration is also nicely illustrated in experiments where an actor wearing black attire is in a completely dark room with only a few sources of light placed along his body. With just a handful of light points, it is possible to infer the actor's motion patterns. Related studies have shown that it is possible to dynamically group and segment information purely based on temporal integration.

Not all visual tasks are so fast. Finding a needle in a haystack is famously challenging. Searching for Waldo can be somewhat infuriating and takes several seconds or more during which the observers will typically move their eyes multiple times, sequentially scrutinizing different parts of the image. Even without making eye movements, certain visual tasks require more time. One example task that requires more time, even

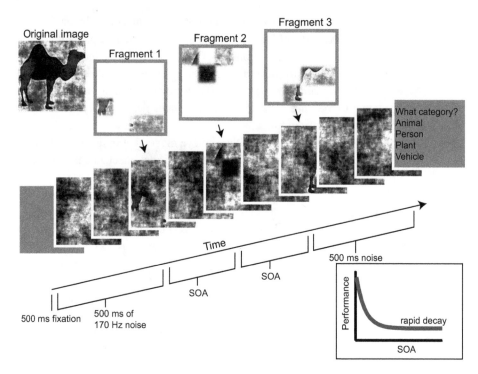

Figure 3.9 Spatiotemporal pattern completion: subjects can integrate asynchronously presented object information. Subjects were presented with different parts of an object asynchronously (in this example, a camel). The middle part of the diagram shows the sequence of steps in the experiment. Subjects fixated for 500 milliseconds and then observed a sequence of frames in which the object fragments were separated by a stimulus onset asynchrony (SOA). Subjects performed a five-alternative forced-choice categorization task. Subjects could integrate information up to asynchronies of about 30 milliseconds.

in the absence of saccades, is the pattern completion problem described in the previous section. Experiments where subjects have limited time to process an image show that completion of heavily occluded objects requires more time than recognition of the fully visible object counterparts. The simplest of these experiments are time-forced tasks, where identification of heavily occluded objects typically lags recognition of fully visible objects by 50–150 milliseconds.

Another situation where subjects have limited computational time is *priming* experiments. Priming refers to a form of temporal contextual modulation whereby an image, A, is preceded in time by another image, P, called the prime. If the perception of A depends on P, then P is said to prime perception of A. For example, the presentation of the prime P might influence how well or how fast subjects recognize the stimulus A. Priming is not restricted to the visual domain. For example, consider the following planets in the solar system: Mercury, Venus, Earth, Mars, Jupiter. Now try to complete the following word: M _ _ N. It is quite likely that you thought about "moon," although the word "mean" would be as good an answer. In fact, according to Google's Ngrams, the word "mean" is three times for frequent in the English language compared to the word "moon."

Therefore, it should be more likely for people to think of "mean" rather than "moon"; the previous sentence listing several planets primed the reader to think about the moon.

Similar experiments can be done in the visual domain by showing a picture as a prime instead of a list of words. By changing the amount of exposure to the prime, we can assess whether the prime image was recognized or not by evaluating its influence on subsequent perception. When the prime P is a heavily occluded object, the magnitude of the priming effect depends on the time interval between P and A. If this interval is less than 50 milliseconds, the priming effect vanishes, suggesting that 50 milliseconds was not enough to complete the pattern and therefore to have any impact on subsequent recognition.

Finally, another common tool to limit processing time in the psychophysicist's arsenal is *backward masking*. In backward-masking experiments, a stimulus, A, is closely followed by a noise pattern, B. If the interval between A and B is very short, typically less than 20 milliseconds, the initial stimulus A is essentially invisible. With longer intervals, subjects can still see the initial stimulus A, but recognition is impaired. When A is a heavily occluded object, and a noise pattern B is introduced about 50 milliseconds after A, it becomes challenging to complete the pattern in A. Investigators argue that the noise pattern interrupts the computations required for pattern completion. If the interval between A and the noise pattern B is longer than approximately 100 milliseconds, the effect of backward masking disappears. These different types of experiments show converging evidence that putting together the parts to infer the whole, during a single fixation, requires additional computational steps manifested through longer reaction times.

3.7   Spatial Context Matters

In addition to temporal integration, visual recognition also exploits the possibility of integrating spatial information. Essential aspects of recognition are missed if we take vision out of context.

Several visual illusions demonstrate strong contextual effects in visual recognition. In a simple yet elegant demonstration, the perceived size of a circle can be strongly influenced by the size of the neighboring stimuli (Figure 3.10). Another example is the Müller-Lyer illusion: the perceived length of a line with arrows at the two ends depends on the directions of the two arrows. These strong contextual dependencies show that the visual system spatially integrates information, and the perception of local features can also depend on the surround and even on global image properties.

Such contextual effects are not restricted to visual illusions and psychophysics demos like the one in Figure 3.10. Everyday vision capitalizes on contextual information. Consider Figure 3.11 (and do *not* peek into Figure 3.12 yet): what is the object in the white box? It is typically hard to answer this question with any degree of certainty. If you are not sure, take a guess. Write down your top five wild guesses. Now, turn your attention to Figure 3.12. What is the object in the white box? Recognizing the same object in Figure 3.12 is a much easier question! Even though the pixels inside the white box are identical in both figures, the surrounding contextual information dramatically

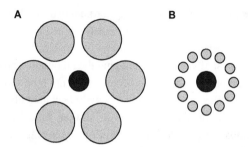

Figure 3.10 Context matters. The dark circle in the center appears to be larger on the right than on the left, but they are actually the same size.

Figure 3.11 Context matters in the real world too. What is the object in the white box? Warning: do not peek into the next figure before trying to answer this question!

changes the probability of correctly detecting the object. One could imagine that the observer may examine multiple different parts of the image before fixating on the white box to deduce what the object is. However, in laboratory experiments where we can precisely monitor eye gaze, subjects show a notable and rapid improvement in recognition performance even when they are only fixating on the white box and the image disappears before subjects can move their eyes. These contextual effects are fast, depend on the amount of context, and can be at least partly triggered by presenting even simpler and blurred version of the background information. These effects also emphasize that perception constitutes an interpretation of the sensory inputs in the light of temporal and spatial context.

3.8   The Value of Experience

Our percepts are influenced by previous visual experience at multiple temporal scales. The phenomena that we have described so far – including the ability to discriminate animals from non-animals, to detect faces, and to integrate spatially discontinuous object fragments – span temporal scales of tens to a few hundred milliseconds. We also considered two examples of temporal integration that also span tens to hundreds of milliseconds: priming and backward masking.

Figure 3.12 Context matters in the real world too. What is the object in the white box?

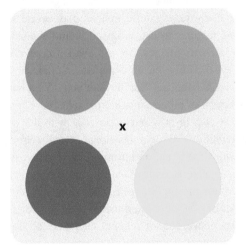

Figure 3.13 Color aftereffect. Fixate on the center x without moving your eyes, and count slowly to 30. Then move your eyes to a white surface. What do you see?

Several visual illusions and phenomena show the powerful effects of temporal context on longer time scales spanning several seconds. One example is *visual adaptation*. A famous example of visual adaptation is the waterfall effect: after staring at a waterfall for about 30 seconds, shifting the gaze to other static objects, those objects appear to be moving upward. The visual system is adapted to downward movement, and things that are not moving appear to be moving upwards, in the opposite direction to what we are adapted to. Adaptation is not restricted to motion. Similar aftereffects can be observed after adapting to colors, textures, or objects like faces. For example, fixate on the x in the center in Figure 3.13 for about 30 seconds; then move your eyes to a white surface. You will experience an aftereffect: the white surface will appear to show blobs of color approximately at the same positions in the retina as the circles in Figure 3.13 but with complementary colors.

The role of experience in perception extends well beyond the scale of seconds and minutes. Even lifelong expertise can play a dramatic effect on how we perceive the visual world. For example, the interpretation of an image can strongly depend on whether one has seen that particular image before or not. In the first exposure to the so-called Dalmatian dog illusion (Figure 10.2B), observers think that the image consists of a smudge of black and white spots. However, after recognizing the dog, subjects can immediately interpret the scene and spot the dog again the next time. Several similar images created by Craig Mooney are commonly used to assess the role of experience in perceptual grouping.

We could say that naïve observers cannot interpret the Dalmatian dog image, but they can learn to understand the image. In this case, the learning process is quite fast: a brief explanation, or briefly tracing the contours of the dog immediately reveals the image's content. Interestingly, once the dog is recognized, the viewer can also interpret other parts of the image as well.

There are many other situations where images may seem unintelligible to the novice observer. You may have seen clinical images such as X-rays or magnetic resonance images. In many cases, those images may reveal nothing beyond strange grayscale surfaces and textures to the untrained brain (as a side comment, note that *the brain is trained* to interpret images, not the *eyes*; it does not make any sense to speak of an untrained eye!). However, an experienced clinician can rapidly interpret the image to come up with a diagnosis. Similarly, if you do not read Chinese, Chinese text may look like a collection of picturesque hieroglyphs.

Another aspect of how our experience with the world influences our perceptions is the interpretation of three-dimensional structure from two-dimensional images. Many visual illusions are based on intriguing three-dimensional interpretations. For example, street artists create striking illusions that convey a stunning three-dimensional scene when a two-dimensional image painted on the street is seen from the right angle. Even when we know that these are illusions, they are so powerful that our brains, laden with years of experience, cannot help but send their top-down cognitive influences to enforce a robust perceptual experience.

Another example of how our preconceived experience-dependent notions with the three-dimensional world influence what we see is the *hollow-face illusion*. A three-dimensional face mask rotates in such a way that in certain angles, it appears convex, protruding toward the viewer, whereas in other angles, it should be concave and appear hollow. However, the concave version is still perceived as a convex face by the viewer. There is a robust top-down bias to interpret the face as convex, probably because we rarely, if ever, encounter concave hollow versions of a face.

Faces have always been a particularly fascinating domain of study for psychologists. Understanding and identifying faces is prone to the same experience-dependent effects as other visual stimuli. For example, psychologists have characterized the "other-race" effect whereby it is harder for people to identify faces from races that they do not have experience with. For example, imagine someone born in Asia who has not had contact with the western world either in person, or in movies, or via any other format. Western faces would all look similar to that person. The converse is also true: western people who have not been exposed to many Asian faces may find it difficult to discriminate among them. As another example switching away from faces, a shepherd who has spent years tending to sheep may be quite good at identifying individual sheep, whereas they may all look similar to the naïve observer.

3.9   People Are Approximately the Same Wherever You Go, with Notable Exceptions

In the previous sections and most of the psychophysics literature, we imagine a generic adult individual as a prototypical subject to discuss properties of human vision. To a good first-order approximation, the basic observations described so far hold regardless of the person's gender, skin color, religion, cultural background, and even age, except for the first few years of life. People see the world in approximately the same way wherever we go.

There are exceptions to this rule. One exception discussed in the last section is due to the role of experience. Doctors may see structure when examining an X-ray image, and a shepherd can identify individual sheep. Other obvious exceptions include cases where the hardware is different or malfunctions. For example, as discussed in Section 2.5, many males only have two types of cones in the retina. Several other distinct eye conditions have been described, including amblyopia (reduced vision in one eye) and nystagmus (repetitive, uncontrolled eye movements). Many people require corrective glasses to fix problems in accommodation by the eye lens. Albinism also leads to vision challenges under bright lighting conditions. As we will discuss in Chapter 4, there are also cortical lesions that lead to abnormal visual perception.

Age matters too. As people age, accommodation by the eye lens might change; some people develop cataracts; others suffer macular degeneration (Figure 2.8). Infants and very young children also see the world differently, not only because of their expertise with the world but also because their visual system is not fully mature. Humans are not born with their fully developed visual system. The visual acuity of newborns is approximately between 20/200 and 20/400, which means that what they see 20 feet away is comparable to what adults see at 200 or 400 feet. In the United States, a person with a visual acuity of 20/200 or less is considered to be legally blind.

Once we take out all these factors, let us consider two people of approximately the same age, with approximately the same visual experience, without any visual deficit. How different are their perceptions of the world? Recently, there has been increased interest in understanding individual differences in visual perception among normally sighted individuals. Although the general principles outlined in this chapter apply, there remains an interesting amount of variation in perception. An example of such variations has been recently brought to the forefront during the rather passionate discussion about the color of a dress (Chapter 1, Figure 1.7). There was an approximately bimodal distribution of the color names used by people to describe the dress.

Additionally, there have also been studies documenting variability in other visual domains. For example, there is considerable variability in the ability to recognize faces, with some people being particularly good and others particularly bad. Moving into higher psychological territory, beauty is in the brain of the beholder: there is considerable variation in visual aesthetic preferences.

3.10   Animals Excel at Vision Too

In the next chapters, we will delve into the brain to enquire about the neural computations responsible for visual perception. It is easier to investigate the insides of non-
human animals' (henceforth animals) brains rather than the human brain. Therefore,
most of the discussion in the next three chapters will focus on animals' brains. The
converse is true about behavior: it is easier to study visual behavior in humans than in
other animals. This chapter has focused on human visual behavior. Before we scrutinize
brain circuits, it is important to ask whether animals share the amazing properties of
vision described so far.

Almost every existing animal species, from flies to fish to birds to rodents and primates,
has capitalized on the advantages of visual processing. Nocturnal animals like bats,
coyotes, or mice have a well-developed visual system. Many subterranean species like
moles still have vision. A recent study of so-called blind moles, presumed to be blind
because the eyes are permanently closed under the skin during their entire life, has shown
that they have rods, cones, and retinal ganglion cells that project to the rest of the brain.
The investigators even showed that these moles have light-directed behavior! There are a
few animal species that are entirely blind – including some types of spiders, fish, and
flatworms. However, blindness is the exception in the animal kingdom.

Diversity rules in biology: there is an extraordinary repertoire of variations in the
visual system. We cannot do justice here to the flamboyant arsenal of visual capabilities
displayed in the animal kingdom. Animals have adapted to their niche and survival
needs by evolving specialized uses for visual processing. We will only mention a few
examples of similarities and differences between vision in animals and humans.

Some properties of animal vision are distinct from human visual capabilities. Humans
are limited to the visible part of the spectrum (defined as visible by humans!), whereas
other species can sense ultraviolet light (e.g., mice, dogs, many types of birds) and also
infrared light (e.g., many types of snakes). While (most) humans have three types of
cones (Section 2.5), the number of cones varies widely across the animal kingdom.
Some species have only one type of cone (e.g., various bats and the common raccoon),
other animals have two types of cones (e.g., cats and dogs), and there are even species
with 16 (the mantis shrimp) or up to 20 types of cones (some species of dragonflies).
Cuttlefish can also sense light polarization, which humans cannot.

Even the number and position of eyes show wide variation. Spiders have between
8 and 12 eyes, five-arm starfish have 5 eyes, and horseshoe crabs have 10 eyes. The
position of the eyes dictates what regions of the visual field are accessible to the animal.
Snails have eyes in their tentacles; starfish have their eyes located in each of their arms.
Even for species with two eyes, the position of the eyes plays a critical role in vision and
shows variability. Approximately forward-facing eyes imply that the central parts of the
visual field are accessible to both eyes, enabling the capability of estimating depth from
stereopsis (the small difference in sampling between the two eyes). On the other hand,
more laterally facing eyes provide a wider field of view. In an extreme example of
laterally positioned eyes, rabbits have a blind spot at the center of the visual field.
Humans have approximately 120 degrees of binocular field and a total visual field of

approximately 180 degrees. In contrast, other animals with two eyes positioned so that they face the sides can have more than 300 degrees of visual field (e.g., cows, goats, horses). The two eyes in humans are essentially yoked together so that their positions are strongly correlated (except in certain conditions like amblyopia). In contrast, other species like the chameleon can move each eye independently, and they can therefore focus on two completely different locations in the visual field.

The resolution of the visual system also shows enormous diversity from animals like the starfish that represent the entire visual scene with approximately 200 pixels all the way to species like preying birds that surpass human acuity. Nocturnal predators have higher sensitivity than humans in low light conditions than humans (e.g., owls, tigers, lions, jaguars, leopards, geckos).

The ability to detect movement is perhaps one of the few universal properties of visual systems, probably a testament to the importance of responding to moving predators and prey, as well as to other imminent looming danger. Many species are specialized to rapidly detect motion changes. For example, wing movements triggered by visual stimuli can be evoked in dragonflies in about 30 milliseconds after stimulus onset, faster than the time it takes for information to get out of the human retina.

Thus, the human visual system, as amazing as it is, is certainly not unique. There exist multiple species that display "better" vision in terms of the ability to detect ecologically relevant features, where what is ecologically relevant depends on the species, of course. Our sense of vision largely dictates how we perceive the world around us. Without the aid of other tools, we are confined to an interpretation of the world based on our senses, and we are often arrogant or unimaginative enough to think that the world *is* precisely as we see it. The short list of visual system properties outlined before emphasizes that our view of the world is but one limited representation, that we can see things that others cannot, and vice versa. We are missing much exciting visual action in the world.

What about the perceptual properties described earlier in this chapter? What do the gestalt rules look like for other species? Can animals also perform pattern completion? Deciphering what animals perceive is not an easy task and requires well-designed experiments and careful training. Monkeys, particularly rhesus macaque monkeys, constitute one of the main species of interest to study the visual system. Their eyes are quite similar to the human ones, and it is possible to train them to perform sophisticated visual tasks. Chimpanzees and bonobos have a visual system that is even more similar to the human one, but they have been less explored, particularly in terms of their brain properties.

Monkeys can be trained to perform multiple visual tasks, including discriminating the presence or absence of visual stimulation, reporting the direction of a moving stimulus, and detecting whether two stimuli are the same or not. Monkeys have been trained to discriminate complex objects, including faces as well as numeric symbols. They can trace lines and contours. They can even learn that the symbol 7 corresponds to seven items on the screen and is larger than the number 3. Monkeys can also learn to play simple video games.

How well can monkeys and other animals extrapolate to novel stimuli that they have not been trained on? For example, to what extent are their recognition abilities tolerant of the type of image transformations described earlier in this chapter (Figure 3.6)? We can define multiple levels of increasingly more complex sophistication and abstraction in the ability to perform visual discrimination tasks: (1) discrimination, as in evaluating the presence or absence of a light source; (2) rote categorization, as in the ability to memorize a few exemplars within a class of objects and distinguish those exemplars from a few exemplars in a different class; (3) open-ended categorization, extending the previous ability to situations where there is an extensive and perhaps continuous number of exemplars within a category; (4) concepts, where animals can draw inferences across different exemplars; (5) abstract relations, dealing with relationships between exemplars as well as relations between concepts. Macaque monkeys do seem to be capable of a relatively sophisticated level of abstraction, including transformation-tolerant visual categorization. After training with a set of visual object categories, their performance and pattern of mistakes resemble those of humans when tested under the same conditions. However, some tasks call into question how abstract monkeys' internal representations of the visual world are. For example, monkeys excelling at a visual discrimination task in the upper-left visual hemifield may have to be retrained extensively to perform the same task in the bottom-right visual hemifield, whereas humans would rapidly transfer their learning across stimulus locations. This lack of extrapolation may not strictly reflect visual differences between species, but perhaps it is more related to task instructions and the communication between researchers and monkeys.

Over the last decade, there has also been increased interest in using rodents, particularly mice and rats, to investigate visual function. There are multiple exciting advantages and opportunities when considering the rodent visual system, including the number of individuals that can be examined, and the availability of an extraordinary repertoire of molecular tools. The type of visual discrimination tasks that rodents have been trained on is limited compared to the behavioral repertoire of macaque monkeys. However, rats do seem to be able to perform basic comparisons between visual shapes, even with some degree of extrapolation to novel renderings of the objects in terms of size, rotation, and illumination.

3.11   Summary

- *Psychophysics* is an exciting field that deals with quantifying behavior, including reaction time metrics, performance metrics, and eye movements.
- Brains make up stuff. Subjective perception is a construct that is constrained by sensory information in light of previous experience. Visual illusions illustrate the dissociation between sensory inputs and perception.
- The gestalt rules of perception describe how we typically group image parts to construct objects. Such rules include closure, proximity, similarity, figure–ground separation, continuity, and common fate.
- Visual recognition performance shows tolerance to large transformations of an image.

- It is possible to make inferences from partial information – for example, during recognition of occluded objects.
- Visual recognition is fast. Many visual recognition questions can be answered in approximately 150 milliseconds.
- Subjects can integrate information presented asynchronously but only over a few tens of milliseconds.
- Contextual information can help recognize objects.
- Humans are generally consistent with each other in their visual recognition abilities and visual perception. Yet there is interindividual variability, particularly when it comes to tasks requiring extensive prior experience.
- Animals excel at vision too, and it is essential to study animals in order to elucidate the mechanisms of vision.

Further Reading

See http://bit.ly/38buAhB for more references.

- Eagleman, D. M. (2001). Visual illusions and neurobiology. *Nature Reviews Neuroscience* 2: 920–926.
- Herrnstein, R. J. (1990). Levels of stimulus control: a functional approach. *Cognition* 37: 133–166.
- Nakayama, K.; He, Z.; and Shimojo, S. (1995). Visual surface representation: a critical link between lower-level and higher-level vision. In *Visual cognition*, ed. S. Kosslyn and D. Osherson. Cambridge: MIT Press.
- Thorpe, S.; Fize, D.; and Marlot, C. (1996). Speed of processing in the human visual system. *Nature* 381: 520–522.
- Wolfe, J. M.; and Horowitz, T. S. (2004). What attributes guide the deployment of visual attention and how do they do it? *Nature Reviews Neuroscience* 5: 495–501.

4   Creating and Altering Visual Percepts through Lesions and Electrical Stimulation

Supplementary content at http://bit.ly/3abKBpP

We want to understand how neuronal circuits give rise to vision. We can use microelectrodes and the type of neurophysiological recordings introduced in Section 2.7. In the case of the retina, it is evident where to place the microelectrodes to examine function. However, there are about 10^{11} neurons in the human brain, and we do not have any tools that enable us to record from all of them. How do we figure out what parts of the brain are relevant for vision so we can study them at the neurophysiological level?

To find out how a device works, it is often useful to take it apart, inspect its elements carefully, examine the device's function upon systematically removing individual components, put the device back together, and ensure that the original function is restored. An extraterrestrial coming to Earth intrigued by how cars work might find out that the car can still navigate quite well upon removing the radio but the car fails to start without the battery.

Trying to figure out how the brain works by examining the behavioral consequences of restricted lesions has been a fundamental approach in neuroscience since its very beginnings. The history of brain science can be traced back to the famous Edwin Smith Surgical Papyrus, which dates back to the seventeenth century BC and describes the symptoms of two warriors who suffered wounds in the head. Despite this early description, for centuries, people believed that the heart was the seat of cognition. The erudite philosopher Aristotle (384–322 BC) believed that the purpose of the brain was to cool down the blood and maintained that the heart contains the rational soul. It was the study of head injuries, skull fractures, and spinal injuries that brought back the discussion of mental events to the brain.

Deducing the function of different brain structures by the examination of lesions is easier said than done. First, different components of the system may interact with one another to perform any one particular task, such that removing one of them could lead to indirect functional consequences beyond those directly associated with the loss of the lesioned tissue. Second, there could be a significant amount of redundancy, such that another component could take over, thereby shadowing the actual function of the lesioned area. Third, it is not particularly easy to remove specific parts of the brain. Despite these challenges, much has been learned about visual circuit function through lesions in animals and humans.

In addition to lesions, another approach to evaluating the role of specific brain areas in visually triggered behavior has been the injection of electrical currents to manipulate brain function. Invasive brain stimulation can trigger activity in neurons within circumscribed regions and help test hypotheses about the involvement of those neurons in visual processing.

4.1   Correlations and Causality in Neuroscience

As often stated, correlations do not imply causation (*non causa pro causa*, in Latin). This simple logical statement is often ignored, leading to much confusion and misinterpretation of cause and effect in neuroscience, as well as in many other disciplines. There are plenty of examples of this type of misinterpretation in the news. For example, the following statements extracted from news articles can easily be misinterpreted to imply causality: "smoking is associated with alcoholism"; "girls who watch soap operas are more likely to show eating disorders"; "people who go to museums live longer." Whether these statements are true or not is irrelevant here. These statements reflect correlations reported by journalists, and readers might erroneously infer some form of causality. The medical community is not immune to this fallacy. Consider the following statement: "The majority of children with autism are diagnosed between the ages of 18 months and three years old. That is also the same period when children receive a large number of immunizations. People see the correlation between receiving immunizations and the diagnosis of autism, and assume that the immunizations cause autism." The correlation between the age of immunization and the appearance of autism syndromes does *not* imply any causal relationship between the two.

In the next chapters, we will examine the activity of individual neurons along the visual cortex. Those neurophysiological recordings provide *correlations* between neuronal responses and visual stimuli, or *correlations* between neuronal responses and visually evoked behavior. Moving beyond these correlations to establish causality is not a trivial matter. We will consider here two approaches that can help bring us a step closer toward understanding the relationship between neural activity in specific brain circuits and visual perception: lesions and electrical stimulation.

4.2   A Panoply of Lesion Tools to Study the Functional Role of Brain Areas in Animals

Investigators take advantage of several tools to examine the effect of removing or silencing a brain area, including physical lesions, cooling experiments, pharmacological intervention, cell-specific ablation, molecular tools such as gene knockouts, and optogenetics.

Physical lesions. One of the most widely used tools to study function in the brain has been the behavioral examination of subjects with physical lesions. It is also possible to induce lesions by injecting chemicals like neurotoxins. In non-human animals (henceforth animals), investigators may remove specific brain areas to examine the behavioral deficits. For example, retinal ganglion cells project to the primary visual cortex (via the LGN) and to the superior colliculus. Primates with lesions to the superior colliculus are still capable of solving visual recognition tasks, whereas animals with lesions to the primary visual cortex are not. Subsequent studies examined the function of different parts of the visual cortex through lesions. Lesions to an area known as the middle temporal area (MT, also known as area V5) lead to severe impairment in the ability to discriminate motion direction, whereas lesions to the inferior temporal cortex lead to object recognition deficits.

Lesion studies in animals often provide highly valuable information, but they are not always easy to interpret. First, it is challenging to make anatomically precise lesions. Second, behavioral assessment may not be trivial: unless the animal shows a definite impairment in a battery of often predefined tasks, important deficits could be missed. Finally, by definition, lesions defined by anatomical landmarks impact multiple cell types and multiple connections, including inputs and fibers of passage. As a rough analogy, imagine removing the entire state of Massachusetts from the United States. The loss of economic activity from Massachusetts may have effects on the broader economy that are difficult to predict, the loss of the infrastructure of major highways and rail lines that run through Massachusetts may also impact traffic and other economic activity in New England and other regions, and removing 114 colleges could impact educational opportunities. There would be severe deficits, but some may not be obvious to spot, some may not be unique to Massachusetts, some may not be immediate and may require time to appreciate, and some may require detailed insights about what to look for.

Cooling. Neuronal activity decreases sharply when the temperature of the brain or a given brain region is lowered (Figure 4.1). Cooling devices can be implanted in the brain to lower the local temperature by several degrees. Lowering the temperature can

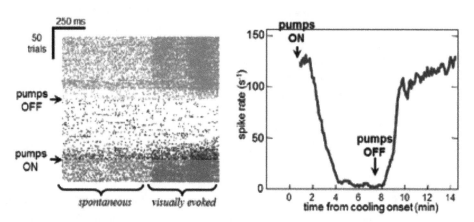

Figure 4.1 Cooling a patch of cortex can essentially abolish activity in the local circuitry. (**A**) Raster plots, showing each action potential as a dot, when a bar was swept repeatedly across the receptive field of a neuron in visual area V2 in an awake macaque monkey. Each row is one sweep lasting 1.5 seconds, and consecutive sweeps are shown from bottom to top. Arrows indicate when a pump is turned on to cool an area in the vicinity of the recording electrode and when the pump is turned off again. Within a few minutes of turning the pump on, activity is reduced. (**B**) Mean visually evoked activity (spontaneous activity subtracted) over time. Visual activity is eliminated within four minutes of turning the pump on. Modified from Ponce et al. 2008

silence activity in the region surrounding the cooling probe. In contrast to physical lesions, cooling is a transient and reversible procedure so that the same animal can be studied before, during, and after the effects of inactivation.

Pharmacology. Pharmacological intervention can also be used to reversibly silence brain regions. The most well-known type of chemical intervention is perhaps general anesthesia, where large parts of the brain are affected, and the patient is "put to sleep." It is also possible to inject neuronal inhibitors to affect activity in *local* circuits. Pharmacological silencing procedures are often reversible, and the silencing effects disappear when the drugs wash out. One of the most common forms of pharmacological intervention is the use of *muscimol*. Muscimol is a potent activator of a specific type of receptor for the brain's main inhibitory neurotransmitter, GABA. It is also one of the main psychoactive components of several types of psychedelic mushrooms. Muscimol has been extensively used to induce local silencing of neural activity. Another common example is the use of *lidocaine*, which acts by extending the inactivation of the fast voltage-gated sodium channels, leading to a reduction or elimination in the possibility of triggering action potentials.

Cell ablation. In a few heroic studies, investigators have used high-resolution imaging tools to identify specific cell types and then ablated those cells one by one to examine the behavioral consequences. Cell ablation is not a reversible procedure, it is difficult to inactivate large areas with this protocol, and it is a particularly challenging experiment because of the requirement to manually go through the cells to be inactivated. The effort is rewarded by a unique ability to remove individual cells from the circuit.

Gene knockouts. To describe gene knockouts, let us first briefly summarize the central tenets of molecular biology. Genetic information is stored in DNA. Each cell can *express* different genes along the DNA, meaning that those genes are converted into a messenger molecule called RNA and subsequently translated into proteins. Powerful molecular biology tools allow silencing expression of specific genes through *knockouts* and *knockins*. These techniques allow researchers to study the consequences of removing specific genes, adding specific genes, or altering the timing or spatial pattern of expression of specific genes.

Furthermore, a recent technique known as *CRISPR* allows investigators to edit individual nucleotides in specific genes. These techniques can be applied in such a manner that animals are born with the modified gene expression patterns. Alternatively, these manipulations can also be programmed in an inducible format so that the changes only take effect when the investigator turns them on. Such molecular manipulations have traditionally been the domain of work in mice, and it remains difficult, though not necessarily impossible, to use these techniques in primate research. More recently, primate researchers have turned their attention to virus injection techniques that could achieve high molecular specificity without having to incur the time and cost of developing knockouts.

Optogenetics. A particularly exciting and promising novel tool to silence – or activate – a specific population of neurons is *optogenetics* (Figure 4.2). Introduced by Ed Boyden and Karl Deisseroth, optogenetics constitutes a transformative technique to manipulate neural activity of cell types of interest with unprecedented resolution and

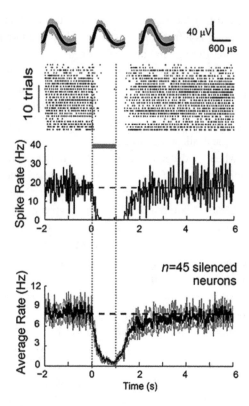

Figure 4.2 Silencing specific neuronal populations via optogenetics. Activity of a silenced neuron during and after 1 second of light illumination in an optogenetics experiment. Top: Action potential waveforms elicited before illumination (left), during illumination (middle), or after illumination (right); shown is the mean (black) as well as the overlay of raw waveforms (gray). Middle: Single neuron activity, shown as a spike raster plot, and as a histogram of instantaneous firing rate averaged across trials (bottom; bin size 20 milliseconds). Bottom: Histogram of instantaneous firing rate, averaged across all silenced single units recorded upon 1 s green light exposure. Black line, mean; gray lines, mean ± standard error (SE); $n = 45$ silenced single units. Modified from Han et al. 2011

control. Briefly, neurons are genetically modified by injecting a virus to express a light-sensitive ion channel. This ion channel is expressed only in specific neurons and not others by virtue of the *promoter* that drives its expression. The promoter is a region of DNA, typically sitting right upstream from the gene itself, which is responsible for controlling when and where a given gene will be activated. Once the neurons of interest express this light-sensitive ion channel, the cells are ready to be manipulated by shining light on the tissue. The opening of some ion channels can lead to excitation (depolarization of the neuronal membrane), whereas the opening of other ion channels can lead to inhibition (hyperpolarization of the neuronal membrane). By injecting a virus carrying an inhibitory channel, expressing that channel only in a subpopulation of neurons and shining light on the tissue, it is possible to turn off only certain types of neurons, in a temporally restricted and reversible manner.

Several distinctions need to be made while considering studies involving lesions and silencing. First, as noted before, many of the techniques like physical lesions involve removing (or silencing) large amounts of tissue. Therefore, an often-encountered discussion in the literature concerns the separation of local effects from "fibers of passage" effects. Imagine that axons going from area A to area C happen to pass near area B. A lesion to area B may also cut through the A→C axons. An investigator performing a lesion in area B may draw conclusions about the functional roles of area B. However, it may turn out that the behavioral consequences of the lesion may not be due to the function of area B at all but instead to the function of areas A or C, whose communication was severed while removing B.

Another distinction to be made concerns immediate versus long-term effects. The brain has a remarkable degree of plasticity. Over time, the behavioral effects of lesions to a given brain area could be overcome through compensatory adjustments in other brain areas. One such potential compensatory mechanism is the presence of a "copy" of the same brain area in the other hemisphere. Many (but not all) parts of the brain have analogous counterparts in the other hemispheres. The effects of unilateral lesions (lesions in only one hemisphere) can be masked by activity in the other hemisphere (unless specific precautions are taken in the experimental design).

4.3   Some Tools to Study the Functional Role of Brain Areas in Humans

Due to obvious ethical reasons, most of the techniques discussed in Section 4.2 cannot be used in studies in human subjects. There are, however, a wide variety of neurological conditions that provide important insights about functional neuroanatomy of the human brain. These cases typically come from a variety of neurological conditions, accidents, and wounds. We mentioned Oliver Sacks in Chapter 2; he was an influential neurologist who wrote extraordinary and intimate accounts of patients visited with a wide variety of mental conditions. In the prologue to one of his books describing the consequences of lesions in the human brain, he wrote, "... feeling in part like a naturalist, examining rare forms of life, in part like an anthropologist, a neuroanthropologist, in the field .... These are tales of metamorphoses, brought about by neurological chance, but metamorphoses into alternative states of being, other forms of life, no less human for being so different."

Bullets and wounds inflicted by other weapons have provided critical insights about function in the visual cortex. Carbon monoxide poisoning, as well as certain viral infections such as encephalitis, often produce severe visual deficits, especially when occurring in the temporal lobe. Head trauma, partial asphyxia during the first weeks of life, tumors, and hydrocephalus (accumulation of cerebrospinal fluid) can also result in visual deficits.

To study the consequences of lesions, it is always important to design the experiments carefully. Otherwise, even remarkable behavioral deficits associated with lesions could be missed. Consider, for example, the case of split-brain patients. These are patients with pharmacologically resistant epilepsy who undergo severance of the primary fibers that connect the two hemispheres, the corpus callosum fibers, as a treatment for epilepsy. For a long time, it was assumed that there was nothing out of the ordinary with these subjects who had their two hemispheres mostly disconnected (not completely disconnected because there are a few other smaller fiber tracts that also connect the two hemispheres). It was not until Roger Sperry (1913–1994) designed careful experiments based on his scientific understanding of the neuroanatomy of the visual system that some of the deficits became apparent.

Sperry knew that the right visual hemifield maps onto the left hemisphere in the visual cortex and vice versa. As described in Section 2.10, it is essential to distinguish between the right and left *eyes* and the right and left *visual hemifields*: the right and left visual hemifields are defined by the position in a visual scene with respect to the fixation point. Thus, every time you move the eyes and fixate on a new location, the location of each hemifield changes. Most of the information from the right hemifield reaches both the left and right eyes (and most of the left hemifield reaches other parts of the retina in both the left and right eyes). By using a simple divider, Sperry designed an experiment where visual information about an object reached only the right hemisphere (information from the left hemifield). Thus, information about the object was not accessible to the left hemisphere. Because for most right-handed people, the left hemisphere is critical for language, Sperry demonstrated that the subjects were unable to name the objects. Conversely, when object information reached only the left hemisphere, subjects had no problem in naming the objects. Sperry was awarded the Nobel Prize for this work in 1981. Previous studies in these subjects had failed to uncover any deficit because visual information was presented to both hemispheres, and therefore the investigators had not been able to observe the problems associated with lack of communication between the two hemispheres.

The study of "natural lesions" in patients encounters other challenges in addition to many of the ones discussed in the previous section for animal work. Many human studies may be unique and hard to reproduce, depending on the exact nature of the lesion. There are plenty of single case studies. These studies are fascinating and highly informative. Yet, without reproducibility, it is not always easy to follow up or investigate the deficits in further detail, as can be done in studies in animals. Additionally, natural lesions do not necessarily respect any boundaries established by anatomical, cytoarchitectonic, or neurophysiological criteria. Therefore, many neurological lesions encompass large parts of the cortex and multiple regions that are functionally distinct. The accidental nature of these lesions can make it challenging to interpret the findings due to the combination of multiple direct, indirect, and non-specific lesion effects. Another difficulty in human lesion studies is that it is not always easy to localize the lesion or brain abnormality. Magnetic resonance imaging (MRI) and computed tomography (CT) can only detect certain types of relatively large-scale brain transformations, but more subtle effects are typically missed.

Despite the limitations in researching human lesions, an advantage of human neurological studies over animal studies is the accessibility of subjective behavioral reports. In some cases, specific visual deficits after lesioning or silencing experiments in animal models may be hard to detect due to the limited nature of the behavioral assessment paradigms. Behavioral evaluation is often more straightforward in humans. In fact, human subjects may even come to the doctor and directly report the deficits in full detail.

4.4 Partial Lesions in the Primary Visual Cortex Lead to Localized Scotomas

The scientific study of the visual cortex is arguably the only positive outcome of the nefarious wars at the beginning of the twentieth century. The discovery of the primary visual cortex can be traced back to the careful examination of bullet trajectories through the human brain and their behavioral consequences during the Russo-Japanese War and World War I. In the late nineteenth century, Hermann Munk (1839–1912) reported that damage to the occipital lobe in one hemisphere in monkeys rendered the animals blind in the contralateral visual hemifield (contralateral means the opposite side). During the early wars of the twentieth century, a Japanese physician named Tatsuji Inouye (1881–1976) and two British physicians named Gordon Holmes (1876–1965) and George Riddoch (1888–1947) described clear and delimited visual field deficits contralateral to the lesion in the occipital cortex. New weapons introduced during these wars caused bullets to penetrate the skull at high speeds without completely shattering the skull. Certain bullet trajectories going through the occipital lobe caused the soldiers to lose consciousness momentarily but ultimately recover.

Methodical scrutiny showed that patients suffering from wounds in the occipital cortex were essentially blind within a delimited part of the visual field, resulting in a *visual scotoma*, a black patch at a specific location with respect to the fixation location. Because positions are described with respect to the fixation point, the location of the scotoma in the world changes when the subject moves his/her eyes. Local damage in the primary visual cortex gave rise to blind regions in the visual field, and the effects were quite similar to the ones observed due to local lesions in parts of the retina. Shape, color, and, to a lesser extent, motion discrimination were typically absent within the scotoma. Similar effects are often encountered through vascular damage, tumors, and trauma studies of the occipital cortex. By correlating the visual deficits with brain damage, it was possible to establish a map of the visual field in the posterior part of the occipital lobe, an area that is now known as the *primary visual cortex* or V1 (Figure 4.3). Biologists like to come up with names for genes, cell types, and brain areas; it is not unusual to have multiple names refer to the same thing. Visual area V1 is sometimes referred to as primary visual cortex, striate cortex, calcarine cortex, area 17 (in cats), and also Brodmann area 17, based on the cytoarchitectonic maps subdividing the cortex into multiple areas by the German neurologist Korbinian Brodmann (1868–1918) at the beginning of the twentieth century. A rose by any other name would smell as sweet.

The discovery of the primary visual cortex was inspiring in many ways. First, it documented how a concrete function could be represented in a specific location in the cortex. Together with localization studies for language functions dating back to the seminal work of Paul Broca (1824–1880), these findings provided ammunition to the idea that the cortex is not merely an amorphous distributed sheet of computational elements but, rather,

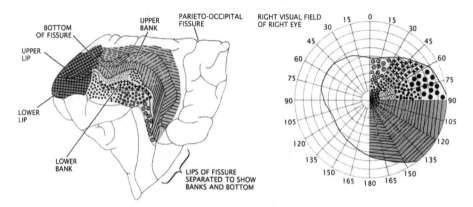

Figure 4.3 Local blind spots (scotomas) caused by lesions in the primary visual cortex. (Left) Flattened map of the primary visual cortex, in the occipital lobe, around the calcarine fissure. The map highlights different locations with different colors for reference to the visual field mapping on the right. (Right) Visual field map showing the position from the center of fixation (center of the circle) at different eccentricities. Note the disproportionately large fraction of the cortex devoted to the small foveal area around fixation (red). Reproduced from Glickstein 1988

that it is possible to ascribe specific roles to groups of neurons in specific locations. Second, going well beyond the localization of language functions, lesions in the visual cortex showed a rather detailed topographic map between the outside world and the brain. Third, these lesion studies set the foundation for the detailed neural circuit analyses that would come a few decades later and that continues to this day, to be discussed in Chapters 5 and 6.

The amount of real estate in the cortex devoted to different parts of the visual field is not distributed uniformly. There is a disproportionately larger area of V1 devoted to processing the fovea (red region in Figure 4.3); this enlargement of the foveal representation is known as the cortical magnification effect. The fovea constitutes less than 0.1 percent of the total visual field size, but its representation takes almost 10 percent of the primary visual cortex. There is progressively less amount of cortex per visual degree as we move from the center of fixation to the periphery. Having a high-resolution representation is good, but it comes at a cost. The brain would have to be orders of magnitude larger, hence heavier and more expensive from an energetic viewpoint, to represent the entire visual field with the same resolution as the fovea. The cortical magnification of the fovea, combined with rapid eye movements (Section 2.4) and working memory (the ability to temporarily store information), provides an elegant compromise to obtain high acuity with a manageably sized brain.

The visual field is mapped onto the cortex in a topographical fashion: nearby locations in the cortex represent nearby locations in the visual field. As noted earlier, information from the right hemifield is mapped onto the left visual cortex and vice versa. The *calcarine sulcus* divides the primary visual cortex. A sulcus is a furrow, which gives rise to the convoluted shape of the brain and allows folding the vast expanse of the cortex into a tight volume. The upper hemifield (yellow in Figure 4.3) is mapped onto the lower bank of the calcarine sulcus, and vice versa. Because of this orderly topographical organization, when an investigator lowers an electrode to record the activity of neurons in the primary visual cortex (Section 5.3), the anatomical landmarks provide an approximate guideline to localize the neuron's receptive field (i.e., the part of the visual field that activates the neuron, Figure 2.9). The topographical arrangement, usually referred to as retinotopic mapping in this case, can lead to saving wire, and hence also space, to establish all the connections to and from the primary visual cortex. Additionally, because of this topography, coarse measurements that average the activity of multiple nearby neurons may still reveal interesting properties of the circuit, in contrast to a situation where all the neurons are arranged in a completely random fashion. Such a topographical organization is also a property of most, if not all, of the other visual cortical areas.

There was a considerable degree of excitement in the vision community a few years ago with the description of a phenomenon called *blindsight*. As the name suggests, it was observed that some subjects with profound lesions to the occipital cortex were still capable of certain visual behaviors within the scotoma. Several possibilities were proposed to account for these observations, including anatomical routes that bypass V1 (for example, those connecting the LGN to other visual cortical areas) and the presence of small intact islands in V1 that may not be seen at the coarse scale of magnetic resonance images used to characterize the lesions. Although there is no doubt about the basic phenomenology of residual visual capabilities in patients with damage to V1, the range of visual behaviors in these subjects is limited. Subjects could detect motion (this was also observed in the initial study of soldiers with occipital cortex wounds by Riddoch in 1917), discriminate day from night, approximately localize a light source and describe its color, and other coarse visually elicited behavior. However, in all cases, their capacity for fine visual discrimination was lost.

The profound deficits after V1 lesions in both animals and humans, combined with the challenges in examining visual behavior in animals, led several prominent investigators in the 1950s to argue that V1 is not only necessary but also sufficient for visual perception. In an interesting historical overview, Charles Gross cites several striking demonstrations of this narrow-minded scientific perception that turned out to be completely wrong: "In human subjects there is no evidence that any area of the cortex other than the visual area 17 [this is area V1] is important in the primary capacity to see patterns .... Whenever the question has been tested in animals the story has been the same"; "visual habits are dependent upon the striate cortex [another name for area V1] and upon no other part of the cerebral cortex"; "image formation and recognition is all in area 17 and is entirely intrinsic. ... [T]he connections of area 17 are minimal."

4.5   *What* and *Where* Pathways

The assertion that vision stops in area V1 was proven to be completely wrong. Multiple studies have shown that severe visual deficits can be ascribed to lesions in cortical areas outside of V1. One of the earliest demonstrations that V1 could not be the entire story was the study of the so-called Klüver-Bucy syndrome. After bilateral removal of the temporal lobe in macaque monkeys, the original reports described a variety of behavioral effects, including loss of visual discrimination, but also other symptoms such as increased tameness, hypersexuality, and altered eating habits. The wide variety of symptoms is now thought to be a consequence of massive and poorly circumscribed lesions. Subsequent and more refined lesion studies confirmed that lesions of the inferior temporal cortex lead to deficits in the ability to discriminate colors and shapes, without all the other accompanying non-visual manifestations.

Studies outside of V1 led to a fundamental distinction between lesions to the *ventral cortex* and lesions to the *dorsal* cortex. The ventral cortex leads from V1 into area V4 and the inferior parts of the temporal cortex (mostly along the rightmost part of the diagram in Figure 1.5). The *dorsal cortex* leads from V1 into areas MT, MST, and parietal cortex structures (mostly along the middle and left part of the diagram in Figure 1.5). Ventral visual cortex lesions lead to deficits in shape recognition, and, therefore, this pathway is often referred to as the *what* pathway. Dorsal visual cortex lesions lead to deficits in object localization, and, therefore, this pathway is often referred to as the *where* pathway. As emphasized by the dense connectivity in Figure 1.5, these two pathways are not really independent, and there are multiple interconnections between the two.

4.6   Dorsal Stream Lesions in the *Where* Pathway

The types of deficits associated with lesions along the dorsal visual stream are quite distinct from those associated with lesions along the ventral visual stream. The dorsal pathway is mainly involved in spatial localization of objects within their environment and detecting object movement. Lesions along the dorsal stream can lead to akinetopsia, neglect, hemineglect, optic ataxia, and simultanagnosia.

Akinetopsia refers to the specific inability to discriminate visual motion. This condition has been likened to the perceptions evoked by stroboscopic lights in a discotheque. The subject with akinetopsia can see isolated snapshots but not the movement trajectory. This condition has also been reproduced in monkeys upon lesioning of the MT area in the dorsal path.

Visual *hemineglect* is described as an attentional disorder and is associated with lesions in the parieto-occipital junction. Hemineglect is defined as the inability to attend to a visual hemifield contralateral to the side of the lesions. For example, a subject may eat from only the right half of the plate or may copy only one half of a drawing. The condition is rather curious: the subjects are *not* blind in one hemifield, as demonstrated by the fact that subjects can be made to attend and identify objects in the affected hemifield. Furthermore, and particularly intriguingly, some hemineglect patients also fail in tasks that involve retrieving information from visual memories in a location-specific manner. In a famous experiment, an Italian subject with left-sided hemineglect was asked to imagine standing in the Piazza del Duomo in Milan, facing the famous cathedral, and report what he could recall from this scene. The subject typically omitted to mention places or streets on the left side from that vantage viewpoint.

Simultanagnosia is the inability to see more than one or two objects in a scene. Sometimes subjects are only able to detect small parts of objects. Subjects with simultanagnosia are not able to interpret a visual scene. The impairment is so debilitating that these subjects are often described as being functionally blind despite showing perfect acuity for the object that they are attending to at any given time.

All of these conditions are extremely infrequent in the population. We can argue that in all of these conditions, object shape recognition remains intact. Because of the motion discrimination deficits, and the spatial aspects of neglect, the dorsal visual cortex is described as the *where* pathway. An alternative, but not necessarily mutually exclusive description, refers to the dorsal visual cortex as the *action* pathway. Melvyn Goodale and David Milner described an unusual patient with a lesion primarily restricted to the temporal lobe. This subject had severe impairment in object shape recognition, as we will describe in the next section. However, despite her inability to recognize objects, the subject showed a rather remarkable ability to interact with many objects. For example, she showed an appropriate reach response toward objects that she could not describe. She also showed correct behavioral performance in visuomotor tasks. Goodale and Milner proposed that the dorsal pathway is particularly engaged in "vision for action," the immediate use of visual information to carry out specific visually guided behaviors. In contrast with this action mode, they proposed that awareness about an object requires activity in the ventral stream and the temporal lobe in particular.

4.7 The Inferior Temporal Cortex Is Critical for Visual Object Recognition in Monkeys

The confusions around Klüver-Bucy syndrome illustrate the challenges in interpreting the consequences of large cortical lesions. Making more precise lesions restricted to the inferior temporal cortex (ITC) has shown that bilateral ITC removal leads to impairment in learning visual discriminations as well as deficits in retaining information about visual discriminations that were learned before the lesions. In typical experiments, monkeys have to learn to discriminate between different visual shapes to obtain a reward. Animals with lesions in ITC fail in this task, but they can still perform other visual tasks such as learning which one of two visual locations is associated with reward.

The severity of the deficit is typically correlated with task difficulty. Monkeys can still perform "easy" visual discrimination tasks after bilateral ITC lesions. Deficits apply to objects, visual patterns, object size, color, and other properties. Deficits in recognizing forms defined by motion or luminance have also been described after ITC lesions. The behavioral deficits are restricted to the visual domain and do not affect discrimination based on tactile, olfactory, or auditory inputs. None of the "psychic blindness" or other social effects described originally by Klüver and Bucy were apparent after bilateral ITC lesions, further emphasizing the importance of spatially restricted lesions to adequately interpret the behavioral deficits. These visual shape recognition deficits are long lasting.

Scrutinizing the anatomical pathways described in Figure 1.5, we observe that there are many ways for information to travel from one point to another in the visual cortex. Information could be flexibly routed throughout the visual circuitry, depending on the nature of the task at hand. In the absence of ITC, certain "easy" tasks could be solved by routing information from early visual cortical areas onto decision and motor centers. Other, more "complex" tasks may necessitate the type of computations that take place in higher areas like the ITC.

In the same way that Klüver-Bucy syndrome could be fractionated by more circumscribed lesions, it is quite likely that future, even more specific, lesions within ITC will further fractionate the object recognition deficits prevalent after bilateral ITC ablation. Indeed, hints of this type of specificity are apparent in recent elegant work combining pharmacology, optogenetic manipulation, neural recordings, and behavior in monkeys. Investigators focused on an area of the ITC with an abundance of neurons that respond preferentially to faces compared to other objects (a theme that we will return to when we examine the neurophysiological properties of ITC neurons in Section 6.2). To the extent that the activity of those neurons is instrumental in tasks that depend on understanding face shapes, the authors hypothesized that inhibiting local regions would disrupt behavioral performance in suitable recognition tasks. To evaluate this hypothesis, they trained monkeys in a gender discrimination task based on face images. Once the animals were trained, the authors inactivated small local regions of the ITC. This inactivation was performed using either optogenetic manipulation or pharmacological intervention. Suppressing local neural activity led to an impairment in gender discrimination performance in the monkeys. These behavioral effects were reversible: performance returned to normal levels after the optogenetic or pharmacological silencing was turned off. The effects were also specific: inactivation of other brain regions did not lead to such behavioral impairments. In sum, lesion studies point to an essential function of the ITC in the ability to discriminate different shapes visually. Such studies played an important role in guiding the neurophysiological investigation of the properties of ITC neurons during visual recognition (Section 6.2).

4.8   Lesions Leading to Shape Recognition Deficits in Humans

Due to experimental challenges, much less is understood about the consequences of lesions to the human ventral visual cortex. Along the ventral visual stream, lesions around area V4 lead to *achromatopsia*, a specific inability to recognize colors. Note that this condition is distinct and dissociable from the type of retinal color blindness discussed in Section 2.5, which is associated with a lack of one or more types of cones.

Lesions in higher areas of the temporal lobe can lead to a variety of intriguing forms of *agnosias* (Agnosia means "lack of knowledge" in Greek). Figures 4.4–4.6 illustrate the type of behavioral deficits encountered in one type of visual agnosia in three different tasks. These figures illustrate the behavior of a 25-year-old patient who was

Figure 4.4 A patient with visual form agnosia who struggles to draw shapes. The patient was asked to draw (**A**) His name; (**B**) Letters W, V, L, X, and A; (**C**) Numbers 1 through 11; (**D**) a circle, square, and triangle; (**E**) A man. Reproduced from Benson 1969

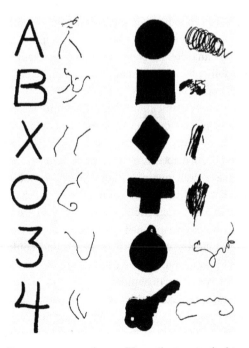

Figure 4.5 The same patient cannot copy shapes. The patient was asked to copy the letters and numbers in column 1 and the shapes in column 3. Reproduced from Benson 1969

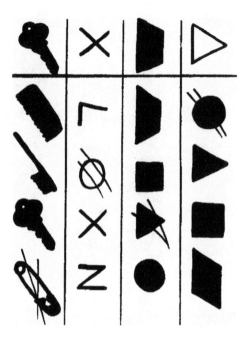

Figure 4.6 The same patient fails to perform a visual shape-matching task. The patient was asked to indicate which of the objects matched the one on top in each column. Reproduced from Benson 1969

examined seven months after accidental carbon monoxide poisoning. The patient was able to navigate the hospital where he was admitted, he could follow moving objects, and he could name colors. There were no abnormalities in the retinae. His visual fields – that is, his ability to detect flashes of light in different locations with respect to fixation – were mostly normal.

Although those elementary visual functions were intact, the patient was unable to name objects placed in front of him. He could still name objects by using tactile, olfactory, or auditory cues, suggesting that the deficit was not associated with an inability to produce speech or to retrieve semantic information about objects. He was unable to make drawings of specific shapes, including writing his name or drawing a man (Figure 4.4). The inability to draw specific shapes upon request could potentially be ascribed to a specific deficit in retrieving visual memories. However, the patient was also unable to copy shapes using templates presented in front of him (Figure 4.5). The patient could clearly understand language and could also execute motor commands. One may still argue that the tasks in Figures 4.4 and 4.5 rely on the ability to draw, and people may have different abilities to draw. However, the same patient was able to make better drawings, and certainly to write his name, before the accident. Furthermore, the patient also struggled in a visual shape-matching task that did not require any drawing (Figure 4.6).

As noted earlier, Figures 4.4–4.6 describe a single case study. Not all subjects with agnosias have the same deficits. For example, some patients can do an excellent job in the copying task (Figure 4.5), but not in the drawing-from-memory task (Figure 4.4). It is not clear whether this type of deficit should be described as a visual impairment or, rather, a language deficiency, a visual imagery challenge, or a difficulty in retrieving shapes from memory. The type of generalized deficit with shapes combined with normal visual field and adequate language and memory function in other sensory modalities, as illustrated by the patient in Figures 4.4–4.6, is rare but seems to suggest a bona fide visual impairment.

These types of studies often involve single subjects or a handful of subjects, and the lesions are necessarily not well circumscribed. Shape-recognition agnosias have been subdivided into multiple groups depending on whether they are thought to be mostly visual, whether the deficits also involve language, and whether the deficits affect object manipulation or recognition through other sensory modalities. One variant is called *associate visual agnosia*. This label is assigned to cases where copying a drawing and matching complex shapes remain intact, but drawing from memory and object identification are significantly impaired. As mentioned before, in many of these studies, it is not entirely clear that the deficits are strictly associated with the visual recognition machinery. Patients may show deficits in naming the stimuli, describing them, using them, drawing them from memory – all tasks that may depend on or relate to language abilities – but not necessarily matching two similar objects based on visual appearance or copying them. Another variant is called *aperceptive visual agnosia*. These subjects cannot name, copy, or match simple shapes. Because they cannot copy or match shapes, these cases may be closer to visual recognition challenges, such as the specific patient considered in Figures 4.4–4.6.

Importantly, in many of these visual agnosia cases, basic visual function remains intact. Visual acuity, the ability to recognize colors, the ability to detect motion, and other visual functions do not seem to be affected. This double dissociation between "basic" visual functions and "higher-level" visual abilities is consistent with the idea of a hierarchy of computations that progressively extracts more complex features from an image – from early image processing in the retina, LGN, and primary visual cortex all the way to structured shape information in the inferior temporal cortex. Indeed, the visual agnosias are typically associated with bilateral damage to visual areas beyond area V1, typically including the inferior temporal cortex. As noted in the previous section, it is likely that many of these basic visual functions can be implemented via connections in Figure 1.5 that bypass ITC.

Would subjects with visual agnosia struggle with the drawing and shape-matching tasks for *any* type of object? How specific are the agnosias? Intriguingly, several studies have reported cases of category-specific agnosias. For example, some studies report a more significant deficit in recognizing "living things." Other studies describe an inability to recognize animals, tools, words, or landmarks. One study reported a patient with an inability to name fruits or vegetables presented through line drawings or photographs. The literature on human lesion studies relating to visual symptoms points to remarkable and sometimes highly specific deficits in visual shape recognition.

One specific form of agnosia has received particular attention in the literature. *Prosopagnosia* (*proso* is Greek for face) refers to the inability to visually recognize faces with intact ability to identify other objects and shapes. Face agnosia is also very rare and typically occurs after brain damage caused by strokes in the right posterior cerebral artery. Some studies have also described a congenital form of prosopagnosia. The fusiform and lingual gyri are typically affected. Oliver Sacks emphasized the extreme nature of prosopagnosia in his book *The Man Who Mistook His Wife for a Hat*. Prosopagnosic subjects are often able to recognize people based on their voices, clothes, gait, and other characteristics but not from photographs of the face. The extent to which the effects should be described as face specific has been debated extensively. Some authors argue that the impairment in face recognition can be better understood as a general difficulty in identifying exemplars from a class with many similar stimuli and the degree of expertise with those stimuli.

4.9   Invasive Electrical Stimulation of the Human Brain

Lesions are not the only way to study the causal function of a given brain area. We switch gears now to consider another way of interfering with brain function: injection of electrical currents. Wilder Penfield was one of the key figures in the invasive study of the human brain through his work with epilepsy patients. As a neurosurgeon, he realized that he had direct access to the inner workings of the human brain through his neurosurgical approach to epilepsy. He worked extensively with patients suffering from pharmacologically resilient epilepsy. In these patients, seizures cannot be stopped by current methods of pharmacological intervention. In these cases, one of the best approaches to eliminate seizures is to remove the epileptogenic focus – that is, the part of the brain where seizures originate. In order to perform this type of resection, the neurosurgeon has to be able to localize the epileptogenic focus and also functionally map the area to ensure that there will not be any other adverse cognitive symptoms as a consequence of the procedure. Guided by these clinical needs, neurosurgeons invasively implant multiple electrodes in these patients; the patients stay in the hospital for about one week, with their electrodes in place in order to accumulate sufficient data. During this week, it is possible to interrogate human brain function with a much better signal-to-noise ratio, much better spatial resolution, and much better temporal resolution than any other method to study human brain activity from the outside.

Because the epileptogenic focus is resected in most of these patients, it is also possible to study the behavioral consequences of removing a part of the brain. One of Penfield's seminal studies described the role of the medial temporal lobe in memory consolidation in patients that underwent bilateral removal of the hippocampus and surrounding areas. Removal of the hippocampus on both hemispheres leads to severe problems in memory consolidation: the patient can see and visually interpret the scene normally, can hold a normal conversation, can reason, and perform a variety of cognitive tasks. In fact, after talking with such a patient for a few minutes, it would be hard to detect anything out of the ordinary. Even though the hippocampus appears at the pinnacle of the anatomical diagram of the visual system in Figure 1.5, all the evidence to date suggests that the hippocampus is not a visual area. The distinct characteristics of patients with bilateral excisions of the hippocampus are only manifested when considering the memory system. If you were to talk to the same patient the next day, the patient would have no recollection of what had happened during your first meeting. Because of those studies, only unilateral resections are performed nowadays.

Penfield was also one of the pioneers in performing neurophysiological recordings from intracranial electrodes in the human brain. Furthermore, he also extensively studied the behavioral effects triggered by electrical stimulation through subdural electrodes while the subjects were awake and readily reported their percepts. Electrical stimulation is a standard procedure that is used routinely in hospitals throughout the world. Because there are no pain receptors in the brain, this is not a painful procedure, and subjects can be awake during brain surgery, which often turns out to be quite useful from a clinical standpoint. It is quite important in these cases to work with subjects who are awake to be able to map cognitive function before resection. In particular, neurologists and neurosurgeons are concerned about language functions, which often reside close to epileptogenic areas. The goal is to treat epileptic seizures without affecting any other cognitive computation. One of the most famous discoveries from Penfield based on these electrical stimulation studies is the *cortical homunculus*, a mapping of the human body in the motor and somatosensory areas around the precentral gyrus.

Upon stimulating a given location, he asked the subjects to report their sensations verbally. Penfield would identify the stimulation locations by numbers. For example, the first time he stimulated electrode 5, the patient did not reply. Upon a second stimulation pulse in the same location, the patient said, "Something." The fourth time, he reported hearing, "People's voices talking." Penfield switched to electrode 7. The first pulse in electrode 7 elicited the following response: "Like footsteps walking – on the radio." Upon the third stimulation pulse in electrode 7, the subject explained, "it was like being in a dance hall, like standing in the doorway – in a gymnasium – like at the Lenwood High School." Twenty minutes later, Penfield moved back to electrode 5, and the subject reported, "People's voices."

Some of the observations are transcribed here verbatim to illustrate the exciting opportunities in terms of the questions that we can ask by obtaining direct verbal reports from stimulating the human cortex. At the same time, the example illustrates how challenging it is to interpret the output of these fascinating but anecdotal reports. What exactly is being stimulated in these studies? How many neurons are activated? What type of neurons are activated? How reproducible are the effects over multiple repetitions? How does the answer to these questions, and the ensuring behavioral reports, depend on the parameters of stimulation like the pulse duration and intensity? How do the conclusions depend on the metrics used to assess the behavioral output? What does the subject feel during electrical stimulation? To what extent is the subjective report influenced by the environment (doctors, nurses, hospital)? How can we map these fascinating reports obtained via electrical stimulation to our understanding of the functions of the cortex? There is a rich experience lost in translation.

In some cases, electrodes are placed in parts of the visual cortex. Particularly when electrodes are placed in early occipital cortex, several investigators have demonstrated that it is possible to elicit perceptual light flashes denominated "phosphenes." An example of such an experiment is illustrated in Figure 4.7. Upon injecting currents, the subject was asked to report the shape and location of what he or she perceived. In most cases, the subject reported seeing approximately circular flashes of light; in a few cases, like electrode 9, the subject reported seeing elongated lines. We briefly alluded to neurons in the primary visual cortex (V1) showing tuning for lines of different orientations in Chapter 1, and we will discuss neuronal tuning preferences in more detail in Sections 5.4 and 5.5. Based on the idea that V1 neurons are excited by oriented bars, one may expect to see more lines in Figure 4.7. However, these coarse stimulation experiments probably activate an enormous number of neurons – probably encompassing many, if not all, orientations. Therefore, it is not too surprising that the main report does not show much feature specificity.

Interestingly, the perceptual experience triggered by stimulating the early visual cortex is consistent with our understanding of the topographic organization derived from lesion studies described earlier (Figure 4.3). This organization is also consistent with the neurophysiological recordings that we will discuss in Section 5.6. First, the location of phosphene experiences in the visual field depends on the exact area of stimulation. Those phosphenes are localized, which is consistent with the idea that multiple neurons with overlapping and constrained receptive field sizes are being activated. Second, injecting currents through nearby electrodes (e.g., electrodes 27, 31, 34, and 35 in Figure 4.7) triggers phosphene sensations in nearby locations in the visual field, as we would expect based on the topographical organization of the visual cortex. Third, the approximate size of the experienced phosphene increases as we move away from the fixation, which is consistent with the increased receptive field sizes as a function of eccentricity.

Following up on the seminal studies of Penfield, several other investigators used electrical stimulation in epilepsy patients to map function in the human cortex. For example, investigators have described multiple subjective experiences elicited after stimulation of the temporal lobe – including visual illusions, both elementary visual hallucinations (phosphenes), and complex visual hallucinations. In addition to visual illusions, electrical stimulation in the temporal lobe elicits a large number of other experiences – including fear, thirst, familiarity, the feeling of déjà vu, and memory reminiscences.

An elegant study by Murphey and colleagues further examined the relationship between electrical stimulation and neurophysiological recordings. They examined an area that responded to colors – more specifically, to the blue color, according to neural recordings. They subsequently used a psychophysical task to ask whether subjects could determine the effects of electrical stimulation. Subjects reported perceiving a blue hue upon electrical stimulation, which is consistent with what the authors predicted based on their neurophysiological findings.

Phosphenes, visual hallucinations, and perception of color are examples of a novel perceptual sensation elicited by the injection of current in the absence of concomitant visual stimulation. Many other studies have focused on evaluating the effects of stimulation over a concomitant visual stimulus. In such cases, results show that

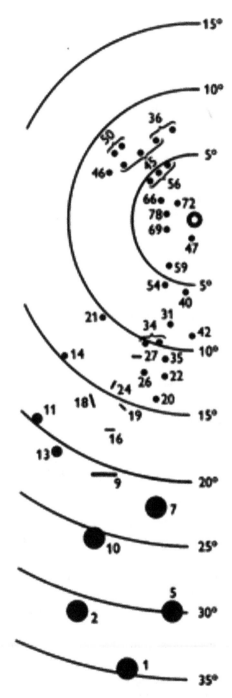

Figure 4.7 Creating visual percepts by injecting currents into the visual cortex. Position of phosphenes (light flash sensation) in the visual field elicited by electrical stimulation in the human occipital cortex. The center circle indicates the fovea, and the numbers identify the electrodes through which electrical stimulation pulses were delivered. The symbols coarsely denote the size and shape of the elicited phosphenes. Reproduced from Brindley and Lewin 1968

electrical stimulation typically interferes with the current percept. For example, several studies have shown that applying electrical stimulation through electrodes near the fusiform gyrus distorts or impairs the ability to perceive faces.

4.10   Electrical Stimulation in the Primate Visual Cortex

While the possibility of electrically stimulating the human cortex is quite exciting, a lot of the observations have been fascinating, yet mostly anecdotal, due to the difficulties inherent to a low number of trials and large electrodes with coarse mapping to neuronal responses. Many investigators have used electrical stimulation through microelectrodes in the macaque monkey visual cortex. The type of microelectrodes used in animal studies is smaller (about 50 microns in diameter) than the ones used in humans (about 2 millimeters in diameter; only a handful of cases have used microelectrodes for stimulation in the human brain). Thus, the number of neurons activated via electrical stimulation in animal studies, though still very large, is smaller than the number of neurons excited in human studies.

One of the seminal studies in monkeys involved electrical stimulation of the MT area – which we introduced in Section 4.2, as an area critical for motion discrimination based on physical lesions in monkeys, and in Section 4.6, as the likely area responsible for impaired motion perception in akinetopsia. Area MT receives direct input from area V1 (and also inputs from other areas like V2), coming from the magnocellular layers in the LGN. Neurons in area MT are selective for motion direction within the receptive field; for example, a neuron may respond strongly to a bar moving to the left and not to a bar moving to the right (Figure 4.8A).

A typical stimulus used to drive MT neurons is a display consisting of many dots moving in random directions (Figure 4.8B). A given percentage of the dots is set to move coherently in one direction. Depending on the percentage of coherent motion, the stimulus can elicit a strong motion percept. A typical sigmoid psychometric curve can be plotted (both for humans as well as for monkeys), showing the proportion of trials in which the subject reports that the dots are moving in one direction as a function of the degree of coherence of the dots in the display. If 100 percent of the dots move coherently in one direction, subjects report movement in that direction in all the trials. If 0 percent of the dots move coherently (all dots are moving randomly), then subjects report random movement in one direction or the other (Figure 4.8C).

William Newsome's team at Stanford trained monkeys to report their perceived direction of motion while recording the activity of neurons in area MT. Recording from neurons in area MT, the investigators started the experiment by mapping a neuron's preferred direction of motion. In a typical experiment, a fixation spot comes up, the monkey is required to fixate, the visual stimulus is displayed for one second, the stimulus disappears, and the monkey needs to indicate the direction in which the dots were moving in a two-alternative forced-choice paradigm (e.g., by making a saccade to one of two possible targets). The direction of motion in each experiment is aligned to

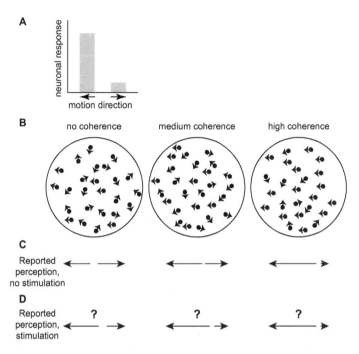

Figure 4.8 Schematic representation of an electrical stimulation experiment in area MT of the macaque monkey. (**A**) Schematic responses of a neuron that responds selectively to leftward motion. (**B**) Random dot stimuli with no coherence (left), high leftward motion coherence (right), and medium leftward motion coherence (center). (**C**) Reported perception in the absence of electrical stimulation. (**D**) Hypothesized perceptual reports when stimulating neurons around the one shown in part A. Based on the work of Salzman et al. 1990

the neuron's preferred direction so that the dots move either in the preferred direction or in the anti-preferred direction.

Based on the neurophysiological recordings, the investigators asked whether electrical stimulation through the same microwire would bias the monkey's visually evoked behavior in the motion discrimination task and whether this bias would be consistent with the neurophysiological preferences. To answer this question, they applied very brief electrical pulses (10 microamperes biphasic square pulses with 200 hertz frequency and 0.2 millisecond duration). Electrical stimulation was applied in the center of regions where there was a cluster of neurons with similar motion preferences within ~150 micrometers. As in other parts of the neocortex, there is a topographical organization of neuronal preferences in area MT; that is, nearby neurons in MT typically have similar motion direction preferences. This topography is presumably important in terms of understanding the effects of electrical stimulation because activating many local neurons with similar tuning properties may lead to stronger behavioral effects than activating neurons that are spatially organized in a completely random fashion with respect to their tuning properties. Monkeys were rewarded on correct responses. The results of such experiments are illustrated

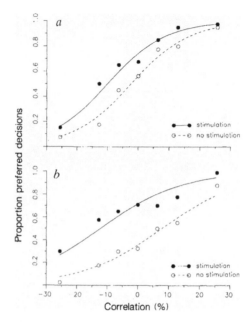

Figure 4.9 Results of an electrical stimulation experiment in area MT of the macaque monkey. The plots show the behavioral psychometric function in discriminating the neuron's preferred motion direction in the presence (filled circles) or absence (empty circles) of electrical stimulation (see text for details). Reproduced from Salzmann et al. 1990

in Figure 4.9. In the absence of microstimulation (empty circles), monkeys showed the typical approximately sigmoid psychometric curve. Monkeys reported the preferred direction of motion in >80 percent of the trials when the dots had 30 percent correlation in the preferred direction, and they reported the anti-preferred direction of motion in >80 percent of the trials when the dots had 30 percent correlation in the anti-preferred direction. In the 0 percent correlation condition, monkeys reported one or the other direction with close to 50 percent performance. Remarkably, upon applying electrical stimulation (filled circles), there was a shift of the psychometric curve. Monkeys reported movement in the preferred direction more often (~15 percent more often) than in the absence of electrical stimulation. This causal increase due to electrical stimulation is a significant finding because it provided compelling evidence that the neurophysiological recordings revealed a signal that could translate into behavioral decisions upon electrical stimulation of the relevant neuronal circuits.

In a similar experiment, Arash Afraz and colleagues stimulated the macaque inferior temporal cortex during a visual recognition task. The lesion studies indicate that the ITC area is important for visual shape recognition (Section 4.7). The experiment followed the structure of the Newsome study in Figures 4.8 and 4.9. Because neurons in ITC are more interested in complex visual shapes rather than motion direction, the investigators compared responses to faces against responses to other shapes. The choice of faces as one of the two stimuli may have been an important methodological point. First, it may be easier to train monkeys to recognize two-dimensional renderings of faces compared to other shapes.

Second, there may be a larger cluster of neurons responding to similar faces compared to other shapes. The investigators presented faces and other non-face images embedded in noise. The noise level changed from 100 percent (pure noise stimulus) to 20 percent; noise in this experiment plays a similar role to coherence in the Newsome experiments.

As we will discuss in Section 6.2, ITC neurons show visually selective responses; the investigators focused on sites that revealed consistent enhanced responses to faces within an area of approximately ±150 micrometers. The investigators applied electrical stimulation in those regions and evaluated the extent to which the monkeys reported seeing faces or not for stimuli with different levels of noise. On average, the investigators were able to elicit a ~10 percent change in the monkey's behavior, increasing the number of times that the monkeys reported seeing faces (even in cases where information about faces was minimal due to the noise). Furthermore, the behavioral effects elicited by electrical stimulation were correlated with the degree of selectivity of the neurons: stimulation of more selective sites led to stronger behavioral biases.

In sum, across different areas within the visual cortex, injecting currents into many neurons that show selectivity for specific stimulus features can bias a monkey's responses toward reporting seeing those specific features. Even in cases where the stimulus consists of random noise, it is possible to bias behavior in a way that can be predicted by the neurophysiological responses. These experiments provide a strong causal link between specific and selective neural activity and visual perception. Additionally, these experiments constitute an intriguing form of injecting specific visual thoughts into the brain.

4.11   Summary

- Inactivating areas of the visual cortex leads to specific visual deficits ranging from localized *scotomas* (primary visual cortex) all the way to impairment in recognition of complex shapes (inferior temporal cortex).
- Without the primary visual cortex, subjects are essentially blind. Very limited and basic visual capabilities remain in the absence of the primary visual cortex.
- Lesion studies have delineated two main processing streams: (1) a *dorsal/where/ action path* that is particularly relevant to detecting motion, interpreting stimulus locations, and spatially acting on visual stimuli and (2) a *ventral/what path* that is more concerned with discriminating colors and shapes.
- Although brain lesions in humans are difficult to fully interpret due to their rarity and accidental nature, they have revealed a plethora of fascinating observations mapping visual deficits to localized circuits in the brain.
- Several cases have been reported of *agnosias* where subjects have specific visual discrimination challenges while maintaining otherwise normal vision.
- Electrical stimulation in the early human visual cortex leads to the perception of *phosphenes*. The location and size of those phosphenes are consistent with our understanding of the topographical organization of the early visual cortex.

- Stimulating other parts of the human visual cortex during concomitant presentation of a visual stimulus can lead to specific perceptual disruption.
- Microstimulation experiments in monkeys have shown that it is possible to bias the animal's behavior in a way that is consistent with predictions based on the neurophysiological responses of neurons in the stimulated area.

Further Reading

See http://bit.ly/3abKBpP for more references.
- Boyden, E. S.; Zhang, F.; Bamberg, E.; Nagel, G.; and Deisseroth, K. (2005). Millisecond-timescale, genetically targeted optical control of neural activity. *Nature Neuroscience* 8: 1263–1268.
- Penfield, W. (1958). Some mechanisms of consciousness discovered during electrical stimulation of the brain. *Proceedings of the National Academy of Sciences of the United States of America* 44: 51–66.
- Sacks, O. (1995). *An anthropologist on Mars*. New York: Alfred A. Knopf.
- Sperry, R. (1982). Some effects of disconnecting the cerebral hemispheres. *Science* 217: 1223–1226.
- Ungerleider, L.; and Mishkin, M. (1982). Two cortical visual systems. In *Analysis of Visual Behavior*, ed. D. Ingle, M. Goodale, and R. Mansfield. Cambridge: MIT Press.

5 Adventures into *Terra Incognita*
Probing the Neural Circuits along the Ventral Visual Stream

Supplementary content at http://bit.ly/2TpAg3w

Around the 1950s, a wealth of behavioral experiments had characterized many phenomenological aspects of visual perception that begged for a mechanistic explanation (Chapter 3). Lesion studies had provided a compelling case that damage to circumscribed brain regions led to specific visual processing deficits (Chapter 4). These lesion studies pointed to specific brain areas to investigate visual processing, especially the primary visual cortex in the back of the brain. In addition, the successful use of microelectrode electrical recordings had led to direct insights about the function of neurons within the retinal circuitry (Chapter 2). The time was ripe to open the black box of the brain and begin to think about how vision emerges from the spiking activity of neurons in the cortex.

Retinal ganglion cells project to the lateral geniculate nucleus (LGN) in the thalamus, and the principal output projection from the LGN conveys visual information to primary visual cortex (V1; see Section 2.10), the first stage of cortical processing for visual information. From V1, information is propagated into a large number of visual cortical areas that are responsible for transforming a pixel-like representation of sensory information into rich and complex visual percepts (Chapter 1, Figure 1.5). The exploration and computational modeling of the visual cortex is an ongoing adventure, where courageous conquistadors dare to peek inside the inner workings of the most complex system ever examined by science. Fundamental structural and functional principles of computation are beginning to emerge out of the sometimes seemingly enigmatic *terra incognita* of visual cortex. These basic principles are introduced in this chapter and the next one and form the basis of the computational models of vision discussed in Chapters 7–9.

5.1 About the Neocortex

The neocortex is the outer structure of the neural tissue in the brain and is thought to be responsible for cognition. The prefix "neo" stands for new, which should be understood in evolutionary time scales and contrasts with the older paleocortex, which includes the olfactory system and the hippocampus. The human neocortex is about 2–4 millimeters thick, comprises about 40 percent of the brain mass, and contains on the order of 10^{10} neurons. The cortex shows a large number of folds such that it can fit about 2,600 square centimeters, into the size of the brain. Because of its extensive surface and relatively shallow depth, many investigators think of neocortex as a quasi-two-dimensional structure. The most prominent fold is the longitudinal fissure separating the right and left hemispheres. The human neocortex has more folds than that of many other mammals; for example, the mouse cortex appears relatively smooth in comparison to the human cortex. Mechanical tension, combined with the strong constraint to save wiring and space, is likely to have been an important factor in determining the shape and folds of cortex throughout evolution.

To a pretty reasonable first-order approximation, *cortex is cortex*: staining of cortical tissue appears at a gross level to be very similar across different parts of the brain. Furthermore, cortical staining also appears quite similar across different species. It takes a connoisseur to distinguish a section of mouse cortical tissue from human cortical tissue. This similarity is perhaps remarkable to some people. Egocentric or anthropomorphic considerations might lead some people to think that the human cortex might be substantially different; after all, mice do not play chess, nor do they read Shakespeare. The coarse similarities in the basic cortical structure suggest that approximately the same pieces of hardware can be combined in different and exciting ways to account for the cognitive capacities of different species. As a rough analogy, similar transistors can be used to build an electronic calculator, a smartphone, and a laptop.

Upon further scrutiny, specialists can distinguish between different species by examining cortical tissue. Furthermore, it is also possible to demarcate different brain regions by examining cortex. The German neuroanatomist Korbinian Brodmann (1868–1918) devised a parcellation of the human and monkey brains – as well as many other species – based on morphological cytoarchitectonic criteria. Many parts of the neocortex are still referred to by their Brodmann area number (Figure 5.1). For example, the primary visual cortex corresponds to Brodmann area 17. Neurophysiological and lesion studies have shown that several of the structural subdivisions proposed by Brodmann, as well as subsequent neuroanatomical work, correlate with functional specialization. Attempts to

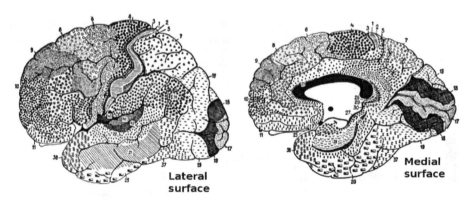

Figure 5.1 The cortex can be subdivided into multiple brain areas based on cytoarchitectonic criteria. Brodmann subdivided the neocortex into multiple areas based on cytoarchitectonic criteria. The primary visual cortex corresponds to Brodmann area 17 in this diagram. From Wikipedia

separate cortical regions, particularly combined with attempts to attach cognitive functions to different regions, have a long and rich history that continues to current days.

5.2   Connectivity to and from the Primary Visual Cortex

The primary visual cortex is the first stage where information from the two eyes converges onto individual neurons. Each hemisphere in V1 represents the contralateral visual field. The part of the retina that is closer to the nose is called *nasal*, while the other half of the retina is called *temporal*. The left visual hemifield (left of the center of gaze) is represented by the nasal part of the retina on the left eye and by the temporal part of the retina on the right eye. Information from the nasal retina on the left eye will cross the brain and end up represented in the right hemisphere in the primary visual cortex. Information from the temporal retina on the right eye will turn at the *optic chiasm* and also end up represented in the right hemisphere in the primary visual cortex.

Like most other aspects of neuroanatomy, the first drawings of the primary visual cortex were made by Santiago Ramón y Cajal, who was introduced in Chapter 2. The basic architecture of the primary visual cortex turned out to be approximately similar to that of other parts of the visual neocortex. The neocortical sheet is characterized by six layers that can be distinguished with Nissl staining, a technique used to sparsely introduce a dye into many neurons in a given area for visualization. Sparse staining is important here because the density of neurons in the cortex is so large that it would be hard to see much upon staining all neurons using standard microscopy. The six layers are characterized by a stereotypical connectivity pattern that is often referred to as the *canonical cortical microcircuit*. With some exceptions – it is biology after all – this canonical connectivity pattern is shared across different visual areas and also across different sensory modalities.

Connections among different areas of cortex are often described as "bottom-up," "top-down," or "horizontal" connections, a nomenclature that is also used to describe connectivity in artificial neural network architectures (Section 7.3, Figure 7.4). A given individual neuron will only project in a bottom-up manner, or horizontally, or provide top-down signals, but not all of these. These different types of connections are defined based on the specific layer of the pre- and postsynaptic neurons. The connections between and within visual cortical areas follow a stereotypical pattern that has been used to define what area is "upstream" or "downstream" and, therefore, which connections are bottom-up or top-down (Figure 5.2). Bottom-up connections arrive at layer 4 – the LGN projects to pyramidal neurons in layer 4 in primary visual cortex. Layer 1 is the most superficial and contains mostly dendrites and few neuronal cell bodies; the neuron cell bodies for those dendritic arbors are mostly located in layers 2 and 3. Top-down connections from other visual cortical areas typically end in the deep layers 5 and 6 and also, to a lesser degree, in layers 2 and 3. After the LGN input (or input from a "lower area") arrives onto layer 4, information flows from layer 4 to layers 2/3 and then on to layer 5 and layer 6. Information from layer 6 provides back projections to the LGN (or to a "lower" visual area) and is also fed back to layer 4.

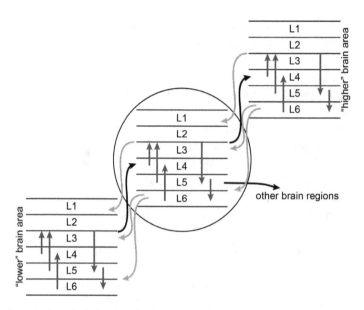

Figure 5.2 Canonical cortical circuits. Cortical connectivity across the visual cortex follows stereotypical connectivity patterns illustrated here. L1 through L6 refer to the six cortical layers. "Bottom-up" connectivity between areas is shown in black, "Top-down" connectivity between areas is shown in light gray, and connections within an area are shown in medium gray.

An important aspect of connectivity in the visual cortex is that connections between areas are almost invariably reciprocal. If area A provides bottom-up input into area B, area B provides top-down inputs to area A. Furthermore, these reciprocal connections are quantitatively comparable: the number of projections from A to B and from B to A are approximately similar.

By scrutinizing the connectivity patterns across layers in multiple brain areas, investigators have come up with an approximate map of the anatomical paths through which different visual areas communicate with each other (Chapter 1, Figure 1.5). Based on the separation of connections into bottom-up and top-down, it is possible to arrange the multiple different visual brain areas into an approximately hierarchical structure. The diagram in Figure 1.5 provides a semi-hierarchical description of the anatomical flow of information in the visual system.

The more we study connectivity in visual cortex, the more we realize that this stereotypical pattern is full of exceptions. There are differences across species, differences between visual cortex and motor cortex, and even differences between different visual cortical areas. To make matters more complicated, these layers can, in turn, be subdivided into sublayer structures, and the connectivity patterns may be different depending on the types of neurons being considered. For example, we started this section by stating that the primary visual cortex is *approximately* similar to other visual cortical areas. Perhaps because of its unique position in receiving more direct thalamic inputs than all other visual areas, V1 is actually thicker, layer 4 has different numbers of sublayers, and the pattern of inputs and outputs is also distinct from other visual areas.

In addition to the variations in the canonical microcircuit across cortical areas and across species, the hierarchical nature of visual cortex should not be interpreted too strictly. For example, numerous "bypass" connections send information from area A to area C without going through the intermediate area B (e.g., information flows from V1 to V2 to V4, but there are also direct connections from V1 to V4). Despite the subdivisions, exceptions, and refinements, the basic principles of connectivity in the visual cortex have played an important role in imposing method to the apparent madness and have inspired the development of the best computational models that we have today (Chapters 7 and 8).

A word of caution about nomenclature is pertinent, particularly for computer scientists used to thinking about neural networks. Biologists talk about different cortical *areas* – such as V1, V2, and V4. Each of these areas has six *layers*, as described earlier. In Chapters 7 and 8, we will discuss computational models of visual processing, which often refer to computational steps instantiated in different "layers." Those computational layers should not be confounded with the cortical layers described here. A layer in a neural network is not necessarily directly linked to one of the six layers in the neocortex in any given brain area. The exact mapping between computational layers and brain areas is not always well defined by modelers. In fact, in many cases, people think about a layer in a neural network as potentially equivalent to a whole brain area in the cortex. We will come back to the question of making a commitment in the mapping between computational models and biological anatomy. For the moment, here we refer to layers in the biological sense discussed in the previous paragraph and in Figure 5.2. In addition to information flowing from one layer to another layer within a visual area and information flowing between brain areas, there are extensive *horizontal* connections whereby information flows *within* a layer. Some investigators use the term *recurrent* connections to refer both to horizontal and top-down connections, but it is conceptually clearer to keep different terms for these two distinct types of signal paths.

5.3 The Gold Standard to Examine Neural Function

Every problem has an appropriate scale of study: a Goldilocks scale, so to speak – not too coarse, not too fine. For example, it is particularly tedious and challenging to attempt to read the newspaper using a microscope (too fine a resolution). It is also extremely challenging to read a newspaper from a distance of 200 meters away (too coarse). A plethora of methods are available to study the brain, ranging from elucidating the three-dimensional structure of specific types of ion channels, all the way to indirectly measuring signals that show some degree of correlation with blood flow, averaged over coarse spatial scales.

In the case of neocortical circuits, this Goldilocks scale is the activity of individual neurons. Studying the three-dimensional structure of each protein inside a neuron is equivalent to trying to read the newspaper with a microscope – but it can be extremely useful for other questions such as understanding the kinetics and properties of ion channels in the neuronal membrane. Studying the average amount of blood flowing through half a cubic centimeter of cortex over several seconds is equivalent to attempting to extract ink tones from the newspaper from 200 meters away – but it can be useful for other questions such as differentiating general and coarse properties of a part of cortex.

In addition to this spatial scale, there is also a natural time scale to examine neuronal activity. Most neurons communicate with each other by sending electrical signals called action potentials lasting about two milliseconds. For most purposes, it is sufficient to study neuronal activity at the millisecond level. With a few exceptions (e.g., small differences in timing between signals arriving at the two ears), microsecond resolution time scales do not provide additional information. One day has 1,440 minutes, and, therefore, the analogy for studying brains at the microsecond instead of millisecond scale (a factor of 1,000) would be to reread the same newspaper every minute. At the other end of the spectrum, techniques that average activity over many seconds are too coarse to elucidate cortical computations. The analogy for studying brains at the scale of several seconds instead of milliseconds (a factor of 1,000) would be to average the newspaper over three years.

Studying the activity of neocortical circuits at the neuronal resolution at a scale of milliseconds is not trivial and requires inserting thin microelectrode probes into the areas of interest. Neuronal action potentials lead to changes in the electrical potential in the extracellular milieu. It is possible to amplify and measure this electrical potential in the extracellular space and measure the action potentials emitted by individual neurons. The methodology was established by Edgar Adrian (1889–1977), and we already introduced example measurements of single-neuron activity in the retina in Section 2.7.

5.4   Neurons in the Primary Visual Cortex Respond Selectively to Bars Shown at Specific Orientations

Human primary visual cortex consists of about 280 million neurons arranged in a 2-millimeter-thick sheet that encompasses a few square inches in surface. There are more papers examining the neurophysiology of the primary visual cortex than the rest of the visual cortex combined. Neurons in the primary visual cortex – as well as those in the retina and LGN (Section 2.7) and also neurons in other parts of visual cortex – show spatially restricted receptive fields; that is, they respond only to a specific part of the visual field (Figure 2.9). The ensemble of all the neurons tiles the entire visual field. On average, the receptive field size of neurons in the primary visual cortex is larger than the receptive field sizes in the retina and LGN, typically encompassing about 0.5 to 1 degree of visual angle. A typical neurophysiology experiment often starts by determining the receptive field location of the neuron under study. After determining the location of the receptive field, a battery of stimuli is used to probe the neuron's response preferences.

The initial and paradigm-shifting strides toward describing the neurophysiological responses in the primary visual cortex were introduced by Torsten Wiesel (b. 1924) and David Hubel (1926–2013). The history of visual neuroscience revolves around the history of visual stimuli. Before the Hubel-Wiesel era, investigators had examined the responses in the primary visual cortex using diffused light or the type of point sources that had successfully elicited activity in the retina and LGN. By a combination of inspiration, perspiration, and careful observation, Hubel and Wiesel realized that neurons in the primary visual cortex responded most strongly when a bar of a particular orientation was presented within the neuron's receptive field. The story of how this discovery came about is particularly fascinating and is recounted in David Hubel's Nobel Lecture. Hubel and Wiesel did not have particularly grandiose hypotheses about the function of neurons in the visual cortex before they embarked on these investigations but rather intuited that compelling principles would emerge by courageously placing electrodes in V1. After a particularly long day recording the activity of a V1 neuron, they were frustrated by how little the neuron seemed to care about the presence of a light or dark annulus inside the receptive field. In those days, they did not have computers to present stimuli; instead, they used slides inserted into a projector. Suddenly, their careful power of observation led them to realize that the neuron would show a burst of activity every time they inserted the slide into the projector. It was the edge of the slide moving in and out of the projector that triggered activation, much more than the content of the slide. Excited by this finding, they went on to discover that the orientation of an edge placed within the receptive field mattered for the neuron: specific orientations led to much larger activation than others.

A typical pattern of responses obtained from V1 recordings is illustrated in Figure 5.3. In this experiment, an oriented bar was moved within the receptive field of the neuron under study. The direction of movement was perpendicular to the bar's orientation. Different orientations elicited drastically distinct numbers of action potentials. While the number of action potentials (or spike count) is not the only variable that can be used to define the neuronal response, it provides a simple and adequate starting point to examine neuronal preferences. When the bar was approximately at a −45-degree angle (Figure 5.3D), the neuron emitted more spikes than for any other orientation. Moreover, the activity of this neuron was also dependent on the direction of motion. When the bar was moving toward the upper right, the neuron was vigorously active, whereas there was minimal activation in the opposite direction of motion.

Hubel and Wiesel went on to characterize the properties of V1 neurons in terms of their topography, orientation preference, ocular preference, color, direction of motion, and even how those properties arise during development. Their Nobel Prize–winning discovery inspired generations of neurophysiologists to examine neuronal responses throughout the visual cortex.

5.5   Complex Neurons Show Tolerance to Position Changes

In the example shown in Figure 5.3, the V1 neuron responds preferentially to a moving bar. Neurons in V1 also respond to flashes of static stimuli. When flashing a stimulus, how precise does the position of the oriented bar within the neuron's receptive field have to be to trigger a response? A distinction has been observed between two types of neurons in V1 based on how picky they are with respect to stimulus position within the

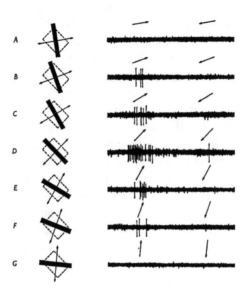

Figure 5.3 Example responses of a neuron in the monkey primary visual cortex. Physiological responses of a neuron in the primary visual cortex to bars of different orientations. In these examples, the bar was moved in a direction perpendicular to its orientation. The dashed lines on the left indicate the receptive field, the black rectangle is the oriented bar, and the arrows indicate the direction of motion. The neuronal response traces are shown on the right. Reproduced from Hubel and Wiesel 1968

receptive field: *simple* and *complex* V1 neurons. Complex neurons are less sensitive to the exact position of the bar within the receptive field. When using gratings containing multiple oriented bars at a given spatial frequency, complex neurons tolerate larger changes in the spatial frequency than simple cells. Simple and complex neurons are often distinguished by the ratio of the "DC" maintained response to their "AC" response elicited by a moving grating. Complex neurons show a small AC/DC ratio (typically <10), whereas simple neurons have a larger AC/DC ratio (typically >10). In other words, complex neurons show a higher degree of *tolerance* to the exact position of an oriented bar within the receptive field compared to a simple neuron whose response magnitude decreases when the bar is shifted away from the preferred position (Figure 5.4). This progression from a simple neuron to a complex neuron showing increased tolerance has inspired the development of hierarchical computational models of object recognition that concatenate operations reminiscent of simple and complex cells as a way of keeping selectivity while achieving tolerance to transformations in the stimulus (Section 8.5).

Some complex neurons also show "end-stopping," meaning that their optimum stimulus includes an end within the receptive field, as opposed to very long bars whose ending is outside of the receptive field. The end-stopping phenomenon can be understood as a form of contextual modulation where the patterns in the region surrounding the receptive field (in this case, whether the line continues or stops) influence the responses to the stimulus inside the receptive field. Such influences from

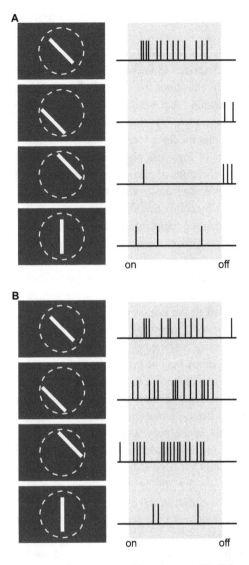

Figure 5.4 Complex neurons show tolerance to position changes. (A) Schematic diagram showing responses from a simple neuron that responds maximally to a −45-degree oriented line when it is positioned in the center of the receptive field (top) but not when the position is shifted (rows 2, 3) or when the orientation changes (bottom). (B) Schematic diagram showing responses of a complex neuron that shows tolerance to position changes.

outside the receptive field are not restricted to end-stopping. V1 neurons also show surround suppression, similar to the suppressive effects of light around the receptive field center for on-center retinal ganglion cells described in Section 2.8 (Figure 2.10). In sum, V1 neurons are particularly sensitive to spatial changes, detecting edges indicative of a discontinuity in the visual field, and some neurons also detecting where the edge stops.

5.6   Nearby Neurons Show Similar Properties

Neurons in the primary visual cortex are topographically organized, in a similar fashion to the situation described in the retina in Section 2.7. The V1 topography is inherited from the LGN: the connections from the LGN to the primary visual cortex are topographically organized, meaning that nearby neurons in the LGN map onto nearby neurons in the primary visual cortex. V1 neurons cover the visual field, with a much higher density of neurons covering the foveal region. These neurophysiological observations are consistent with the types of scotomas observed in cases of localized V1 lesions (Section 4.4) and also with the locations of phosphenes reported upon stimulation in V1 (Section 4.9).

Hubel and Wiesel discovered another aspect of the topographical arrangement of neurons in V1 by comparing the tuning preferences of different neurons recorded during the same electrode penetration. In addition to sharing properties with their two-dimensional neighbors along the cortical sheet, neurons also share similar response patterns with their neighbors in the third dimension representing cortical depth. Advancing the electrode in a direction approximately tangential to the cortical surface, different neurons along a penetration share similar orientation tuning preferences. This observation led to the notion of a *columnar structure*: neurons within a column have similar preferences; neurons in adjacent columns show a continuous variation in their orientation tuning preferences.

Such topography may be critical for saving wires by virtue of arranging neurons with similar properties that need to be connected near each other. In particular, interneurons that have short dendrites may require having their targets nearby. However, if we keep the neuron-to-neuron connectivity intact, we could, in principle, rearrange the geometry of the neurons in arbitrary ways while keeping the computations intact. Topography may thus be mostly dissociated from function. Therefore, the smooth map of tuning properties within V1 is probably not a requirement for V1 computations. In fact, recent work has shown that this level of organization may not be a universal property. The primary visual cortex in mice does not have such a precise topographical mapping of orientation preferences; the geometrical arrangement of tuning preferences is described as "salt-and-pepper."

Even if this topography is not strictly required for computational purposes, it may come in quite handy for investigators. For example, recording techniques with a reduced spatial resolution that average the activity of many neurons may depend strongly on topography (because average responses from completely randomly arranged neurons may yield nothing). For similar reasons, as discussed in Section 4.10, stimulation of many neurons via current injection may also be dependent on topography.

5.7   Quantitative Phenomenological Description of the Responses in the Primary Visual Cortex

Let $D(x,y)$ denote the responses of a neuron at position x, y. The receptive field structure $D(x,y)$ of orientation-tuned simple V1 neurons is often mathematically

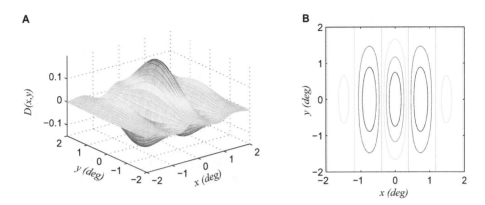

Figure 5.5 The spatial structure of receptive fields of V1 neurons is often described by a Gabor function (Equation (5.1)). (**A**) Illustration of a Gabor function. (**B**) Contour plot.

described by a *Gabor* function – that is, the product of an exponential and a cosine function:

$$D(x, y) = \frac{1}{2\pi\sigma_x\sigma_y} e^{\left[-\frac{x^2}{2\sigma_x^2} - \frac{y^2}{2\sigma_y^2}\right]} \cos(kx - \phi), \tag{5.1}$$

where σ_x and σ_y control the spatial spread of the receptive field, k controls the spatial frequency, and ϕ the phase. The Gabor function is characterized by an elongated excitatory region whose angle corresponds to the orientation preference of the V1 neuron, as well as a surrounding inhibitory region. An example illustration of a Gabor function is shown in Figure 5.5.

In addition to the spatial aspects of the receptive field, it is important to characterize the temporal dynamics of responses in V1. In most cases, the spatial and temporal aspects of the receptive fields in V1 can be considered to be approximately independent; that is, they can be separated without considering complex interactions between space and time. The temporal aspects of the receptive field can be fitted by the following phenomenological equation:

$$D(t) = \alpha e^{-\alpha t}[(\alpha t)^5/5! - (\alpha t)^7/7!] \tag{5.2}$$

for $\tau >= 0$ and 0 otherwise. This equation is a fancy way of fitting the rapid and transient increase in firing rate upon flashing a stimulus at time 0 (Figure 5.6). The parameter α controls the latency and width of the temporal receptive field.

5.8   A Simple Model of Orientation Selectivity in the Primary Visual Cortex

Equation (5.1) provides a phenomenological description of the receptive field structure. In a remarkable feat of intuition, Hubel and Wiesel proposed a simple and elegant biophysically plausible model of how orientation tuning could arise from

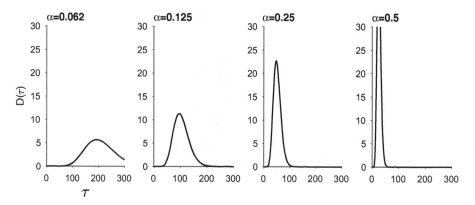

Figure 5.6 The temporal structure of receptive fields of V1 neurons. Equation (5.2) is shown for different values of the parameter α.

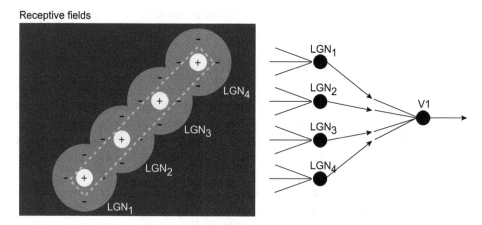

Figure 5.7 Building orientation tuning by combining circular center-surround neurons. Schematic diagram showing how multiple LGN neurons with a circular center-surround receptive field structure can be combined to give rise to a V1 simple neuron that shows orientation tuning when those receptive field centers are adequately aligned. Modified from Hubel and Wiesel 1962

the responses of neurons with LGN-type receptive fields (Figure 5.7). In their model, multiple LGN neurons with circularly symmetric center-surround receptive fields (Figure 2.10) arranged along a line project onto a V1 simple neuron. Orientation tuning is thus constructed in a bottom-up fashion by combining the inputs of the right set of LGN neurons.

Subsequent work gave rise to a plethora of other possible models, and there is still an ongoing debate about the extent to which the purely bottom-up Hubel-Wiesel model represents the only mechanism giving rise to orientation selectivity in area V1. Still, this simple and elegant interpretation of the origin of V1 receptive fields constitutes a remarkable example of how experimentalists can provide reasonable and profound models that account for their data. Furthermore, the basic ideas behind this model have been extended to explain the buildup of neuronal preferences for more complex shapes in other areas (Section 8.5).

In addition to orientation selectivity, there are many other properties of V1 neurons that are also arranged topographically including their spatial receptive fields, their ocular dominance (stronger responses to inputs coming from one or the other eye), their direction selectivity (stronger responses for specific directions of motion), and their retinal disparity (sensitivity to shifted positions between the right and left eyes used for stereopsis). It turns out that all of these other properties can also be mapped onto the specific arrangements of inputs from the LGN.

Extending their model for orientation selectivity in simple neurons by combining the output of LGN neurons (Figure 5.7), Hubel and Wiesel proposed that the responses of complex neurons could originate by the nonlinear combination of responses from multiple simple neurons with similar orientation preferences but slightly shifted receptive fields. These pioneering ideas of a linear filtering operation bringing about the responses of simple neurons in V1 followed up by a nonlinear pooling operation giving rise to complex neurons in V1 has played an influential role in inspiring computational models of visual processing (Section 8.5).

Figure 5.8 summarizes schematically how a V1 simple neuron would respond in a real-world image. This neuron has a receptive field in the upper right part of the visual field (black circle). Two fixations are shown in this figure. In the first fixation (**A1**), the image inside the receptive field is similar to the neuron's preferred orientation (**B**). After a nonlinear activation function (**C**), the neuron shows a strong response (**D1**). When the subject makes a small eye movement to the right, landing on fixation 2 (**A2**), the image inside the receptive field does not resemble the neuron's preferred features anymore, and the response is weak (**D2**).

5.9   Many Surprises Left in V1

Despite significant amounts of work investigating the neuronal properties in primary visual cortex, much remains to be explained. Multiple biases contribute to a partial view of V1 function. First, many of the recording procedures to date tend to focus on neurons that have higher firing rates and that are easier to pick up through extracellular recordings. Interneurons are smaller and harder to record from than the larger pyramidal cells. Additionally, there could be "shy" neurons that may be overlooked. Second, the types of stimuli that we use to probe neuronal responses also have biases (Section 5.11, Figure 5.10). Perhaps there are neurons in V1 that respond strongly to purple triangles with a sunflower on top, but, not surprisingly, nobody has tested this. Why would anyone test such a stimulus? None of our theories suggest that such a stimulus would be particularly relevant for V1 neurons. However, our theories may also be biased. Another important point to keep in mind is that neuronal responses in V1 are often probed in monkeys that are not performing any visual task other than fixating. Spatial context, temporal context, internal expectations, and task demands can modulate the responses of V1 neurons.

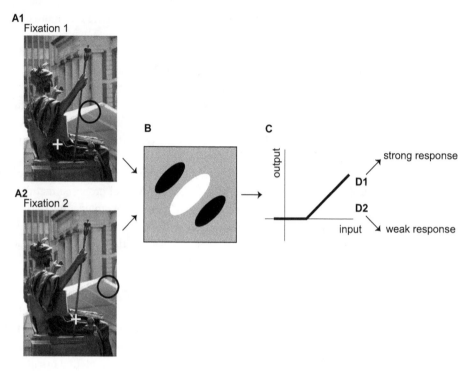

Figure 5.8 Beyond gratings and into the real world. Schematic example of how a V1 simple neuron might respond in the real world. "+" indicates the fixation location, and the black circle indicates the receptive field location. In **A1**, the image inside the receptive field is similar to the neuron's preferred orientation (**B**), eliciting a high response (**D1**), whereas the reverse is true in the bottom case.

The last decade has seen an exciting increase in studies of mouse V1, many of which have opened our eyes to a world full of surprises, even at the heart of the most studied cortical area. Many of the experiments in mice are performed while the animal is running on a ball, a sort of treadmill exercise, while the mouse is watching a flashed stimulus or a movie. One of the most shocking findings in V1 in the last decade is that the running speed strongly modulates V1 neuronal responses. The same visual stimulus can trigger very distinct responses depending on whether the animal is still, trotting slowly, or sprinting. If this is not astounding enough, the responses of those V1 neurons can also be modulated by running in the dark, in the absence of any visual stimulation. Continuing with the list of intriguing observations in mice, there are direct connections from the primary auditory cortex onto V1, and it is possible to trigger responses in V1 neurons with auditory tones! These responses are weaker than visually triggered ones, but it is an auditory signal driving the most visual part of cortex. Whisker deflections can also modulate V1 neurons. And head movements too.

It remains unclear whether any of these observations extend to monkeys, let alone humans. It is not easy to do neurophysiological recordings in monkeys running around, and it is very challenging to perform neurophysiological recordings in human V1.

To the best of our knowledge, there is no report of auditory stimuli modulating V1 responses in monkeys (after controlling for eye position, attention, and visual stimulus). The rodent brain is much smaller than the macaque monkey brain (the *Mus musculus* and *Macaca mulatta* diverged about 75 million years ago), which is – in turn – smaller than the human brain (*Macaca mulatta* and *Homo sapiens* diverged about 25 million years ago). Introspectively, our visual world does not seem to change when we are walking or running around. However, there could be compensatory mechanisms that account for modulatory responses in V1 during running (remember that we are not even aware of the massive and pervasive visual changes caused by blinks and eye movements, Chapter 2). The auditory cortex, somatosensory cortex, and motor cortex are closer to V1 in mice than in monkeys, and there are more convolutions that could isolate brain areas in the macaque brain, and even more so in the human brain. Of note, this is all speculation, and we will need to evaluate all of these possibilities in neurophysiological recordings in monkeys and humans. We should keep our brains open and expect many exciting surprises ahead.

5.10   Divide and Conquer

Leaving the primary visual cortex and ascending through the hierarchy of cortical computations, we reach the fascinating and bewildering cortical areas that bridge low-level visual features into the building blocks of perception. In the primary visual cortex, there are neurons that respond selectively to lines of different orientations (Figure 5.3). At the other end of the visual hierarchy, there are neurons in the inferior temporal cortex (ITC) that respond selectively to complex shapes and help us identify chairs, faces, and planets (to be discussed in Section 6.2). In between V1 and the representation of complex object shapes, there is a vast expanse of cortex involved in the seemingly magical transformations that convert oriented lines into complex shapes. How do we go from oriented lines to recognizing chairs, faces, and planets (Figure 5.9)?

Despite heroic efforts by a talented cadre of investigators to scrutinize the responses between the primary visual cortex and the highest echelons of the ITC, the ventral visual cortex remains mostly *terra incognita*. Visual information flows along the ventral visual stream from V1 into areas V2, V4, posterior, and anterior parts of the ITC. The cortical real estate between V2 and the ITC constitutes a mysterious, seductive, and controversial ensemble of neurons whose functions remain unclear and are only beginning to be deciphered. Courageous investigators – armed with computational models, electrodes, and intuition – are beginning to describe the neuronal turning preferences of neurons in areas V2, V3, and V4, in terms of features including curvature, disparity, color, texture, and shapes.

To solve the complex task of interpreting a scene, the visual system seems to have adopted a *divide-and-conquer* strategy. Instead of trying to come up with a single function that will transform lines into complex shapes in one step, the computations underlying visual cognition are implemented by a cascade of multiple approximately sequential computations. Each of these computations may be deceptively simple, and

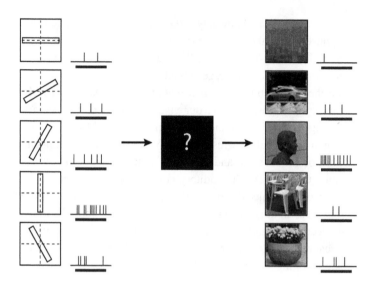

Figure 5.9 How does the cortex convert pixels to percepts? Through the cascade of computations along the ventral visual stream, the brain can convert preferences for simple stimulus properties such as orientation tuning into sophisticated features such as faces.

yet the concatenation of such steps can lead to interesting and complex emergent results. As a rough analogy, consider a factory making cars. There is a long sequence of specialized areas, departments, and tasks. One group of workers may be involved in receiving and ordering different parts; others may be specialized in assembling the carburetor; others in painting the exterior. The car is the result of all of these sequential and parallel steps. To understand the entire mechanistic process by which a car is made, we need to dig deeper into each of those specialized sub-steps without losing touch with the overall objective that each of these sub-steps contributes to – that is, the final product.

5.11   We Cannot Exhaustively Study All Possible Visual Stimuli

It would be nice to be able to describe the tuning preferences of neurons along the ventral visual stream in an analogous way to orientation tuning and Gabor functions for V1 neurons. There have been many empirical attempts to characterize the neuronal preferences of V2, V4, and ITC neurons, yielding exciting insights. As in the famous parable of blind men trying to describe an elephant by touching separate parts, different investigators have come up with several examples of how neurons respond to angles, colors, curvatures, and other shapes.

One of the main challenges to investigate the function and preferences of neurons in cortex is that there are too many possible images and we only have a limited amount of recording time for a given neuron. Given current techniques, it is simply impossible to exhaustively examine the large number of possible combinations of different

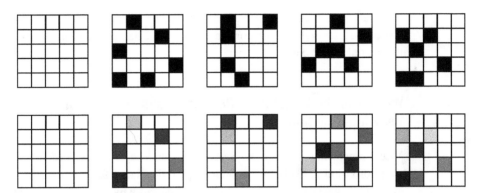

Figure 5.10 The curse of dimensionality in vision. With current techniques, we cannot exhaustively sample all possible stimuli. Here we consider a 5 × 5 grid of possible binary images (top) or possible grayscale images (bottom). Even for such simple stimuli, the number of possibilities is immense.

stimuli that might drive a neuron. Consider a simple scenario where we present image patches of size 5 × 5 pixels, where each pixel is either black or white (Figure 5.10, top). There are 2^{25} (more than 33 million) such stimuli. If we present each stimulus for 100 milliseconds and we do not allow for any intervening time in between stimuli, it would take more than five weeks to present all possible combinations. There are many more possibilities if we allow each pixel to have gray tones from 0 to 255 (Figure 5.10, bottom): 256^{25} such images (about 10^{60} such images!). Moreover, the problem becomes even worse if we allow three colors (red, green, and blue) and if we allow images larger than a mere 5×5 pixels. Even after restricting our analyses to the ill-defined subset of natural images (Section 2.1), we would still have an astronomically large number of possible images. We can typically hold extracellular recordings with single (non-chronic) electrodes for a couple of hours. Recent extraordinary efforts have managed to track the activity of a given neuron for up to a year. However, even with such chronic electrodes, it is challenging to keep an animal engaged in a visual presentation task for more than a few hours a day. Thus, we cannot record the responses of a neuron to all images.

Because of the severe limitations in the number of stimuli that can be tested, investigators often recur to several astute strategies to decide which stimuli to use in order to investigate the responses of cortical neurons. These strategies typically involve a combination of (i) inspiration from previous studies (past behavior of neurons in other studies is a good predictor of how neurons will behave in a new experiment); (ii) intuitions about what types of images might or might not matter for neurons (for example, many investigators have argued that real-world objects such as faces should be important); (iii) statistics of natural stimuli (as discussed in Section 2.1, it is reasonable to assume that neuronal tuning is sculpted by exposure to images in the natural world); (iv) computational models (to be discussed in more detail in Chapters 7–9); (v) serendipity (the role of rigorous scrutiny and systematic observation combined with luck should not be underestimated). Combining these approaches, several investigators have probed the neural code for visual shapes along the ventral visual cortex.

5.12   We Live in the Visual Past: Response Latencies Increase along the Ventral Stream

Visual processing is very fast (Section 3.6). Indeed, as we argued in Chapter 1, the speed of vision is likely to have conferred critical advantages to the first species with eyes and may well constitute one of the key reasons why evolution led to the expansion of visual capabilities. However, even though the world seems to materialize in front of us upon opening our eyes, as we noted in Section 2.6, processing in the retina takes time. The intuition that vision is instantaneous is nothing more than an illusion. It takes about 30 to 50 milliseconds for signals to emerge from retinal ganglion cells into the thalamus, and it takes further time for signals to propagate through the cortex.

A small fraction of this time has to do with the speed of propagation along dendrites and axons within a neuron. However, within-neuron delays are relatively short. In particular, action potential signals within axons that are insulated by myelin can propagate at speeds of about 100 meters per second. Thus, signals from a single myelinated axon could, in principle, traverse the entire length of the human brain of approximately 15 centimeters in about 1.5 milliseconds. Dendrites tend to be shorter than axons, and propagation speeds within dendrites are also quite fast. The main reason why vision is far from instantaneous is the multiple computations and integration steps in each neuron combined with the synaptic handoff of information from one neuron to the next executed throughout the multi-synaptic circuitry of cortex.

At each processing stage in the visual system, it is possible to estimate the time it takes for neurons in that area to realize that a flash of light was presented. Response latencies to a stimulus flash within the receptive field of a neuron increase from ~45 milliseconds in the LGN to ~100 milliseconds in the inferior temporal cortex (Table 5.1). There is an increase in the average latency within each area from the retina to the LGN to V1, to V2, to V4, to the ITC. This progression of latencies has further reinforced the notion of the ventral processing stream as an approximately hierarchical and sequential architecture. Each additional processing stage along the ventral stream adds an average of ~15 milliseconds of computation time.

It should be emphasized that these are only coarse values, and there is significant neuron-to-neuron variability within each area. An analysis of neural recordings in anesthetized monkeys by Schmolesky and colleagues showed latencies ranging from 30 milliseconds all the way to 70 milliseconds in the primary visual cortex. Because of this heterogeneity, the distributions of response latencies overlap, and the fastest neurons in a given area (say V2) may fire before the slowest neurons in an earlier area (say V1). Not only is there heterogeneity in response latencies from one neuron to another within a given visual area, but even the same neuron can also show different latencies depending on the nature of the stimulus. For example, response latencies tend

Table 5.1 Response latencies in different areas in the macaque monkey. From Schmolesky et al. 1998.

Area	Mean (ms)	S.D. (ms)
LGNd M layer	33	3.8
LGNd P layer	50	8.7
V1	66	10.7
V2	82	21.1
V4	104	23.4
V3	72	8.6
MT	72	10.3
MST	74	16.1
FEF	75	13

to be inversely proportional to the stimulus contrast. The notion of sequential processing is only a coarse approximation. However, the response latencies constitute an important constraint to the number of possible computational steps along the visual system.

Because of these latencies, we continuously live in the past in terms of vision. The notion that we only see the past events is particularly evident when we consider distant stars. The light signals that reach the Earth left those stars a long time ago. Although much less intuitive, the same idea applies to visual processing in the brain. Of course, the time it takes for light to bounce on a given object and reach the retina is negligible, yet signal propagation in the brain takes on the order of a hundred milliseconds, as discussed earlier. Through learning, the brain might be able to account for these delays by predicting what will happen next. For example, how is it possible for a Ping-Pong player to respond to a smash? The ball may be moving at about 50 kilometers per hour (apparently, the world record is about 112 kilometers per hour), and thus, the ball traverses the ~3-meter length of the table in about 200 milliseconds. By the time the opponent has to hit the ball back, his or her visual cortex is processing sensory inputs from the time when the ball was passing the net in the best-case scenario, not to mention the fact that orchestrating a movement also takes time (signals need to propagate from vision to the decision centers of the brain, and then from there to the muscles; all of these steps cost time). The only way to play Ping-Pong and other sports is to use the visual input combined with predictions learned through experience. Because of these predictions, players not only capitalize on smashing speed but also recur to other strategies such as embedding the ball with spinning effects to confuse the opponent.

5.13   Receptive Field Sizes Increase along the Ventral Visual Stream

Concomitant with the prolonged latencies, as we ascend through the visual hierarchy, receptive fields become larger (Figure 5.11). Receptive fields range from less than one degree in the initial steps (LGN, V1) all the way to several degrees or even tens of degrees in the highest echelons of the cortex. Each area has a complete map of the visual

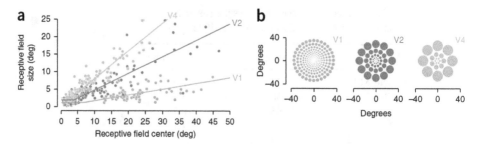

Figure 5.11 Receptive field sizes increase with eccentricity and along the ventral stream. Receptive field size increases with eccentricity for a given area. Additionally, receptive field size increases along the ventral visual stream at a fixed eccentricity. (A) Experimental measurements based on neurophysiological recordings in macaque monkeys. (B) Schematic rendering of receptive field sizes in areas V1, V2, and V4. Reproduced from Freeman and Simoncelli 2011

field; thus, the centers of the receptive fields go from the fovea to the periphery. As discussed for the primary visual cortex, within each area, the size of the receptive field increases as we move farther away from the fovea. There is always better resolution in the fovea, across all visual areas. The range of receptive field sizes within an area also increases with the mean receptive field size. The distributions are relatively narrow in primary visual cortex, but investigators have described a wide range of receptive field sizes in V4 and inferior temporal cortex. The scaling factor between receptive field size and eccentricity is more pronounced in V4 than in V2 and more pronounced in V2 compared to V1.

The increase in receptive field size from one area to the next may be a natural consequence of pooling-like operations in a hierarchical network, as we will discuss in more detail when we introduce computational models of visual cortical processing in Section 8.2. The increase in receptive field size provides several interesting properties: (i) a specific mechanism of discarding precise positional information in favor of (ii) extracting visual features that show progressively larger degrees of invariance to the exact position or scale of relevant visual features, and (iii) the ability to combine shapes from slightly shifted locations to build progressively more complex visual feature descriptors.

5.14   What Do Neurons beyond V1 Prefer?

There have been a few systematic parametric studies of the neuronal preferences in areas V2 and V4. These studies have opened the doors to investigate the complex transformations along the ventral visual stream. Even though multiple interesting studies compared responses in V1, V2, and V4, we do not yet have a clear, unified theory of what neurons "prefer" in these higher visual areas. Of course, the term "prefer" is an anthropomorphism. Neurons do not prefer anything. They fire spikes whenever the integration of their inputs exceeds a given threshold. Investigators often speak about neuronal preferences in terms of what types of images will elicit high firing rates.

The notion that V1 neurons show a preference for orientation tuning is well established, even if this only accounts for part of the variance in V1 responses to natural stimuli. There is significantly less agreement as to the types of shape features that are encoded in V2 and V4. There have been several studies probing responses with stimuli that are more complex than oriented bars and less complex than everyday objects. These stimuli include sinusoidal gratings, hyperbolic gratings, polar gratings, angles formed by intersecting lines, and curvatures with different properties, among others. Simple stimuli such as Cartesian gratings can certainly drive responses in V2 and V4. As a general rule, neurons in V2 and V4 can be driven more strongly by more complex shapes. As discussed earlier in the context of latency, there is a wide distribution of stimulus preferences in V2 and V4.

Perhaps one of the challenges is that investigators seek an explanation of neural coding preferences in terms of colloquial English expressions such as orientation, color, or curvature. An attractive idea that is gaining momentum is the notion that neurons in these higher visual areas filter the inputs from previous stages to produce complex tuning functions that defy language-based descriptions. A neuron may be activated by a patch representing complex shapes and textures that cannot be simply defined as an angle or a convex curve. Ultimately, the language of nature is mathematics, not English or Esperanto. Neuronal tuning properties do not have to map in any direct way to a short language-based description; we will come back to this idea in Chapters 7 and 8 when we discuss computational models of vision.

5.15   Brains Construct Their Interpretation of the World: The Case of Illusory Contours

A pervasive illusion is the notion that our senses contain a veridical representation of precisely what is out there in the world. This notion can be readily debunked through the study of visual illusions. In Section 3.1, we argued that our brains make up stuff by constructing an interpretation of the outside world. Our brains "making up stuff" implies that there should be neurons that explicitly represent those constructs. Let us revisit the Kanizsa triangle (Figure 5.12), where we have the strong illusion of perceiving an equilateral triangle in the midst of the three Pacman icons. The small parts of the sides of the triangle near the vertices are composed of real black contours. However, the center of each side is composed of a line that does not really exist. These lines represent illusory contours – that is, edges created without any change in luminance.

It is relatively easy to "trick the eye," except that the eye is typically *not* tricked in most visual illusions. Visual illusions represent situations where our brains construct an interpretation of the image that is different from the pixel level content. In most such illusions, the responses of retinal ganglion cells (RGC) follow the pixel-level content in the image relatively well. Consider recording the activity of an RGC whose receptive field center corresponds to position A in Figure 5.12, right along one side of the Pacman. There is a luminance change inside the receptive field, and we expect the neuron to fire vigorously at this location upon flashing the Kanizsa figure. Now consider an RGC with

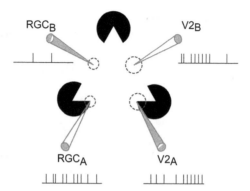

Figure 5.12 V2 neurons can represent lines that do not exist except in the eyes of the beholder. The figure shows the Kanizsa triangle visual illusion and a schematic rendering of neurophysiological recordings from four neurons: two retinal ganglion cells (RGC) and two V2 neurons. When the receptive fields (gray dotted circles) encompass locations that have a real contour (**A**), both RGC and V2 neurons fire vigorously. In contrast, when the receptive fields encompass an illusory contour (**B**), the V2 neuron fires vigorously, but the RGC neuron only fires a few baseline spikes.

a receptive field center located at position B, smack in the middle of the illusory contour. We do not expect this neuron to fire above baseline levels because there is no stimulus inside the receptive field. In other words, the activity of RGCs does not correlate with our perception. If the retina does not reflect perception, then who does? It seems reasonable to conjecture that there must be neurons somewhere that explicitly represent the contents of our perception – in this case, the illusory contours. This explicit representation is a critical postulate that we will discuss again in more depth when we take up the question of the neuronal correlates of consciousness in Section 10.3.

Indeed, neurons in area V2 respond to illusory contours (Figure 5.12). A V2 neuron that prefers horizontal edges would fire strongly if its receptive field is at location A because there is a real horizontal line there. Remarkably, a V2 neuron that prefers leftward edges would also fire if its receptive field is at position B, where there is an illusory edge. V2 neurons respond almost equally well to an illusory line or to a real line. The responses to illusory contours are remarkable because there is no contrast change within the neuron's receptive field. Hence, these responses indicate a form of context modulation that is consistent with the subjective interpretation of borders. There are also neurons in V1 that respond to illusory contours, but there are more such neurons in V2. Interestingly, the responses to illusory contours show a short delay with respect to the responses to real lines. These delays may reflect the need for additional computational steps required to infer the presence of a line when there is none.

5.16   A Colorful V4

Neurons in the retina (cones), LGN (parvocellular neurons), and primary visual cortex (particularly those within so-called blobs in V1) are all sensitive to the color of the stimulus within their receptive field. Neurons in area V4 demonstrate sensitivity to color properties that are more complex than those in earlier areas. A notable property is that neurons in V4 have been implicated in the phenomenon of color constancy whereby an object's perceived color is relatively insensitive to large changes in the overall illumination, in contrast to the responses earlier in the visual system.

There are many visual illusions based on the phenomenon of color constancy. A banana typically appears to be yellow to our eyes, whether we see it at noon, or in the early evening, or under the kitchen light. The actual spectrum of light reaching the eyes depends quite strongly on the environment illumination, and cones in the retina signal the actual wavelengths reflected off the banana. However, our perception discounts the background illumination and interprets the banana to be yellow. The integration of color signals emanating within the receptive field with those in the surround to perform this type of discounting is thought to take place in V1, and even more clearly in V4 neurons. The responses of V4 neurons better correlate with how primates perceive colors. Furthermore, the rare condition of cortical color blindness known as achromatopsia has been associated with damage to area V4 (Section 4.8).

5.17   Attentional Modulation

As noted earlier in this chapter, neurons along the ventral visual cortex receive numerous top-down signals in addition to their bottom-up inputs. Through these top-down signaling mechanisms, the activity of neurons along ventral visual cortex can be strongly modulated by signals beyond the specific visual content within their receptive fields – including spatial context, temporal context, expectations, and higher-level cognitive influences such as task goals.

Despite keen interest in such top-down signals, there have been many more studies about the role of bottom-up inputs on neuronal responses. At least partly, this imbalance is due to the fact that it is much easier to change what is shown on the screen than to change an animal's internal expectations and goals.

A prime example of the study of top-down modulatory signals in visual processing involves *spatial attention*. One way to allocate attention to one part of the visual field is by moving the eyes. However, spatial attention effects can also be demonstrated outside of the fixation focus. A subject can be looking at one location and paying attention to another place, a phenomenon known as *covert* attention (as opposed to *overt* attention, which is the more common scenario where attention is allocated to the fixation area). Through a series of astute training paradigms, investigators have been able to train animals to deploy covert spatial attention, thus enabling them to investigate the consequences of spatial attention on neurons with receptive fields outside the fovea.

An animal is trained to fixate in the center of the screen, and its eye movements are strictly monitored to ensure that attentional effects are not driven by saccades. In some trials, the animal is rewarded for detecting a visual stimulus in a certain location on the right, and that tells the animal to allocate attention to that region of the visual field without breaking fixation. Compliance can be checked by randomly probing a stimulus presented at another location and showing that performance is better (faster, more accurate) in the attended area.

Under these experimental conditions, neurons typically show an enhancement in the responses when their receptive field is within the focus of attention, particularly upon presentation of a visual stimulus. In other words, imagine a neuron in V2 with a receptive field location that is right at the center of the attended area in some trials and outside the attended area in other trials. The neuron will respond to an identical visual stimulus with more spikes in those trials when attention encompasses the receptive field. The effect of spatial attention is not all-or-none. Neurons still respond vigorously to a stimulus placed within their receptive field regardless of whether or not the animal is paying attention to that location. Attention leads to about 5 to 30 percent increased firing rates. The magnitude of this attention effect follows the reverse hierarchical order, being significantly stronger in area V4 compared to area V1.

Neuronal responses can also be modulated in a feature-specific manner. Instead of paying attention to a particular location, the animal can be trained to pay attention to a specific stimulus feature such as the color red or vertical lines. When the animal is paying attention to the neuron's preferred features, the neuron shows an enhanced firing rate.

5.18   Summary

- Visual computations transpire in the six-layered neocortical structure.
- The cortex is characterized by stereotypical connectivity patterns from one area to the next, forming approximately canonical microcircuits.
- The gold standard to study cortical function is to scrutinize the activity of individual neurons.
- Neurons in the primary visual cortex detect edges and show orientation tuning, responding more strongly to a bar in a specific orientation within the receptive field.
- Complex neurons in the primary visual cortex show tolerance to the exact position of the preferred stimulus within the receptive field.
- A Gabor function can phenomenologically fit the responses of V1 neurons.
- A mechanistic model posits that V1 simple cell receptive fields can be created by adequately combining the outputs of center-surround neurons from the lateral geniculate nucleus positioned to create the desired orientation.
- A model posits that V1 complex cell receptive fields can be created by adequately combining the outputs of V1 simple cells with the same orientation preferences but slightly shifted receptive fields.
- The visual cortex uses a divide-and-conquer strategy, subdividing visual processing into a sequence of computations in tens of different brain areas arranged into an approximate hierarchy.

- Ascending through the visual hierarchy, neurons show increased receptive field sizes, more complex tuning preferences, and longer latencies.
- Neurons in area V2 respond to illusory contours.
- Spatial context, temporal context, and task demands like attention can modulate neuronal responses along ventral visual cortex.

Further Reading

See http://bit.ly/2TpAg3w for more references.

- Carandini, M.; Demb. J. B.; Mante, V.; Tolhurst, D. J.; Dan, Y., et al. (2005). Do we know what the early visual system does? *Journal of Neuroscience* 25: 10577–10597.
- Hubel, D.H.; and Wiesel, T. N. (1968). Receptive fields and functional architecture of monkey striate cortex. *The Journal of Physiology* 195: 215–243.
- Kremkow, J.; Jin, J.; Wang, Y.; and Alonso, J. M. (2016). Principles underlying sensory map topography in primary visual cortex. *Nature* 533: 52–57.
- Markov, N.T.; Ercsey-Ravasz, M. M.; Ribeiro Gomes, A. R.; Lamy, C.; Magrou, L., et al. (2014). A weighted and directed interareal connectivity matrix for macaque cerebral cortex. *Cerebral Cortex* 24: 17–36.
- Schmolesky, M.; Wang, Y.; Hanes, D.; Thompson, K.; Leutgeb, S.; et al. (1998). Signal timing across the macaque visual system. *Journal of Neurophysiology* 79: 3272–3278.

6   From the Highest Echelons of Visual Processing to Cognition

Supplementary content at http://bit.ly/364H8WR

The inferior temporal cortex (ITC) is the highest echelon within the visual stream concerned with processing visual shape information. The Felleman and Van Essen diagram (Chapter 1, Figure 1.5) places the hippocampus at the top. While visual responses can be elicited in the hippocampus, people with bilateral lesions to the hippocampus can still see very well. A famous example is a patient known as H. M., who had no known visual deficit but gave rise to the whole field of memory studies based on his inability to form new memories. The hippocampus is not a visual area and instead receives inputs from all sensory modalities (Chapter 4).

The history of how the inferior temporal cortex became accepted and described as a visual area is fascinating and follows the refinements in the ability to make more precise lesions and controlled behavioral experiments. In stark contrast to the hippocampus, bilateral lesions to the ITC are associated with impairment in visual object recognition in macaque monkeys (Section 4.7), and with several object agnosias in humans (Section 4.8). We are beginning to decipher the neural code that represents how visual scenes are interpreted.

6.1   A Well-Connected Area

The inferior temporal cortex (ITC) spans Brodmann's cytoarchitectonic areas 20 and 21 (Figure 5.1). The ITC is a vast expanse of cortex that is usually subdivided into a posterior area (PIT), a central area (CIT), and an anterior area (AIT). Biologists are fond of confusing people by using different names for the same thing, a phenomenon that can be partly explained by independent investigators working on related topics in parallel and coming up with new nomenclature to describe their findings. The ITC is also referred to in the literature as areas TEO and TE. The degree of functional specialization among different parts of the ITC remains poorly understood, and it is extremely likely that we will have to subdivide the ITC into many different subareas beyond the current coarse subregions, based on connectivity, neurophysiological, and computational properties.

Like most other parts of cortex, the connectivity patterns of the ITC are extensive and complex. When we describe computational models of vision in Chapters 7 and 8, it will be apparent that most models represent a major simplification of the actual connectivity diagram. The ITC receives feedforward topographically organized inputs from areas

V2, V3, and V4 along the ventral visual cortex. The ITC also receives fewer inputs from areas V3A, MT, and MST, highlighting the interconnections between the dorsal and ventral streams (Section 4.5). The ITC projects back to V2, V3, and V4. There are also interhemispheric connections between the ITC in the right and left hemispheres through the main set of fibers connecting the two hemispheres, the corpus callosum.

The ITC also has extensive projections to and receives signals from non-visual regions, including (i) areas that provide critical inputs to the medial temporal lobe memory system such as the perirhinal cortex, parahippocampal gyrus, and entorhinal cortex; (ii) areas involved in processing emotions such as the amygdala; and (iii) areas in prefrontal cortex that are relevant for decision making, planning, and working memory. Thus, from an anatomical standpoint, the ITC is ideally situated to interpret visual inputs in the context of current goals and previous history, and to convey this information to make behavioral decisions and create episodic memories.

6.2   ITC Neurons Show Shape Selectivity

Over the last five decades, a heroic school of investigators has studied ITC responses in monkeys due to the overall similarity between their visual system and that of humans. Most, if not all, ITC neurons show visually evoked responses, firing vigorously to color, orientation, texture, direction of movement, and shape. Posterior portions of the ITC show a coarse retinotopic organization and an almost complete representation of the contralateral visual field. The receptive field sizes of posterior ITC neurons are about 1.5–4 degrees; on average, the receptive fields are more extensive than those found in V4 neurons.

In more anterior locations along the ITC, there is a weaker retinotopic organization. The receptive field sizes in more anterior parts of ITC are often large. Estimates vary widely, ranging from ~2 degrees receptive fields to neurons with receptive fields that span several tens of degrees. Most receptive fields in anterior ITC include the foveal region.

Example responses from three ITC neurons in response to five pictures are shown in Figure 6.1. In this figure, each picture was repeated 10 times, and the stochasticity of the neuronal responses is evident in the heterogeneous patterns from one trial to the next. This trial-to-trial variability is not specific to ITC and is prevalent throughout the visual cortex. There is considerable discussion in the field about the origin of this variability – which does not seem to be intrinsic to neurons but may constitute a network phenomenon that reflects different levels of attention, expectations, eye positions, and other changes across trials.

Despite this trial-to-trial variability, there are several consistent features that are evident in the neuronal responses in Figure 6.1. All three neurons show an increased firing rate that commences approximately 100 milliseconds after stimulus onset (approximately near the end of the white horizontal line denoting the duration of stimulus presentation). This latency should not be interpreted as a response triggered by the stimulus offset; if the stimulus duration were longer, the neurons would still start to fire at around 100 milliseconds after stimulus onset. These 100 milliseconds reflect

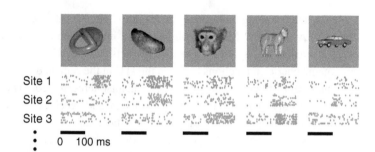

Figure 6.1 ITC neurons are picky. Example responses from three neurons in inferior temporal cortex (labeled "Site 1", "Site 2", "Site 3") to five different grayscale images. Each dot represents a spike, each row represents a separate repetition (10 repetitions per object), and the horizontal white lines denote the duration of the image (100 milliseconds presentation time). Data from Hung et al. 2005

the latency for all the computations that transpire throughout the ventral visual cortex before reaching these ITC neurons (Section 5.12). The neurons are picky in their stimulus preferences. The "Site 1" neuron showed a stronger response to the first two pictures (toy, food) compared to the last two pictures (synthetic rendering of a cat, car). In contrast, the "Site 3" neuron showed an increased response to the third and fourth pictures (monkey face, cat).

Investigators have effectively tested the responses of ITC neurons to a wide range of visual stimuli. For example, some studies have used parametric descriptors of abstract shapes. Logothetis and colleagues trained monkeys to recognize paperclips forming different three-dimensional shapes and subsequently found neurons that were selective for specific three-dimensional object configurations. ITC neurons can be driven by pictures of cars, toys, faces, and fruits.

This wide range of response preferences might seem puzzling at first. Perhaps one would like to conjecture that an area that plays a vital role in object recognition would have neurons that respond specifically to objects in the real world. There could be banana neurons (i.e., a neuron that responds if and only if investigators show a picture of a banana to the monkey), peanuts neurons, chair neurons, face neurons, paperclip neurons, hand neurons, and spaghetti with meatball neurons. Indeed, if we ignore momentarily the "if and only if" part, it is possible to find neurons activated selectively by these types of images. As illustrated by the examples in Figure 6.1, the responses are *not* all-or-none. ITC neurons do not seem to be activated *only* upon presentation of one specific type of object in the real world with baseline level responses to everything else. Instead, ITC neurons show graded activations with stronger responses to some stimuli compared to others.

It is unclear whether ITC neurons show any special treatment to naturally occurring objects like bananas or faces. ITC neurons may represent a sufficiently rich dictionary of complex features. These features can be used to represent any number of naturally occurring objects in an analogous way to forming words by combining different letters or sentences by combining words. Those features can be found in fractal patterns, in paperclips, in faces, and chairs. We will come back to a more quantitative description of these properties and the responses of ITC neurons when we describe current computational models of visual processing in Chapters 7 and 8.

As discussed in the case of neurons in earlier visual areas (Sections 2.7 and 5.6), there is a clear topography in the ITC response map. By advancing the electrode in a trajectory that is approximately tangential to cortex, investigators find neurons that have similar tuning. This level of organization can be represented by "columns" of neurons with similar preferences. Moving horizontally, neighboring neurons in the ITC also show similar, but not identical, preferences.

6.3   Selectivity in the Human Ventral Visual Cortex

Less is known about the internal machinery that processes visual information in the human brain. The primary source of information about the inner workings of human ventral visual cortex comes from invasive neurophysiological recordings in epilepsy patients, which were introduced through the work of Penfield in Section 4.9. A fraction of patients with epilepsy can be treated pharmacologically. In cases of focal epilepsies that do not respond to current drug treatments, an important approach has been to surgically remove the epileptogenic focus. In most cases, this surgical procedure requires first carefully mapping brain activity to discern where seizures are coming from and also to ensure that the brain excisions do not interfere with future cognitive function. For this purpose, neurosurgeons typically implant electrodes inside the human brain. Because current noninvasive techniques are too coarse to map the origin of seizures, the neurosurgeons typically implant many tens of electrodes in different brain areas with the hope of pinpointing the seizure onset. After implantation, the patients stay in the hospital for about one week for observation, granting investigators a rare and unique opportunity to scrutinize human brain function at high spatiotemporal resolution and with high signal-to-noise ratio compared to anything that can be done from outside the brain.

The location of the electrodes is strictly dictated by clinical needs. Sometimes, those electrodes are placed along ventral visual cortex. An example of visually selective responses in human ITC is shown in Figure 6.2. The human intracranial field potentials – that is, the voltage recorded at these electrodes – show many of the hallmarks of the macaque ITC responses. Signals along the human ventral visual cortex also show circumscribed receptive fields, which increase in size from the fovea to the periphery, and from one area to the next. Field potentials along the human ventral visual cortex are also selective and graded (Figure 6.2A). The intracranial field potential signals also show trial-to-trial variability, yet the visually evoked responses can be readily appreciated in single trials (Figure 6.2B). There have been many more neurophysiological studies scrutinizing responses in monkeys compared to humans. Many details about the response properties along the human ventral visual cortex remain unexplored. For example, to the best of our knowledge, nobody has investigated responses in the human ventral visual cortex to fractal patterns or paperclips, as shown in monkey studies.

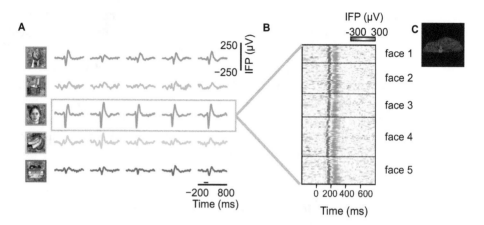

Figure 6.2 The human ITC also shows shape selectivity. Example electrode describing the physiological responses to 25 different exemplar objects belonging to five different categories. (**A**) Responses to each of 25 different exemplars (each color denotes a different category of images; each trace represents the response to a different exemplar). (**B**) Raster plot showing every single trial in the responses to the five face exemplars. Each row is a repetition; the horizontal lines separate the exemplars; the color shows voltage (see scale bar on the right). (**C**) Electrode location. Reproduced from Liu et al. 2009

However, the absence of evidence does not imply evidence of absence. As far as we can tell, responses along the human ventral visual cortex show selectivity to a wide variety of visual shapes like their macaque monkey counterparts.

Response latencies in the human brain seem to be slightly longer than those in macaque monkeys, perhaps because of the larger brain size, or perhaps because there might be more computational steps before the information reaches the human ITC. Within the scarce and preliminary neurophysiological evidence available today and, to a reasonable extent, many of the properties of the macaque ITC are recapitulated in the human ITC.

It should be noted that it is not entirely clear how to meaningfully compare brain areas and functional responses between humans and monkeys (or any other pair of species separated by long evolutionary timespans). First of all, we should be cautious about comparing spikes in monkeys to intracranial field potential signals in humans. It turns out that field potential signals show similar selectivity patterns to spiking signals in monkey ITC. The coarser field potential responses are somewhat less picky than spikes in terms of their ability to distinguish different stimuli, perhaps due to averaging over many neurons.

A more challenging consideration involves establishing rigorous homologies between species. It seems evident that the eyes in monkeys are homologous to the human eyes. Additionally, although the neuroanatomical connections in humans remain unclear, it is quite tempting to assume that the monkey primary visual cortex may be homologous to the human primary visual cortex. As we go deeper into the ventral visual cortex beyond V1, homologies become murkier. Regardless of whether we can establish a unique evolutionarily rigorous one-to-one map between specific structures in different species, it is nevertheless clear that human ventral visual cortex shows rapid and selective responses to complex shapes that are qualitatively similar to those observed in monkeys.

6.4   What Do ITC Neurons *Really* Want?

ITC neurons seem to respond to a wide variety of different shapes that investigators have used to probe their stimulus preferences. Recording time is limited, and investigators need to make choices about which stimuli to use in an experiment; we introduced this problem in Section 5.11. Typically, investigators choose stimuli based on a combination of inspiration from previous studies (if a particular type of stimulus worked before to drive neurons in a given area, it should work now too) or intuitions based on the prevalence of natural stimulus statistics (it seems logical to assume that neurons may represent the types of inputs that the animal experiences daily), or arguments about the presumed evolutionary importance of certain classes of stimuli. Additionally, important advances about neuronal tuning properties have been based on semi-serendipitous discoveries.

These types of experiments carry the potential biases injected by the investigators in selecting the stimuli. Obviously, we can only find tuning for those stimuli that we probe. Even the title of this section has a strong anthropomorphic spin. Neurons do not really "want" anything. The question is meant to allude to what types of visual stimuli maximally activate a given neuron (in the sense of triggering more spikes). As emphasized in Section 5.11, the critical difficulty in elucidating the response preferences of neurons involves the *curse of dimensionality*: too many possible images and too little time.

A promising line of research to elucidate the feature preferences in ITC involves changing the stimuli in real time, dictated by the neuron's preferences. Recent work based on this approach suggests that we may need to rethink the neural code for features in ITC (and perhaps earlier visual areas as well). One of the first applications of this approach was developed by Charles Connor's group to let neurons themselves reveal what they like rather than impose a strong bias in the stimulus selection. Recent work by Will Xiao involved developing a computational algorithm that is capable of generating images guided by neuronal firing rates (Figure 6.3). The investigators combined an image generator and a genetic algorithm based on the neuron's firing rate as a fitness function to guide the evolution of stimuli in real time. In a given generation, the investigators probe the responses to a set of images. Images that trigger high firing rates are kept, and the rest are modified and recombined by the genetic algorithm in combination with the image generation algorithm.

In Section 8.5, we will introduce deep hierarchical models of vision that start with pixels and yield a high-level feature representation of the image. Additionally, in Sections 9.8 and 9.9, we will introduce generative adversarial networks that create images by inverting a deep hierarchical model. The generative algorithm deployed by Xiao and colleagues, inspired by work in machine learning to build image generators, is

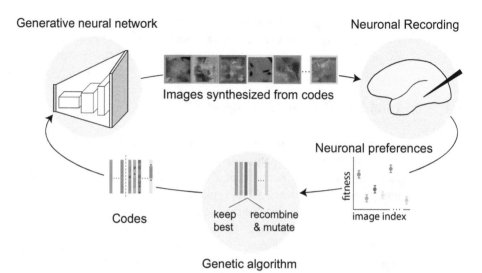

Figure 6.3 Letting neurons reveal their tuning preferences. An approach to investigate neuronal tuning in an unbiased manner. A generative neural network is used to create images by inverting a model of visual recognition (Section 9.9, Figure 9.10). The synthetic images are presented while recording neuronal activity. The neuronal responses are used as a fitness index to guide a genetic algorithm to select a new generation of improved images. Reproduced from Ponce et al. 2019

essentially an inverted version of deep hierarchical computational models, starting with high-level features and ending up with the generation of an image.

By running this generative computational algorithm while recording the activity of a neuron in ITC, Xiao and colleagues discovered images that elicited higher firing rates than natural images that had been used before to test the responses of the neurons. The investigators refer to these synthetic images as "super-stimuli." These super-stimuli contain naturalistic combinations of textures and broad strokes, which have been likened to impressionist renderings of abstract art. The fundamental novel concept here is that neurons may be optimally activated by combinations of sophisticated features that cannot be easily described in words. In contrast to anthropomorphic descriptions of feature preferences in ITC ("this neuron likes faces," "this neuron likes chairs," "this neuron likes curved shapes"), the new line of work suggests that neurons might be activated by complex shapes that defy a language-based definition. A rich basis set of neurons tuned to such complex features is capable of allowing the organism to discriminate real-world objects, but the basis set does not have to be based on icons of real-world objects.

6.5   ITC Neurons Show Tolerance to Object Transformations

As emphasized in Sections 1.4 and 3.4, an essential property of visual recognition is the capacity to recognize objects despite the transformations of the images at the pixel level (Figure 3.6). It is therefore interesting to ask whether the visual selectivity at the neuronal level, as described in the previous sections, is maintained across image transformations. For example, would the neuron shown in the top row in Figure 6.1 continue to respond selectively to the first two objects if they are shown at a different scale, in a different position with respect to fixation, or in a different color?

ITC neurons show a significant degree of tolerance to certain object transformations. ITC neurons have larger receptive fields and therefore show more tolerance to object position changes compared to neurons in earlier parts of the ventral visual cortex. ITC neurons also show similar responses in spite of substantial changes in the retinal size of the stimuli. Tolerance does not necessarily imply that the firing rate in response to a given object should be *identical* across different transformations. Even if the absolute firing rates are affected by a transformation, like changing the stimulus size, the rank-order preferences among different objects – and, therefore, the relative stimulus preferences – are maintained. ITC neurons also show a certain degree of tolerance to depth rotation. Additionally, while luminance changes typically define most shapes, ITC neurons also respond to shapes defined by other cues. For example, shape can be defined by noise patterns that move in a coherent fashion or by texture changes without luminance edges.

An extreme example of tolerance to object transformations was provided by recordings of single-neuron responses from the medial temporal lobe (not the ITC) in human epilepsy patients. Recording from the hippocampus, entorhinal cortex, amygdala, and parahippocampal gyrus, investigators found neurons that show responses to multiple objects within a semantically defined object category. They also found some neurons that show a remarkable degree of selectivity to individual persons or landmarks. For example, one neuron showed a selective response to images where the ex-president Bill Clinton was present; another neuron preferred pictures of the famous actress Jennifer Aniston. Remarkably, the images that elicited a response in these neurons were quite distinct from each other in terms of their pixel content ranging from a black-and-white drawing to color photographs with different poses and views. Such an extreme combination of selectivity and tolerance has not been described in ITC areas but rather in areas of the medial temporal lobe. As noted at the beginning of this chapter, these medial temporal lobe structures receive visual inputs but are not strictly visual areas. In fact, damage to medial temporal lobe structures does not seem to be associated with any apparent visual impairment, or any other perceptual deficit, but rather with memory problems. Therefore, it is likely that this combination of selectivity and tolerance reflects a *readout* of activity from a population of ITC neurons to transform sensory inputs into episodic memories.

6.6   Neurons Can Complete Patterns

During natural vision, objects are often only partially visible due to poor illumination or because there are other objects in front of them (Section 3.5). In early visual areas with small receptive fields, occlusion may cover the entire part of the visual field that a given neuron is interested in. In contrast, in higher visual areas with larger receptive fields, occlusion may only obstruct part of the input to a given neuron. The degree of tolerance to object transformations described in the previous section suggests that neurons might potentially also tolerate inputs that only contain some of the preferred features.

Indeed, the ITC shows a large degree of robustness to occlusion. The neural responses in the ITC can complete patterns and maintain their selectivity even when more than half of the preferred object features are invisible. At both the behavioral level (Section 3.5) and the neurophysiological level, pattern completion requires additional computation time: the latencies of the visually selective evoked responses elicited by partially visible objects are about 50 milliseconds longer than those triggered by fully visible objects. These observations suggest the need for additional processing to make inferences from partial information. We will come back to this point in Sections 7.6 and 8.16 when we discuss the computational mechanisms of pattern completion.

In the previous section, we noted that tolerance to object transformations does not necessarily imply that the neural responses to transformed versions of an object should be identical. Scaling, rotation, color changes, and other transformations can alter a neuron's firing rate, and tolerance refers to the maintained neural selectivity. In the same fashion, completing patterns does not imply that neural responses to heavily occluded objects are identical to the responses to the fully visible counterparts; pattern completion at the neuronal level indicates that selectivity is maintained.

Whereas certain image transformations, such as scale or position changes, maintain the same object features visible (albeit in different places or sizes), other image transformations like three-dimensional rotation or heavy occlusion alter which features are visible and which ones are not. Therefore, it is perhaps unsurprising that the disappearance of certain object features and the appearance of new features during rotation may lead to different firing rates. What is remarkable is that some of the relative stimulus preferences are maintained under these conditions that carry substantial changes at the pixel level.

6.7   IT Takes a Village

The observation that individual neurons can show a high degree of selectivity and tolerance to image transformations should not be taken to imply that there is a one-to-one map between the activity of a single neuron and recognition of a specific object. The idea of a one-to-one map between neurons and specific objects is erroneously referred to as the "grandmother cell" theory. A one-to-one system would be extremely unwieldy and fragile. Losing that one neuron might lead to an inability to recognize that particular object. Additionally, in most cases, readout neurons depend on inputs from hundreds to thousands of other neurons and cannot be reliably or exclusively driven by a single input.

As noted in Section 6.2, nearby neurons in the visual cortex tend to show similar feature tuning properties. Even if we cannot currently monitor the activity of every neuron in a local area, finding a neuron with a specific tuning function is likely to imply the existence of a large number of other nearby neurons with similar tuning properties. In fact, the idea of a "grandmother cell," as coined by Jerry Letvin in 1969,

referred to a whole population of cells with identical selectivity and tolerance properties (in the original description, he referred to a "mother cell" rather than a "grandmother cell"). Understood as in the original definition, the idea of a grandmother cell –
that is, a population of probably nearby neurons that show selectivity and tolerance to
related stimulus properties – is an adequate description of neuronal tuning throughout
the visual cortex. Retinal ganglion cells are grandmother cells for changes in illumination at sparse and specific locations in the visual field, primary visual cortex neurons
are grandmother cells for oriented lines, and ITC neurons are grandmother cells for
complex shape features.

    While each neuron shows a preference for some shapes over others, the amount of
information conveyed by individual neurons about overall shape is limited.
Additionally, there seems to be a significant amount of "noise" in the neuronal
responses in any given trial. The term noise is somewhat of a misnomer, as it refers
to the trial-to-trial variability in the spike timing and spike counts, as noted in
Figure 6.1. Whether this is real noise or part of the signal and what the origin of this
variability is remain topics of debate in the field. For suprathreshold stimuli, perception
is quite robust: you can look at the shape of the letter A a thousand times, and it will
always look like an A. Therefore, somewhere in the brain, a postsynaptic neuron
receiving inputs from capricious presynaptic neurons that emit different responses to
presumably identical inputs in each trial still needs to be able to discount the variability
and decipher what is out there in the world.

    Can animals use the neuronal representation of a population of somewhat capri-
cious ITC neurons to discriminate among objects in single trials? The critical
emphasis is on single trials. Unlike what many investigators do when they analyze
neural recordings, the brain cannot average over trials (we do not need to look at the
letter A 10 times to be able to recognize it). The brain is not constrained to making
inferences from the activity of a single neuron. Any given neuron in cortex receives
input from approximately 10,000 other neurons. Such a population could show
interesting properties that ameliorate or eliminate the challenges associated with
interpreting the output of a single neuron.

    Chou Hung and colleagues addressed this question by recording activity (sequen-
tially) from hundreds of ITC neurons and using machine learning classifiers to decode
the activity of a pseudo-population of neurons in single trials. The term pseudo-
population refers to the notion that these neurons were not simultaneously recorded.
The machine learning decoding approach aims to learn a map between (i) the activity
patterns of a population of neurons in response to a set of images and (ii) the labels of
objects in those images (Figure 6.4). Consider an experiment where we present pictures
of cats or pictures of fish. Let $_jx_i$ represent the activity of neuron i in response to image j.
For example, x could represent the total number of spikes emitted by the neuron in a
given time window. Due to the latency of ITC responses (Figure 6.1), we can consider a
window between 100 and 300 milliseconds after stimulus onset. The population
response of N neurons to image j is $_j\boldsymbol{x} = \left[_jx_1, \ldots, _jx_N\right]$.

    If we imagine that all of these inputs might project to a given postsynaptic neuron, we
can write the total aggregated input to the postsynaptic neuron as the weighted sum of

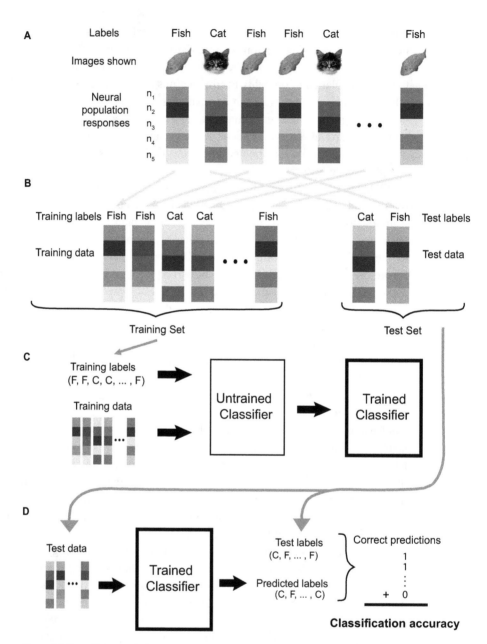

Figure 6.4 Decoding population responses. Basic steps involved in training and testing a classifier. (A) Illustration of an experiment where images of cats and fish were shown in random order to a subject while simultaneous recordings were made from five neurons/channels. The grayscale level denotes the activity of each neuron/channel. (B) Data points and the corresponding labels are randomly selected to be in either the training set or in the test set. (C) The training data points and the training labels are passed to an untrained classifier that "learns" which neural activity is useful at predicting which image was shown – thus becoming a "trained" classifier. (D) The test data are passed to the trained classifier, which produces predictions of which labels correspond to each unlabeled test data point. These predicted labels are then compared to the real test labels (i.e., the actual labels that were presented when the test data were recorded), and the percentage of correct predictions is calculated to give the total classification accuracy. Modified from Meyers and Kreiman 2011

all these inputs: $w_{1j}x_1 + \ldots + w_{Nj}x_N$. Those weights can be thought of as a measure of the synaptic strength, the impact that a given input will have on the postsynaptic neuron. Can such a downstream neuron detect the presence of a cat or a fish? We can build a detector that can read out from the population activity whether the image shown in a given trial contained a cat or a fish. We will set a threshold on the total combined inputs, $g(w \bullet x)$ for short, where g indicates a nonlinear function like a sigmoid, w and x are the vectors defined above of dimension N, and the "$\bullet$" represents a dot product. We can define that if $g >$ threshold, the image contains a cat, and if $g <$ threshold, then the image contains a fish. Machine learning algorithms offer several astute ways of choosing those weights w to minimize the number of classification errors that the algorithm makes. We will not go into the details here, but just to be concrete, we can imagine that we use a support vector machine (SVM) classifier with a linear kernel, which is a robust way of choosing those weights and which is the approach followed by Chou Hung and colleagues. This approach can be extended to many categories, not just binary classification. The key inference is that, if a reliable and simple (e.g., linear) classifier can be learned, then the pseudo-population of neurons contains sufficient information about the stimuli that can be readily extracted by biologically plausible computations (dot product followed by nonlinearity).

Using this approach, Hung et al. found that a relatively small group of ITC neurons ($N \sim 200$) could support object categorization quite accurately: up to ~90 percent accuracy in a task consisting of eight possible categories (where chance is one in eight). Furthermore, the pseudo-population response could extrapolate across changes in object scale and position. In other words, it is possible to fit the w values using the responses x_1 to images at a particular scale, and then subsequently use the responses x_2 to images at a different scale to accurately predict object labels. Thus, even if each neuron conveys only noisy information about shape differences, a small population of neurons can be powerful in discriminating among visual objects in individual trials, even extrapolating to transformed versions of the images used for training.

6.8   ITC Neurons Are More Concerned with Shape than Semantics

In the previous section, we considered whether it is possible to discriminate which object category was presented to the monkey by reading out neural activity from the ITC. Instead of decoding the object category, it is also possible to ask which specific exemplar was presented to the monkey. A population of ITC neurons excels at this question as well. Quantitatively comparing exemplar identification and categorization performance is tricky because the two tasks are not equated in terms of difficulty. First, in the experiment discussed in the previous section, there were eight categories and close to 80 exemplars. Therefore, even by chance, it is easier to get the object category right. Equating chance levels can be easily achieved by randomly subsampling and picking only eight exemplars. Yet this does not quite address a more challenging problem in this type of comparison: it is easier to distinguish a picture of a face from a picture of a house than to distinguish between two different houses.

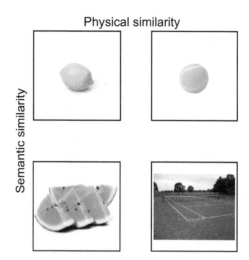

Figure 6.5 ITC neurons are more concerned with shape similarity than semantics. These images share more physical similarity along the horizontal dimension and more semantic similarity along the vertical dimension. Responses in the ITC more closely reflect the physical properties of the stimulus – including color, size, and shape.

Do ITC neurons carry any type of categorical information, or is shape the main variable that is represented in ITC? To answer this question, we need to better define what we mean by "category." The word category is typically associated with semantic labels. One way to dissociate semantic information from pure shape information is to consider objects that are physically similar but semantically distinct and vice versa (Figure 6.5). For example, a lemon is similar to a tennis ball in terms of its color, size, and approximate shape. However, a lemon is *semantically* closer to a watermelon or a tree, and a tennis ball is semantically closer to a tennis court or a tennis racquet. There is no evidence to date that ITC neurons can link a tennis ball to a tennis court, or link a lemon to a watermelon. Instead, there is evidence that ITC neuronal responses to physically similar images are closer than responses to semantically similar but physically distinct objects.

An elegant series of experiments that tackled the question of categorization was conducted by Earl Miller's group. They created synthetic images of cats and dogs and morphed between them in such a way that they could continuously change shape similarity without affecting categorical ownership or change category ownership with small changes in shape similarity. They found that ITC neuronal responses correlated with shape similarity better than with categorical ownership. They also recorded responses from neurons in the prefrontal cortex, which is one of the targets of ITC neurons. In contrast with the ITC neurons, the responses of those prefrontal cortex neurons did reflect the task-dependent categorical boundaries.

Another intriguing case where neuronal responses seemed to be dissociated from pure shape information is the case of those neurons recorded from the human medial temporal lobe discussed earlier (Section 6.5). Those neurons do seem to carry semantic information that transcends physical shape similarity, and those neurons receive either direct or indirect information from the anterior ITC, but they are not part of the ITC.

As repeatedly stated, the absence of evidence should not be interpreted as evidence of absence. It is conceivable that there may be semantic information that can be dissociated from pure shape information in ITC, but there is no clear evidence for this yet. Semantic information is a critical component of how we use language. In addition to the medial temporal lobe and prefrontal cortex, structures responsible for language are likely to contain neurons that represent semantic information. Furthermore, it is plausible that such semantic neurons may project back to the ventral visual cortex and modulate or sharpen visually evoked responses.

6.9   Neuronal Responses Adapt

Neurons throughout visual cortex are particularly sensitive to change. Neuronal responses dynamically depend on the temporal context. Temporal context can dramatically alter visual experience (Section 3.8), as in the illusory perception of upward motion after fixating on a waterfall, due to adaptation. As a consequence of adaptation, the responses of ITC neurons, as those in earlier parts of visual cortex, are transient (Sections 2.9, 5.7, and 5.12). If a constant stimulus is shown for many seconds, the neuronal responses only last a few hundred milliseconds.

Adaptation is an evolutionarily conserved property of visual processing that is also prevalent in other sensory systems. One function of adaptation is probably to save energy by reducing the number of spikes triggered by an unchanging stimulus. At least partly, the biophysical mechanisms underlying such suppression may be due to intrinsic changes in a neuron through transient modulation of its membrane conductance. However, adaptation is also evident at much longer time scales than the presentation of a single stimulus. For example, exposure to an adapter stimulus leads to a reduction in the neural response to subsequent presentations of the same or similar stimuli, a phenomenon known as repetition suppression. The repetitions need not be adjacent in time. Suppression is also evident even when there are other intervening stimuli, though the strength decreases with the time interval between repetitions.

Adaptation is evident at multiple time scales. As discussed in Section 2.9 and Section 5.7 (Figure 5.6), neuronal responses are typically transient and are quickly attenuated during a single trial over scales of hundreds of milliseconds, even if the stimulus remains on the screen. Repetition suppression is a manifestation of adaptation at a scale of multiple trials, typically occurring over several seconds. Figure 6.6 shows an example paradigm where the effects of adaptation can take place over minutes. In the so-called oddball paradigm, a given stimulus is repeated multiple times (high-probability stimulus shown in blue), whereas another stimulus is shown only rarely (low-probability stimulus shown in orange). Figure 6.6B–C shows average population responses from multiple neurons in the rat primary visual cortex (V1) and in a higher

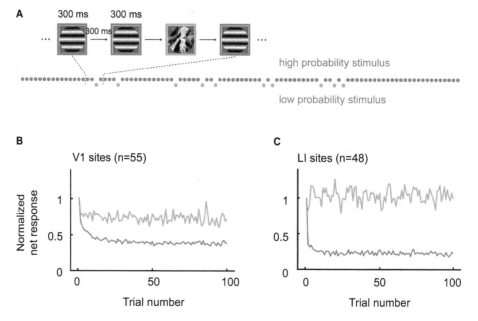

Figure 6.6 Neural adaptation increases the salience of novel stimuli. (**A**) Oddball paradigm where one stimulus is presented with high probability (blue) and another stimulus is presented with low probability (orange). (**B**)–(**C**) Normalized average population responses from neurons in rat primary visual cortex (B) and the latero-intermediate area (C) as a function of trial number for low- and high-probability stimuli. Modified from Vinken et al. 2020

visual area called the latero-intermediate area (LI). Whereas there is general agreement about what constitutes the primary visual cortex across species, it is less evident how to establish homologies between higher visual areas across species, and therefore, the nomenclature diverges across species. Repeated presentation of the high-probability stimulus leads to a sharp reduction in the neural responses over trials (blue). In contrast, the low-probability stimulus evokes a larger response, especially in area LI. This effect can help detect novel stimuli or changes in the environment.

Adaptation occurs throughout the visual system. The consequences of adaptation are stronger in higher areas like the ITC, or area LI in the rat, compared to earlier neurons like those in V1, probably due to the cumulative effects through a hierarchical cascade of neurons, each showing increasingly larger effects of adaptation that impact the next stage. In other words, adaptation leads to a reduction in response in RGCs and in the LGN, which in turn implies a weaker input to V1, and this is compounded with the intrinsic effects of adaptation in V1. The weaker V1 signals lead to a reduced input to V2, which is compounded with the intrinsic adaptation effects in V2, and so on. Another effect that could contribute to the increased adaptation in higher stages is that earlier areas are more sensitive to small eye movements, hence reducing the similarity in the inputs for prolonged stimulus durations or repetitions of the same stimulus.

6.10 Representing Visual Information in the Absence of a Visual Stimulus

Perceptually, prolonged exposure to a stimulus often leads to a temporarily reduced sensitivity to its features. The lingering effects after removal of the stimulus are called aftereffects, which have been described for a wide range of low- to high-level visual stimulus properties, and they are considered to be related to adaptation.

In addition to aftereffects, exposure to a stimulus leaves a memory trace that allows subjects to remember what they have just seen. A classical experiment used to study memory effects at short time scales is the delayed match-to-sample task. Subjects are presented with an image, the image disappears, and there is a delay of several seconds. After this delay, a second image is shown, and subjects have to indicate whether the second stimulus matches the first one (because it is identical, or because it is a scaled or rotated version of the same object, or because they match in color or any other property). Typically, the delay period consists of a blank screen. For subjects to be able to execute this task, neurons somewhere in the brain need to be able to maintain information about the preceding stimulus, even during the blank screen. Such information stored for a few seconds is typically referred to as *working memory*.

It turns out that, although the responses of neurons in the ITC are drastically reduced in the absence of visual stimulation, the activity does not fully return to baseline (Figure 6.7). Instead, ITC neurons maintain a small activation above baseline during the delay. Furthermore, this delay activity is stimulus selective: a neuron will maintain higher delay activity if its response to the preceding stimulus was higher.

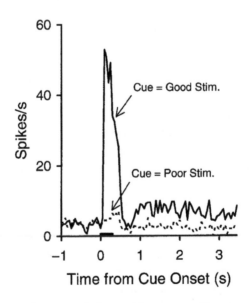

Figure 6.7 Selective neuronal response during working memory. Responses of a neuron during a delayed match-to-sample task when the cue was a good stimulus (solid) or a poor stimulus (dashed). The horizontal black bar denotes the cue duration (300 milliseconds). Reproduced from Chelazzi et al. 1998

Some investigators have interpreted those neuronal responses during the delay period in the absence of visual stimulation as an example of *visual imagination*. They argue that the subjects are imagining the sample stimulus to hold it in memory during the delay. To the extent that this is the case, it would seem that ITC neurons may show a selective response that matches the animal's internally generated percept irrespective of sensory inputs. It is difficult to directly test this idea due to the challenge in eliciting volitional visual imagery in animals. In humans, several investigators have measured neuronal correlates of volitional imagery, but those responses have been investigated in the medial temporal lobe rather than in the ITC.

Taking these ideas a step further, another situation where visual percepts can be generated in the absence of concomitant visual inputs is during dreams. Humans often report vivid visual imagery during dreams. Whether the visual cortex is involved in the representation of those visual percepts remains to be determined. We will come back to this discussion in Section 10.4.

6.11   Task Goals Modulate Neuronal Responses

We have described properties of ITC neuron responses as if they were static and immutable, but this is far from the case. For example, the reduced response to repeated presentation of the same stimulus (Section 6.9, Figure 6.6) shows that temporal aspects of the task can modulate neuronal responses. Beyond the temporal reduction in the response, other aspects of the current task goals can also modulate responses throughout ventral visual cortex.

One of the most studied forms of task-dependent modulation of neural responses is the effect of attention introduced in Section 5.17. A typical paradigm to study spatial attention is to train a monkey to fixate in the middle of the screen while devoting covert attention to either the left or right hemifields. Under these conditions, monkeys show enhanced performance and faster reaction times during visual discrimination tasks when a stimulus is presented within their locus of attention. Furthermore, the same visual stimulus, presented at the same location in the receptive field of the neuron under study, evokes a stronger response when the monkey is paying attention to the location encompassing the stimulus (Figure 6.8). Such attentional modulation is evident throughout the entire range of stimulus preferences.

Other aspects of the task goals can also modulate neuronal responses along the ventral visual cortex. During visual search experiments, the subject is looking for a particular object or a particular feature (e.g., looking for Waldo). For example, Robert Desimone's laboratory trained monkeys to look for red oriented bars. Under these conditions, neuronal responses to red objects were enhanced throughout the visual field. Other typical tasks involve flashing images while subjects have to indicate in a forced-choice yes/no fashion whether a particular target object is present or not. Here again, trials containing the target object or object category trigger enhanced neural responses. In Section 3.7, we described two forms of temporal contextual modulation: priming and backward masking. Both of these manipulations also impact the responses

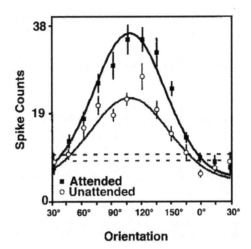

Figure 6.8 Spatial attention modulates responses in area V4. Modulation of the tuning curve of a V4 neuron in response to gratings of varying orientations when the animal attends to the receptive field location (solid squares) or when attention is diverted away from the receptive field location (empty circles). Reproduced from McAdams and Maunsell 1999

in the ITC. In sum, while the contents of what is on the screen at a particular moment are the main determinants of the responses of ITC neurons, current goals, spatial context, temporal context, and other task demands can modulate the responses throughout the ventral visual cortex.

6.12   The Role of Experience in Shaping Neuronal Tuning Preferences

Neuronal responses can be altered during a task as a consequence of adaptation (Section 6.9), memory (Section 6.10), or task-oriented goals (Section 6.11). Neuronal responses can also be altered over longer time scales. Neuronal tuning preferences are malleable and depend strongly on the diet of visual experience that the animal is subject to. A perennial debate focuses on the relative role that nature and nurture play in shaping the architecture of visual cortex and neuronal response tuning functions.

Genetics largely dictates the basic architecture of the visual system. Animals are born with visual structures like the eyes, LGN, and different cortical areas. While there are differences between species, the six cortical layers, as well as their canonical connectivity with each other and between cortical areas, seem to be either already present at birth or formed shortly thereafter. Furthermore, there is a small but clear degree of orientation selectivity that can be measured in primary visual cortex right at the time of eye opening in ferrets, cats, and monkeys.

Mature tuning properties are a consequence of experience. Several experiments have shown that visual inputs shape the mature neural tuning in primary visual cortex. For example, monocular deprivation (i.e., eliminating inputs from one eye) leads to an expansion of neuronal preferences for the active eye at the detriment of neurons responding to inputs from the deprived eye. Dark rearing leads to impaired orientation tuning throughout the primary visual cortex. Furthermore, experiments in which cats are reared in environments where they are predominantly exposed to vertical lines rather than horizontal lines lead to a preponderance of V1 neurons preferring vertically oriented bars rather than horizontal ones.

Given that even the early stages in cortical processing depend on visual experience, it is perhaps less surprising that subsequent stages can also be modified by changing the statistics of the visual inputs. As mentioned earlier, neurons in macaque ITC can respond selectively to shapes like paperclips after the monkey is exposed to those images. It is clear that monkeys are not born with neurons tuned to arbitrary paperclip shapes. Furthermore, monkeys can be trained to recognize symbols, like numbers or letters. After training, ITC neurons can also respond selectively to those novel shapes, and, again, such tuning is not present at birth or without training. The presumed ethological relevance of natural stimuli like faces has led some investigators to suggest that tuning for those shapes could be innate. However, careful experiments have refuted this hypothesis. If monkeys are reared in an environment without any exposure to faces, then investigators do not find clusters of neurons tuned to faces. In sum, current evidence suggests that in the development of visual response functions, genetics provides the underlying architecture and the plasticity rules while environmental statistics guide the learning of tuning functions for neurons throughout visual cortex.

The shaping of ITC neuron tuning happens not only during development but also in adults. The paperclip and numeric symbol experiments were both conducted in adult monkeys who were exposed to those novel images over periods of several months.

Neuronal tuning can also even be changed much more rapidly. For example, it is likely that if we learn to recognize characters in a new language, or if we learn to recognize a new person, we would find changes in neuronal tuning in the ITC. Indeed, elegant experiments in monkeys have shown that it is possible to alter the tuning properties of ITC neurons over the course of a recording session lasting less than an hour.

6.13   The Bridge between Vision and Cognition

The studies discussed here constitute a non-exhaustive list of examples of the type of responses that investigators describe in the highest parts of the inferior temporal cortex. While the field has acquired a considerable number of such examples, there is an urgent need to put together these empirical observations into a coherent theory of visual recognition, which will be the focus of the next chapters.

It is critical to develop more quantitative and systematic approaches to examine feature preferences in extrastriate visual cortex (and other sensory modalities). The methodology described in Section 6.4 provides initial steps toward unbiased ways of interrogating neuronal tuning functions in visual cortex. At the same time, we should aim to describe a neuron's preferences in quantitative terms, starting from pixels.

What types of shapes would a neuron respond to? This quantitative formulation should allow us to make predictions and extrapolations to novel shapes. It is not sufficient to show stimulus A and A" and then interpolate to predict the responses to A'. If we could truly characterize the responses of the neuron, we should be able to predict the responses to any different shape B. Similarly, as emphasized multiple times, feature preferences are intricately linked to tolerance of object transformations. Therefore, we should be able to predict the neuronal response to different types of transformations of the objects. Much more work is needed to understand the computations and transformations along ventral visual cortex. How do we go from oriented bars to complex shapes such as faces? A big step would be to take a single neuron in, say, the ITC, be able to examine the properties and responses of its afferent V4 units to characterize the transformations from V4 to the ITC.

This formulation presupposes that a large fraction of the ITC responses is governed by their V4 inputs. However, we should keep in mind the complex connectivity in cortex and the fact that ITC neurons receive multiple other inputs as well (recurrent connections, bypass inputs from earlier visual areas, back projections from the medial temporal lobe and prefrontal cortex, and connections from the dorsal visual pathway). There is clearly plenty of unexplored territory for the courageous investigators who dare explore the vast land of the extrastriate ventral visual cortex and the computations involved in processing shapes. Another incipient area of active research that is still in its infancy and will require serious scrutiny in the near future is to further our understanding of how high-level visual information interfaces with the rest of cognition.

6.14   Summary

- The inferior temporal cortex (ITC) sits at the pinnacle of the visual cortical hierarchy, receiving strong inputs from both ventral and dorsal cortical areas and projecting widely to areas involved in episodic memory formation, decision making, and cognitive control.
- Monkey and human ITC neural responses are selective for a wide range of shapes, including abstract patterns, bananas, chairs or faces.
- ITC neurons represent an extensive overcomplete dictionary of features, are more concerned with shape rather than semantics, and show invariance to image transformations.
- ITC neurons can complete patterns from partially visible stimuli.
- The activity of neural populations in the ITC in single trials can be used to decode object information with linear classifiers.
- Neural responses continue representing selective visual information even in the absence of a visual stimulus.
- Neuronal tuning properties are the result of experience with the statistics of the visual world.

Further Reading

See more references at http://bit.ly/364H8WR

- Arcaro, M. J.; Schade, P. F.; Vincent, J. L.; Ponce, C. .R.; and Livingstone, M. S. (2017). Seeing faces is necessary for face-domain formation. *Nature Neuroscience* 20: 1404–1412.
- Freedman, D.; Riesenhuber, M.; Poggio, T.; and Miller, E. (2001). Categorical representation of visual stimuli in the primate prefrontal cortex. *Science* 291: 312–316.
- Hung, C. P.; Kreiman, G.; Poggio, T.; and DiCarlo, J. J. (2005). Fast read-out of object identity from macaque inferior temporal cortex. *Science* 310: 863–866.
- Liu, H.; Agam, Y.; Madsen, J. R.; and Kreiman, G. (2009). Timing, timing, timing: fast decoding of object information from intracranial field potentials in human visual cortex. *Neuron* 62: 281–290.
- Logothetis, N. K., and Sheinberg, D. L. (1996). Visual object recognition. *Annual Review of Neuroscience* 19: 577–621.

7 Neurobiologically Plausible Computational Models

Supplementary content at http://bit.ly/2HpAqRm

We have been traveling through the wonderful territory of the visual cortex, examining the properties of different brain areas and neural circuits, learning about how animals and their neurons respond to visual stimuli and what happens when different parts of the visual cortex are lesioned or artificially stimulated. It is now time to put all this biological knowledge into a theory of visual recognition and to instantiate this theory through a computational model that can see and interpret the world. En route toward this goal, here we start by discussing how scientists describe neural circuits using computational models and define the basic properties of neural networks.

7.1   Why Bother with Computational Models?

I have to start by admitting that I am quite biased here. Building quantitative models is *necessary* for understanding. In fact, I would go even further and claim that understanding *means* building quantitative, predictive, and falsifiable models. For computer scientists, physicists, or mathematicians, this statement may be preaching to the converted because computational models are routinely taught in courses, and building such models is a daily endeavor. However, too often, biologists or psychologists look upon computational models with suspicion and wonder why we need models at all. The curricula in biology or psychology tend to lack examples of quantitative models; instead, concepts are often conveyed through language-based frameworks and graphics that aim to describe ideas about how the visual system works.

The progression from verbal ideas to formal quantitative descriptions is a sign of maturity in a field. The language of science is mathematics, not English or Esperanto. Descriptions that are not rigorously substantiated by mathematical thinking are often imprecise, ambiguous, and prone to failure. Another problem with verbal models is that they are usually not falsifiable because word definitions are not sufficiently well articulated, and the meaning of the words may be malleable enough to account for a wide variety of findings. An even more emphatic version of this claim was elegantly articulated by Max Tegmark, a famous MIT astrophysicist, in his argument for a mathematical universe.

In the course of formulating hypotheses, designing experiments, and interpreting the results, scientists implicitly make several assumptions, consider certain intuitions to represent established facts, and jump through presumably logical connections. Quantitative models force us to think about and formalize these hypotheses and assumptions. This process of explicitly stating assumptions can help us design better experiments, discover logical flaws in our thinking, and further understand the results.

It is often the case that the same questions, or closely related questions, are analyzed from different angles, using different experimental systems, or using the same systems in different laboratories. Scientists often use qualitative descriptions of the observations, and the same words can be interpreted in substantially distinct ways, giving rise to useless discussions. Consider statements such as "we recorded high-quality multiunit activity," "the neuron was highly selective," "the neuron responded more strongly to faces than other stimuli," or "the representation was strikingly sparse." These statements are full of ambiguity.

It is not trivial to compare results across different reports. Quantitative models can integrate observations across experiments, measurements, techniques, and laboratories. Seemingly unrelated observations can be linked together using a common theoretical framework. A model can point to critical missing data, critical information, and decisive experiments. A good model can lead to non-intuitive experimental predictions. It is often the case that experimentalists rightly or wrongly believe that they can come up with predictions for the next set of experiments based on their intuitions; however, intuition often fails (unfortunately). Striking examples of how intuition can fail (at the time) include the idea that the Sun rotates around the Earth rather than the other way around, the duality of waves and particles, and the tunnel effect in quantum mechanics. We discussed multiple examples of erroneous intuitions in previous chapters, including the idea that vision is instantaneous, that vision reflects precisely what is out there in the world, and that the entire world around us has the same high resolution. The power of abstraction is critical to be able to extrapolate and push the frontiers of knowledge beyond the limitations imposed by our biases and intuitions.

In addition, a quantitative model implemented through simulations can be useful from an engineering viewpoint (we will come back to this in Section 9.5). For example, consider the problem of building algorithms that will take inputs from a digital camera and recognize objects. As we will soon see, a theoretical model that describes how the primate visual cortex recognizes objects can lead to computational algorithms with broad applicability in the real world.

Sometimes experimentalists are afraid of formulating quantitative models and feel that building such models should be the domain of computer scientists or physicists exclusively. I have often encountered brilliant scientists who seem to be reluctant to venture into the wonderful land of computational models and theoretical neuroscience. One of the reasons may be the perennial fear of mathematics. In other cases, scientists may believe that they have to be "professional theoreticians" to build quantitative models. I would strongly argue against this notion.

Some of the most provocative computational models have come from scientists who probably do not consider themselves to be theoreticians, and who spend most of their lives perfecting insightful experiments. One could provide a long list of neat computational insights put forward by experimentalists. An excellent example of a model suggested by experimentalists is the proposal for how orientation tuning arises in primary visual cortex (V1). Hubel and Wiesel, the Nobel laureates introduced in Section 5.4, discovered that V1 neurons are tuned to the orientation of a bar within their receptive fields. In addition to describing the empirical findings, they went on to propose an elegant model of how orientation tuning could arise. They considered a feedforward model that pooled the activity of multiple units in the LGN with circular center-surround receptive fields (Figure 5.7). Hubel and Wiesel proposed that orientation tuning in simple cells in V1 arises by combining the activity of LGN units with receptive fields that are aligned along the preferred orientation of the V1 neuron. Since then, there has been a large body of computational work to describe the activity of V1 neurons. The insights of Hubel and Wiesel have played a key role in inspiring generations of experimentalists and theoreticians alike: modern computational theories of vision can trace their roots to those models proposed by Hubel and Wiesel.

7.2   Models of Single Neurons

At the heart of computational models of brain function is the fundamental "atom" of computation: the neuron. I reserve the word *neuron* to refer to real biological cells and the word *unit* to refer to a computational abstraction of what a neuron does (but some people in the field use these two terms interchangeably). Many models have been proposed to describe the activity of individual neurons. These models range from the use of filter operations to describe firing rates to simulations that include dendritic spines and even individual ionic channels. We can distinguish several categories of single-neuron models, in increasing order of complexity: filter models, integrate-and-fire models, Hodgkin-Huxley models, multi-compartmental models, models including dendritic subcompartments like spines, and models that incorporate realistic geometries.

As we move from filter operations toward realistic geometries, there is a significant increase in the biological accuracy of the model. Analytical solutions become more challenging, and often nonexistent, as we increase the complexity of the model (an equation is said to have an *analytical solution* if we can explicitly write down a closed-form expression that represents the solution). There is also a concomitant increase in the computational cost of the simulations as we move toward more complex models.

More biologically accurate models are not necessarily better, if the additional realism comes at the cost of too much complexity that is not directly relevant for the task at hand. As the famous fiction writer, Jorge Luis Borges, once said: "To think is to forget a difference, to generalize, to abstract." Borges illustrated this point in a delightful short story about abstraction and maps. A map constitutes a simple everyday example of how abstract models can be extremely useful. By definition, a map abstracts away many details to reveal fundamental properties, such as how to navigate from point A to point B. A city map with a 1:1 scale (where each foot in the city is represented by a foot in the map) would be much more realistic and contain every possible detail. Such a 1:1 scale map would occupy as much space as the city itself and would not be very useful for navigation. Biological systems may seem to be resilient to abstraction; evolution cares about fitness and does not optimize for human interpretability. The random variations that accompany evolutionary time scales lead to biological systems breaking "rules" all the time and the development of complexity that "just works."

There are several questions that we need to address to model the activity of a neuron. The answers to these questions depend on which specific aspects of the neuronal responses we are interested in capturing. Let us consider a simple analogy from fundamental physics. Imagine that we want to understand how an object of mass m – say, a cow – will accelerate as we apply a force F. We can consider a simple model that assumes that the object is a point mass – that is, that the entire mass is concentrated on a point where the force is applied – and write a one-parameter model $F = m \cdot a$. We are well aware that cows are not point masses; this assumption ignores the entire geometry of the cow. Although a trivial point, it should be noted that this one-parameter model does not do a perfect job of describing the movement of the cow in the presence of friction. Nevertheless, this simple model can capture essential ingredients of the problem, and it can even help us understand that the same principles behind the cow's movement also explain the movement of the planets.

In a similar vein, theoreticians often ignore the geometrical shape of a neuron with its dendrites and axons (Figure 7.1A). A simple idealization considers the unit as a single compartment, where inputs are received and integrated and the output is decided. For example, in the Hubel-Wiesel model mentioned earlier (Section 7.1, Figure 5.7), one can model the activity of individual V1 neurons as a filter operating on the visual input and describe aspects of the V1 responses without getting into the details of dendritic computation, biophysics of action potential generation, or other interesting neuronal properties.

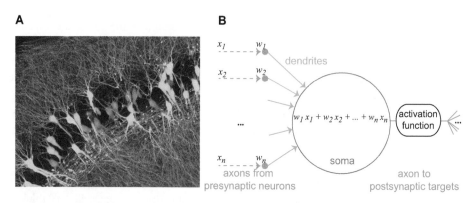

Figure 7.1 From real neurons to computational units. (**A**) Network of hippocampal neurons labeled with soluble tdTomato. Straub and Sabatini 2016. (**B**) A typical computational unit (blue circle) receives inputs from n presynaptic units $x_1, x_2, \ldots, x_n$. Each one of those inputs is multiplied by a synaptic weight w which controls the magnitude of the postsynaptic potential triggered by that specific synapse (orange circles). The dendrites (green) convey the information to the soma (blue), which computes a weighted sum of the inputs. A nonlinear activation function dictates the output for a given summed input level. This output is, in turn, communicated via the axons to other units.

Depending on the question, other times, it may be critical to consider multiple compartments – such as soma, axon, and dendrites. Different computations may take place depending on the location of inputs within a dendrite, and one may need to pay attention to the exact three-dimensional shape of every single axonal branch and the spatial distribution of spines and synapses on each branch. Einstein famously stated: "Make things as simple as possible, but not simpler."

A useful conceptualization of a neuron that is extensively used in neural network models is illustrated in Figure 7.1B. We can subdivide the neuron into three main compartments: dendrites, soma, and axon. Each dendrite receives inputs from another unit in the network. The presynaptic activity is denoted by x_i, with $i = 1, \ldots, n$, where n represents the total number of inputs. The activity of each input unit is a scalar value, which can be coarsely thought of as the firing rate of presynaptic input i. The impact of a given presynaptic input i on the unit of interest depends on a weight factor w_i, which can be coarsely thought of as the synaptic strength between the two units. In the simplest version, each of these inputs is considered to be independent, and their contributions are linearly added into the somatic voltage z:

$$z = w_1 x_1 + w_2 x_2 + \ldots + w_n x_n. \tag{7.1}$$

The summed activity is then passed through a nonlinear activation function to produce the output. This nonlinearity captures the notion that firing rates cannot be less than zero. It may also impose a maximum firing rate, and it may simulate other effects such as neuronal adaptation (Equation (7.2) implements only the first of these constraints). A particularly simple and commonly used activation function is the rectifying linear unit (ReLU), schematically illustrated in Figure 7.2:

$$y(z) = max\,(0, z). \tag{7.2}$$

The resulting activity y is then propagated to all the postsynaptic units. A nonlinearity such as the one in Equation (7.2) plays a critical role. First, there are whole families of functions that cannot be approximated without the introduction of nonlinearities. Second, as we will discuss soon (Section 7.4), we want to

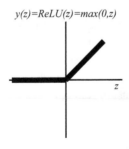

$y(z)=ReLU(z)=max(0,z)$

z

Figure 7.2 The rectifying linear unit (ReLU). A simple nonlinearity that is very popular in neural network models. The unit's activation is represented by a scalar value, loosely thought of as the "firing rate" of a real neuron. The unit receives a total input z, loosely thought of as the total summed voltage in the soma. The unit's output is rectified such that negative inputs lead to no activation, and the output is linearly proportional to z.

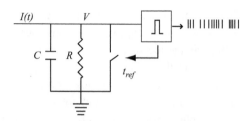

Figure 7.3 The leaky integrate-and-fire unit. The leaky integrate-and-fire model represents a neuron as an RC circuit with a capacitor C that integrates the incoming currents $I(t)$ and a leaky resistor R. When the voltage reaches a certain threshold, a spike is emitted, and the voltage is reset. A refractory period t_{ref} may be imposed before emitting another spike.

combine many units to build neural networks; the output $y(z)$ will constitute the input to another unit, and so on. If all we have at our disposal are linear functions, then instead of having multiple layers of units, each one linearly summing previous inputs, we might as well combine all the steps into a single linear operation (mathematically, if $y = Ax$ and $z = By$, then we might as well write $z = Cx$). Equation (7.2) is undoubtedly an oversimplification, but it is often a useful oversimplification.

The operations illustrated in Figure 7.1 and Equations (7.1) and (7.2) do not have any internal dynamics. A step up in complexity is the *leaky integrate-and-fire model*, which dates back to 1907 and is arguably one of the most often used conceptualizations for single units in computational neuroscience. The simplest instantiation of a leaky integrate-and-fire model is a resistor–capacitor circuit (Figure 7.3). A current $I(t)$ is integrated through a capacitance C and is leaked through a resistance R. The dynamics of the intracellular voltage $V(t)$ can be described by

$$C\frac{dV(t)}{dt} = -\frac{V(t)}{R} + I(t). \tag{7.3}$$

Whenever the voltage crosses a threshold, a spike is emitted, the voltage is reset, and an absolute refractory period is imposed. This oversimplified version of a real neuron captures some of our most basic intuitions about neuronal integration. Synaptic inputs are conveyed from dendrites onto the soma where information is integrated, and an output action potential is generated when the somatic voltage exceeds a threshold. This model does not capture several biophysical phenomena including spike rate adaptation, different computations in multiple compartments, spike generation outside the soma, the sub-millisecond events during an action potential, the neuronal geometry, or other vital nuances of neurons. However, the integrate-and-fire model simulates basic properties of how inputs are integrated to give rise to outputs quite well.

It is quite straightforward to write code to simulate the dynamic behavior of integrate-and-fire units. For example, here is a simple (and not entirely correct for the aficionados) implementation of the integrate-and-fire unit in a programming language called MATLAB.

```
1  V(1)=V_res;                 % Initial resting voltage
2  for t=2:n                   % For each time in the simulation from 2 to n
3          V(t)=V(t-1)+(dt/tau_m) * (E_L - V(t-1) + R_m * I_e(t));
                               % Change in voltage at time t
4          if (V(t)>V_th)      % If V(t) is above threshold V_th
5              spk(t)=1;       % Emit a spike
6              V(t)=V_res;     % And reset the voltage to a value V_res
7          end
8  end
```

In just a few lines, one can simulate this simple first-order differential equation and create spikes (spk) in response to arbitrary input currents (given by I_e(t)). As an example, we can set E_L=−65 mV, V_res=E_L, V_th=−50 mV, tau_m=10 ms, R_m=10 Mohm, n=1000 time steps, and dt=0.1 ms. We can play with different input patterns (e.g., a random input signal like I_e=2+3* randn(n,1)). The integrate-and-fire model can describe some of the basic instantaneous firing properties of cortical neurons. For example, when current is injected into a pyramidal neuron in cat primary visual cortex, the initial firing rate computed from the first two spikes can be well approximated by an integrate-and-fire model. Real neurons are fancier devices. Among other properties, neurons show adaptation, and the firing beyond the first two spikes is not well described by the simple integrate-and-fire model (but adjustments can be made to describe adaptation).

The integrate-and-fire unit does not capture the biophysical processes in the submillisecond dynamics describing the shape of action potentials. In another remarkable example of powerful intuition by experimentalists, Alan Hodgkin (1914–1998) and Andrew Huxley (1917–2012) provided fundamental insights into the generation of action potentials. They received the Nobel Prize for this work, which preceded the biological characterization of different ionic channels. The *Hodgkin-Huxley model* characterizes the shape of the action potential by incorporating the key sodium and potassium currents that are responsible for membrane depolarization and repolarization:

$$I(t) = C\frac{dV}{dt} + \bar{g}_L(V - E_L) + \bar{g}_K n^4(V - E_K) + \bar{g}_{Na}m^3 h(V - E_{Na}). \qquad (7.4)$$

E_L, E_K, and E_{Na} represent the leak, potassium, and sodium reversal potentials, respectively; g_L is the leak conductance; $\bar{g}_K n^4$ describes the time and voltage-dependent potassium conductance; and $\bar{g}_{Na}m^3 h$ describes the time and voltage-dependent sodium conductance.

Again, it is straightforward to write the necessary code to simulate the dynamics in a Hodgkin-Huxley model unit. The Hodgkin-Huxley model provides a significantly richer view of intracellular voltage dynamics compared to the simpler integrate-and-fire models, and is also widely used when exploring the properties of neural networks.

7.3   Network Models

Now that we have briefly described a family of increasingly more sophisticated models of single neurons, we are going to simplify each unit in a substantial way, going back to the representation in Figure 7.1. We are going to shift the focus from individual units to the properties of networks of interconnected units. Even though each individual neuron can perform interesting computations, visual selectivity, invariance, and the ability to solve different visual tasks emerges as a consequence of the interactions that take place at the network level. We will consider networks consisting of millions of units (a recent estimate calculated that there are about 416 million neurons in macaque area V1). Because of the computational cost of studying networks with large numbers of interconnected units when each of those units themselves can perform fancy computations, the vast majority of neural network models deal with elementary units.

Even highly oversimplified units can perform interesting computations when connected in sophisticated ways. Collective computation refers to the emergent functional properties of a group of interconnected neurons. Ultimately, to understand the output of a complex system like the brain, we need to think about circuits of units and their interactions. Intuition often breaks down quickly when considering the activity of the circuit as a whole, and neural network models can help understand those emergent circuit properties. To study fluid mechanics, one can abstract from the details of the collisions and trajectories of individual molecules and instead characterize properties of the fluid such as temperature and viscosity. Similarly, most neural network models idealize and simplify the component units. Networks can be built from simple electronic devices (operational amplifiers replace neurons; cables, resistors, and capacitors replace axons, dendrites, and synapses). The dynamics of neural networks systems can also be readily simulated in computers.

A typical neural network architecture involves arranging units in layers that process information sequentially. The initial layer represents the input, and we often think of the final layer as representing the output (although one might as well read out information from any of the layers). A three-layer network is schematically illustrated in Figure 7.4. Focusing on the middle layer only (gray rectangle), and assuming that the bottom of the diagram represents the input, the connections that go from the bottom layer to the middle layer are referred to as bottom-up or *feedforward* (shown in red). Without any other connections, this type of network is referred to as a bottom-up or purely feedforward network. The simplest version of a feedforward network is the *perceptron*, with a single input layer and an output. Connections between units in the same layer are referred to as *horizontal* (shown in blue, sometimes also referred to as *lateral* connections). Connections from the top layer back to the preceding middle layer are known as top-down or *feedback* (shown in green). Some investigators use the term *recurrent* connections to jointly refer to horizontal and top-down connections, but it is preferable to describe these connections separately since they can be involved in different computations. The connection strengths are characterized by strengths or weights – here denoted as W_{ij} for the

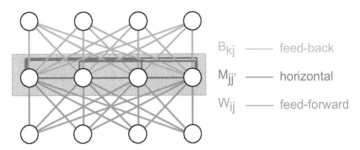

Figure 7.4 Feedforward, horizontal, and feedback connections in neural networks. Neural network models consist of multiple interconnected neuron-like units (circles here), each one of which follows the types of computations illustrated in Figure 7.1. A typical neural network architecture is to arrange units in layers. This diagram shows three layers. Assuming that the input is at the bottom of the diagram and the final output is at the top, we can distinguish feedforward connections (red), horizontal connections (blue), and feedback connections (green).

bottom-up connections, $M_{jj'}$ for the horizontal connections, and B_{kj} for the top-down connections. In the diagram in Figure 7.4, units are connected in an all-to-all fashion; that is, every unit in the bottom layer projects to every unit in the middle layer, and the same holds for all other connection types. Connectivity does not need not be all-to-all; some of the connection strengths can be set to 0 to indicate missing connections. Also, in the schematic in Figure 7.4, there are four units in each layer, and therefore all the indices i, j, and k go from 1 to 4, but this need not be the case; there could be different numbers of units in each layer. The diagram focuses on the connectivity to the middle layer, but in general, there would also be further bottom-up connections from the middle layer to the top layer and top-down connections from the middle layer to the bottom layer. In general, there would not be any horizontal connections in the bottom layer; we often think of the bottom layer as the input image. Similarly, in general, there would not be any horizontal connections in the top layer; we often think of the top layer as the output, indicating perhaps the presence of different classes of objects in the image.

Model units in neural networks may be either excitatory (positive weights) or inhibitory (negative weights). The same model unit could excite some postsynaptic targets and inhibit others. Except for a few counterexamples, this is not the case in biology, where a single neuron either provides excitatory outputs *or* inhibitory outputs, but not both.

Figure 7.4 does not constitute an exhaustive description of all the possible ways in which units can be connected in a neural network. In the most typical scenarios, units are connected within a layer (horizontal connections) or between adjacent layers (in a bottom-up and top-down fashion). However, it is also possible to build in "bypass" connections that skip a particular layer – for example, from the bottom layer to the top layer in Figure 7.4. Figure 7.5 schematically shows a variety of important neural network architectures that have been studied in the literature. This figure highlights some of the most important neural network architectures that have been used to model

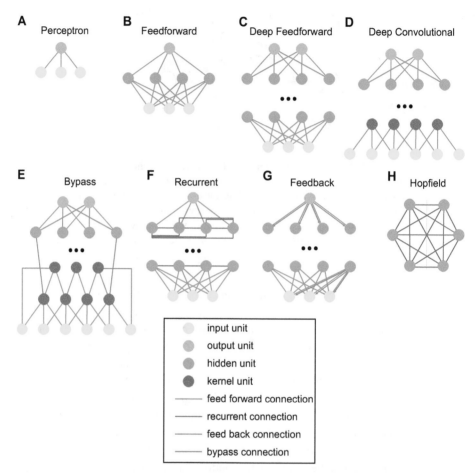

Figure 7.5 A family of neural network models. This figure illustrates a variety of important neural network models. In each diagram, the bottom layer provides the input (yellow), and the top layer provides the output (orange). Only a handful of units or layers are shown for illustration purposes. The "..." indicates that there could be many layers in between. In most cases, information flows from bottom to top via the feedforward connections (red). In **F**, there are additional recurrent connections (blue), and in **G**, there are feedback connections that provide information from an upper layer to a lower layer. The network in **H** is a different type of architecture where the units are all in the same layer, and they are reciprocally connected in an all-to-all fashion.

visual computations, but it is not exhaustive either. In all of those diagrams, only a handful of units are shown for illustration purposes, but there can be many more units.

In Figure 7.5A–E, units are organized in a cascade of layers conveying information from the bottom to the top, similar to the example in Figure 7.4, considering only the red lines. The hierarchical organization in these networks loosely resembles the hierarchical arrangement of computations in visual cortex (Figure 1.5), though even a glance of Figure 1.5 shows that current architectures only capture a small fraction of the complexity of the visual system.

7.4 Firing-Rate Network Models

Firing-rate network models constitute a simple yet instructive class of circuits. In the simplest instantiation, consider a feedforward circuit with N units projecting to a given output unit. The vector x represents the input activity. We can think of the components of x as the firing rate of each input unit. A scalar value y denotes the output firing rate. A synaptic kernel K_s describes how the input firing rate is (linearly) converted into an input current for the output unit. Theoreticians often represent the strength of a given synapse i ($i = 1, \ldots, N$) by a scalar value w_i. This value could represent a combination of the probability of synaptic release from the presynaptic neuron and the amplitude of the postsynaptic potential (positive or negative) evoked by the incoming neurotransmitters. The total input to the output unit I_s is given by

$$I_s = \sum_{i=1}^{N} w_i \int_{-\infty}^{t} d\tau K_s(t - \tau) x_i(\tau), \tag{7.5}$$

where w_i represents the weight or strength of each synapse. Using an exponential kernel, the dynamics of this circuit can be described by

$$\tau_s \frac{dI_s}{dt} = -I_s + \sum_{i=1}^{N} w_i x_i. \tag{7.6}$$

The firing rate of the output unit is usually a nonlinear function of the total input current: $y = F(I_s)$. F could be a sigmoid function or a rectifying threshold function.

7.5 The Convolution Operation

One of the key computational ingredients of visual processing is that the same operation is typically repeated throughout the visual field. For example, we find neurons in primary visual cortex that show orientation tuning with receptive fields tiling the entire visual field. Thus, a computational operation that filters the image to extract orientation information needs to be repeated over and over throughout the image. This type of operation is readily implemented through the *convolution operation*.

Given two functions $f(t)$ and $g(t)$, the operation of convolution (in Latin, *convolvere* means "to roll together"), denoted by the symbol * in the following equation, is defined as the integral of one signal being reflected, shifted, and multiplied by the other:

$$f(t) * g(t) = \int_{-\infty}^{\infty} f(\tau) g(t - \tau) d\tau. \tag{7.7}$$

In image processing, the process of convolution refers to shifting a given filter throughout the entire image (or the entire previous layer) and returning the output at each location. An example of this process is illustrated in Figure 7.6. For simplicity, here the input grayscale image is a handwritten version of the number 3, reduced to

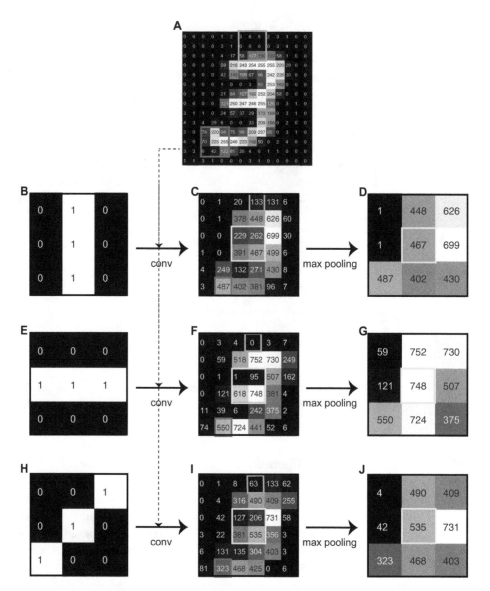

Figure 7.6 Basic operations in neural networks. A grayscale image (14 x 14 pixel image representing number 3) is convolved with three different filters (**B, E, H**). In this case, each of the filters is 3 × 3 pixels and, for simplicity, the values are only 0s and 1s. The convolution operation here has a "stride" of 2, meaning that the filter skips through one pixel as it slides through the image. The green (blue) location in the image (**A**) yields the output highlighted in green (blue) after convolution in (**C, F, I**). A pooling operation takes the output of the convolution and extracts the maximum in blocks of size 2 × 2, also with a stride of 2. The yellow location after convolution corresponds to the yellow location in the final output in **D, G, J**.

14 × 14 pixels. Each pixel has an intensity between 0 (black) and 255 (white). In general, the activation value of each unit does not need to be an integer, and the input image could have three colors, not just one. We consider three possible feature filters, shown in Figure 7.6B (vertical filter), **E** (horizontal filter), and **H** (diagonal filter). To simplify the numbers, here, the 3 × 3 pixel filter weights consist of zeros and ones, but again, in general, these filters would contain real values. The filter is placed at each location, and the filter values are multiplied by the corresponding values in the image. For example, consider the vertical filter and the green square at the top of the image containing the values 3, 6, 5 in the first row, 0, 0, 0 in the second row, and 58, 127, 130 in the third row (Figure 7.6A). We get $\mathbf{0} \times 3 + \mathbf{1} \times 6 + \mathbf{0} \times 5 = 6$ in the first row (bolded numbers come from the filter), $\mathbf{0} \times 0 + \mathbf{1} \times 0 + \mathbf{0} \times 0 = 0$ in the second row, and $\mathbf{0} \times 58 + \mathbf{1} \times 127 + \mathbf{0} \times 130 = 127$ in the third row. Adding these three numbers yields the value of 133 in the corresponding green square in Figure 7.6C. The same process is repeated throughout the entire image to yield the matrix in Figure 7.6C. Because the filter resembles a vertical line, after adequate normalization, the operation highlights regions of the input image that contain pixels that look like short vertical lines. Similarly, the filter in Figure 7.6E highlights horizontal edges, and the one in Figure 7.6H highlights diagonal edges.

We can think of these filters as a coarse approximation to simple neurons in area V1, responding to oriented lines (Section 5.4). The next step in area V1 is to pool signals from multiple simple neurons to create a complex neuron with similar tuning but responding more or less independently of the position of the preferred feature within the receptive field (Section 5.5). Inspired by the idea of simple and complex neurons, after convolution, we implement a *pooling* operation that combines multiple values within a window. This pooling operation increases the receptive field size. A typical pooling operation is to take a maximum of all the input values. For example, consider the yellow square at the center of Figure 7.6C, consisting of a 2 × 2 matrix with values 229, 262 in the first row, and 391, 467 in the second row. These four numbers are combined through the max operation to yield 467 in the corresponding yellow square in Figure 7.6D. The max-pooling operation provides position invariance by allowing high activity in any of the four locations.

The convolution and pooling operations provide a way to develop a system of hierarchical feature extraction steps. In the example shown in Figure 7.6, all the operations are fixed. In general, we are going to be interested in designing adequate filters to solve a particular problem or, even better, to learn those filters automatically. After learning to solve visual tasks, successive convolution and pooling layers in a network learn to extract progressively more complex features from the image, from edges to complex shapes and objects. We will come back to the question of how to train neural networks to learn the weights in Section 8.6.

7.6   Hopfield Networks

The dynamics of feedforward networks are quite simple, with information proceeding from one layer to the next. More elaborate dynamics can be generated in networks with recurrent

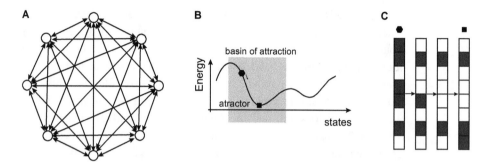

Figure 7.7 Attractor-based recurrent neural networks. (**A**) Schematic of an eight-unit Hopfield network with all-to-all connectivity and symmetric connectivity matrix ($w_{ij} = w_{ji}$). (**B**) The state of the network is characterized by an energy function with attractor states defined by the weight matrix. Starting in a state within the basin of attraction (gray rectangle) like the point represented by the hexagon will lead the network down the energy landscape to the attractor state represented by the square. (**C**) Example evolution of the network state from an initial state (hexagon) toward an attractor (square). Here each square represents the activity of a unit (gray = on, white = off). Three update states are shown here (arrows). The network can perform pattern completion because when it is initiated in a state that is close to but not identical to a memory (attractor), the dynamics will move the state toward the attractor.

connectivity. A simple yet rich example is the case of *Hopfield recurrent networks* (Figure 7.7). What is particularly attractive about these networks is that there are emergent properties of the circuit that are not easy to identify or describe upon considering only individual units without paying attention to the interactions. A Hopfield network can solve rather challenging computational problems and has interesting properties such as robustness to perturbations and the possibility of performing pattern completion.

The most basic version of the Hopfield network is defined by a single layer with binary units that are connected in an all-to-all fashion with symmetric weights. Figure 7.7A shows an example Hopfield network with eight units. Let the state of unit i at time t be represented by $s_i(t)$; this state can take the values 0 or 1 for a binary network. The network state is then represented by the vector $\mathbf{s}(t) = [s_1(t), \ldots, s_N(t)]$, where N is the total number of units (Figure 7.7C). There are no self-connections ($w_{ii} = 0$), and units are connected all-to-all in a symmetric fashion ($w_{ij} = w_{ji}$). Following Equations (7.1) and (7.2), the state of each unit is updated according to the thresholded and weighted sum of inputs from all the other units:

$$s_i(t+1) = sign\left(\sum_{j \neq i}^{N} w_{ij} s_j(t) - \theta\right), \tag{7.8}$$

where θ is a threshold. What is interesting about this type of recurrent architecture is that it is possible to define an energy function (Figure 7.7B) given by

$$E(t) = -\frac{1}{2}\sum_{i,j} w_{ij} s_i(t) s_j(t) + \sum_i s_i(t)\theta_i. \tag{7.9}$$

This energy function can be shown to be bounded below and to decrease monotonically according to the dynamics defined by Equation (7.8). In other words, the network has attractor states that it will converge to upon starting it at arbitrary states. If the network starts at a state represented by the hexagon in Figure 7.7B (state on the left in Figure 7.7C), it will dynamically evolve, always decreasing the energy of the network, until it reaches an attractor state represented by the square in Figure 7.7B (state on the right in Figure 7.7C).

Now suppose that we want to store a series of patterns $\mu = 1, \ldots, m$, defined by the state of each of the units: $\epsilon_1^\mu, \ldots, \epsilon_N^\mu$. We can use a Hebbian learning rule to calculate the weights of the units in the Hopfield network:

$$w_{ij} = \frac{1}{m} \sum_{\mu=1}^{m} \epsilon_i^\mu \epsilon_j^\mu. \tag{7.10}$$

These patterns define attractor states for the network. If we initialize the network at some arbitrary state, as long as that state is within the *basin of attraction* of a given attractor, the network state will evolve toward the corresponding attractor (Figure 7.7B and C).

From an implementation standpoint, a recurrent network with discrete time steps can be "unrolled" to convert it into a feedforward network with shared weights. For example, three time steps of a recurrent network with eight units can be implemented as a four-layer feedforward network with eight units in each layer, with all-to-all connections, and where the weights from one layer to the next are all the same across layers. For the Hopfield recurrent network, the lack of self-connections implies setting the weights from unit i in a given layer to unit i in the next layer to 0, and the symmetric connectivity matrix implies setting the weights from unit i in a given layer to unit j in the next layer equal to the weight from unit j to unit i in the next layer.

Despite this equivalence between recurrent and feedforward networks, the recurrent connectivity offers several advantages. First, the recurrent network requires fewer units (if T is the number of recurrent steps, the number of units in the feedforward equivalent network is $T+1$ times the number of units in the recurrent network). In biology, the size of the brain matters a great deal because of weight constraints and especially because of energetic constraints. The brain is particularly expensive from an energetic standpoint. Size and energy consumption considerations may also be relevant for certain computational applications such as implementing computer vision algorithms in a smartphone. Second, the recurrent network also requires fewer weights (again by a factor of $T+1$). The number of weights is also important in terms of size constraints in biology.

Furthermore, a critical advantage of recurrent networks is their computational flexibility. In a recurrent network, the architecture does not need to specify the number of steps, T, ahead of time. Some problems may be harder and require rumination during more steps, whereas other problems may be easier and require fewer steps. In contrast, the feedforward equivalent network offers a rigid structure where the computations always must traverse all the $T+1$ layers. To add flexibility and circumvent this problem, some feedforward networks include bypass connections where information processing can skip certain layers (Figure 7.5E). Achieving the full flexibility of the Hopfield network via bypass connections would require connecting every layer to every other layer, leading to an enormous increase in the number of weights. Most deep neural network models only include a small subset of all possible bypass connections.

One criticism of Hopfield networks is that there is no evidence of all-to-all connectivity in biological circuits. However, there is extensive evidence of partial horizontal connections between neurons within a given layer in cortex, and these connections can bring the multiple benefits outlined here: efficiency in space and energy requirements, flexible computations, and pattern completion. Another consideration is that reciprocal connections where unit i connects to unit j and unit j connects to unit i are the exception rather than the rule in biology, especially if the strength has to be symmetrical.

7.7   Neural Networks Can Solve Vision Problems

How can neural networks solve any type of vision problem? Let us consider a simple visual recognition task. Imagine that we have a set of images consisting of handwritten versions of the number 3 and handwritten versions of the number 7 (Figure 7.8A). Humans can look at each picture and rapidly tell that the one on the left is a 3 and the one on the right is a 7. Now consider a neural network. The exact architecture of the neural network is not relevant for the moment; we can think of any of the network architectures in Figure 7.5 for now, and we will have more to say about different architectures in Sections 8.3–5. The input to the network is the intensity of every pixel in the image. The size of the examples in Figure 7.8A are 16×16 pixels, so there would be 256 input units (a vector of 256 numbers concatenating all the rows in the image matrix). The activation of each input is an intensity value from 0 (black) to 255 (white). Each image would have a different combination of those 256 values. As we discussed in Section 2.11, we can think of these numbers as a coarse rendering of the firing rates of retinal ganglion cells in response to the image.

We can try to classify the images directly based on those 256 values. Alternatively, we can build a neural network, such as the one in Figure 7.4, with 256 input units (instead of the four inputs shown in that figure). Armed with many examples of 3s and 7s, the neural network can be *trained* to adjust the connection strengths to learn suitable features that may make it easier to separate the two groups of images. In Section 8.6, we will discuss how those connection strengths can be adjusted. For the moment, let us assume that we have already trained the network. After training, the neural network extracts a set of features from each image. We can represent those features and plot all the images in a multidimensional graph like the one in Figure 7.8B, where each point corresponds to a different image. The number of dimensions corresponds to the number of features – that is, the number of units in the neural network, before the classification layer. The output classification layer will have as many units as the number of classes to separate – in this case, two output units: one indicating the presence of a 3 and another one indicating the presence of a 7.

We can think of the cascade of computations that take place from one layer to the next as the set of computations that happen from the retina to visual cortex (Chapters 5 and 6). Using this mapping, we can think of the activation of each of the output units as a coarse rendering of the firing rates of neurons in the visual cortex. The exact area in

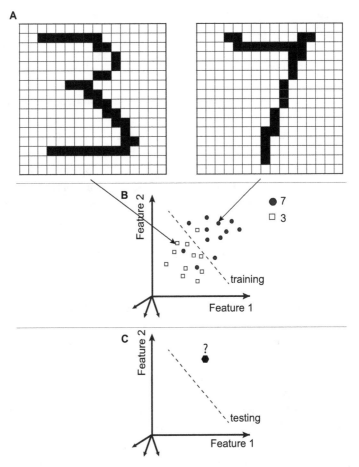

Figure 7.8 Schematic example of a vision problem solved by a neural network. (**A**) Consider a set of many images representing handwritten digits 3 and 7, only two of which are shown here. (**B**) The pixel intensities can be fed onto a neural network that will extract a set of features. Each image can then be represented by a point in a multidimensional space consisting of multiple features. Here all the 3s are represented by white squares and all the 7s by gray circles. The dataset is used to train a classifier (schematically represented here by the dashed line) to separate the two types of images. (**C**) Given a new image that was not used during training, the classifier will label it as 3 or 7, depending on which side of the line it falls.

the visual cortex is not relevant for the current discussion here; we will come back to comparisons between neural networks and the responses of neurons in different parts of the visual cortex in Section 8.14.

In Section 6.7, we illustrated how a classifier can learn to discriminate between different types of pictures based on the firing rates of a population of neurons (Figure 6.4). We can now use the same procedure to classify the images based on the features extracted by the neural network. The dashed line in Figure 7.8B represents the classifier: an image is classified as a 3 if the point falls "below" the dashed line in this graph and as a 7 otherwise. Of course, the dashed line corresponds to a hyperplane in a high-dimensional space because, generally, there are more than just two features. Additionally, the procedure can be readily extended to a classification problem with multiple classes, not just two (for example, classifying all ten handwritten digits, Section 8.10).

If we are now presented with a new image – that is, an image that has *not* been used to train the neural network – we can again compute the activation values and plot the new test image on the same graph (Figure 7.8C). The classifier can thus assign a label of 3 or 7 to the new image. Extending the mapping between units in a network and neurons in the brain, we may think that the activity of a population of neurons in visual cortex is read out by neurons in another brain area that is ultimately responsible for our ability to say "this image is a 3" and "that image is a 7." In Chapter 8, we will dig deeper into the architectures of neural networks (Section 8.5), how well they map onto the cascade of computations throughout ventral visual cortex (Section 8.14), and how well they can explain visual behaviors (Sections 8.12 and 8.13).

7.8   Extreme Biological Realism: The "Blue Brain" Project

Before ending this chapter, we come back to the notion of computational models and abstraction. Many biologists strongly feel that oversimplified networks like the ones described here fail to capture the complexity and richness of neurobiological circuitry. This observation is, of course, completely accurate.

At the other end of the spectrum in network models, one encounters efforts like the "Blue Brain" project. This project aims to introduce a significant amount of biological realism, using sophisticated and intensive network simulations. The ambitious goal is to create an in silico replica of a rodent brain, maybe even a human brain one day. In contrast to the abstractions used in neural networks, the project intends to create biophysically more realistic simulations of individual neurons, and incorporate direct data about neuronal shapes and interconnections between neurons.

Current neural networks, even in the simplified and abstracted format of Figure 7.4, have an enormous number of tunable parameters (Section 8.9). Building biologically detailed models of neural circuitry adds many orders of magnitude of complexity in terms of the numbers of free parameters. For example, should models consider the detailed geometry of every dendrite, the distance between neurons, the amount of myelin surrounding each axon, the distinct biophysical properties of the myriad different types of interneurons? The list of biological properties goes on and on. For many of these additional parameters, we still do not have sufficient data to constrain realistic models. Even if we did have enough experimental data to constrain the enormous parameter space, it is not immediately apparent that we would want to include all the minutia of the biological machinery. The previous brief discussion regarding the appropriate level of abstraction and realism in modeling single neurons is equally applicable here in the context of network models.

7.9 Summary

- To understand vision, it is essential to build quantitative computational models.
- We use models with varying degrees of abstraction, where biological properties are simplified to extract basic computational principles.
- The integrate-and-fire neuron consists of a leaky integrator and captures essential properties of how inputs to a neuron are converted into output activity.
- The convolution operation allows extracting the same visual features throughout the entire visual field.
- Basic elementary computations include filtering, normalization, pooling, and nonlinearities.
- Combining multiple units leads to neural network models with emergent computational properties that ultimately boil down to the combination of simple elementary steps.
- Neural networks typically include feedforward connections, horizontal connections, and top-down connections.
- Mixing these different types of connections, it is possible to construct a wide variety of different neural network architectures.
- Attractor-based recurrent neural networks like the Hopfield network can show interesting dynamic properties that save energy, provide flexible computational power, and show robustness to perturbations.
- Neural networks can solve vision problems.

Further Reading

See more references at http://bit.ly/2HpAqRm
- Dayan, P., and Abbott, L. (2001). *Theoretical neuroscience*. Cambridge: MIT Press.
- Gabbiani, F., and Cox, S. (2010). *Mathematics for neuroscientists*. London: Academic Press.
- Hopfield, J. J. (1982). Neural networks and physical systems with emergent collective computational abilities. *PNAS* 79: 2554–2558.
- Koch, C. (1999). *Biophysics of computation*. New York: Oxford University Press.
- Markram, H. (2006). The blue brain project. *Nat Rev Neurosci* 7: 153–160.

8   Teaching Computers How to See

Supplementary content at http://bit.ly/36RxOGX

We have come a long way since our initial steps toward defining the basic properties of vision in Chapter 1. We started with characterizing the spatial and temporal statistics of natural images (Chapter 2). We summarized visual behavior – that is, how observers perceive the images around them (Chapter 3). Lesion studies helped define specific circuits in the cortex that are responsible for processing distinct types of visual information (Chapter 4). We explored how neurons in the retina, the thalamus, and the ventral visual cortex respond to a variety of different stimulus conditions (Chapters 2, 5, and 6).

In this chapter, we will put all of these separate bits and pieces of phenomenological observations into a coherent theoretical framework to understand how neuronal circuits orchestrate the processing of visual information. We introduce computational models that instantiate this theoretical framework, endowing machines with the possibility of beginnings to see and interpret the visual world around us.

8.1   Recap and Definitions

We start by summarizing key observations from previous chapters to define constraints to solve the problem of vision. A theory of vision, implemented by a computational model, should satisfy the following eight desiderata.

1. *Selectivity*. The visual system shows a remarkable degree of selectivity demonstrated by the ability to differentiate among shapes that appear to be similar at the pixel level (e.g., arbitrary three-dimensional shapes created from paper clips, symbols, letters, and different faces). A model should be able to discriminate among images that are similar in pixel space yet represent different objects (Figure 1.4).

2. *Transformation tolerance*. A trivial solution to achieve high selectivity would be to memorize all the pixels in an image – i.e., a pure template matching algorithm (Figure 1.4). This type of algorithm would not tolerate any changes in the image. An object can cast an infinite number of projections onto the retina (Figure 1.3). These image transformations arise due to changes in an object's position with respect to fixation, its scale, in-plane or depth rotations, variations in contrast, illumination, color, or occlusion, among others (Figure 3.6). The importance of

combining selectivity and tolerance constitutes a critical feature of vision systems and a substantial challenge for computational models.

3. *Speed*. Vision is very fast, as emphasized by many psychophysical experiments, as well as neurophysiological recordings in humans and monkeys (Section 3.6). In approximately 150 milliseconds, we can extract the presence of objects and get a good first impression of what is happening in an image. This speed imposes a constraint on the number of computational steps that the visual system can use for visual recognition tasks.

4. *Generic*. We can recognize a large variety of objects. Estimates of the exact number of object categories that primates can recognize vary widely depending on several assumptions and extrapolations. Certain types of objects that an individual is particularly familiar with may be especially interesting. Those objects may have more cortical real estate associated with them; they could be processed faster and could be independently impaired. However, independently of precise figures of the number of shapes that primates can identify, and independently of a nonuniform distribution over object classes, there exists a generic system capable of distinguishing multiple arbitrary shapes. In fact, we can even discriminate shapes seen for the first time (referred to as one-shot learning).

5. *Implementable in an image-computable algorithm*. A successful theory of vision needs to be described in sufficient detail to be implemented through image-computable algorithms. An image-computable algorithm takes an image as an input – or a sequence of images – and produces an output. The requirement for such a quantitative algorithm is essential because the computational implementation allows us to run simulations and to quantitatively compare the performance of the model against behavioral metrics. The simulations also lend themselves to a direct comparison between the model's computational steps and neurophysiological responses at different stages of the visual processing circuitry. The computational model can be tested with the same images used in behavioral or neurophysiological experiments.

In contraposition to image-computable models, there are various fascinating ideas and theoretical constructs about vision that have not been implemented through computational algorithms. We can refer to these ideas as language-based conceptualizations or verbal models. As a brief, concrete example, a verbal model can state that the visual system has filters that extract color information, image edges, textures, and the presence of faces. Verbal models can be useful for the field and can inspire the development of computational models. However, verbal models are insufficiently specified and are therefore prone to misinterpretation (What exactly is a texture or a face? How is color information extracted?). Verbal models do not provide quantitative predictions (How fast will a subject distinguish between images with different edge orientations? What will be the firing rates of a population of neurons that distinguish one face from another one?). Because verbal models are not well specified, they are not falsifiable. Furthermore, we cannot easily compare different verbal models, or verbal models versus quantitative models, or verbal models and behavioral or neural responses.

An algorithmic implementation forces us to rigorously state assumptions and formalize the computational steps. In this way, computational models can also be readily compared to other models, in addition to behavior and neural responses. The implementation can also help us debug the theory by discovering erroneous hidden assumptions and cases where performance diverges from behavioral or neural metrics.

6. *Restricted to primates.* For simplicity, here we follow the lead of previous chapters, and we restrict the discussion of computational models to primate vision. There are strong similarities in vision at the behavioral and neurophysiological levels between macaque monkeys (one of the prime species for neurophysiological studies) and humans. Some of these models may well apply to other species (e.g., cats and rodents). Some aspects of the model may require refinement and modification for other species. When thinking about invertebrate vision (e.g., flies), there may need to be more drastic changes to the overall models.

7. *Biophysically plausible.* We aim to directly link the theoretical framework for vision to actual brain circuits, thus bridging across the three levels of analyses proposed by David Marr and Tomaso Poggio (Section 1.9). Therefore, the computational implementation should be based on neural networks, meaning that the model must be able to explain how computations take place in terms of the basic elements of computation in neural circuits – that is, neurons. We restrict ourselves to models that are biophysically plausible and, in doing so, skip a vast literature in computer vision where investigators try to solve similar problems without direct reference to cortical circuitry.

    Pure engineering approaches to vision are useful from a practical viewpoint irrespective of whether they have any connection to brain circuits. Ultimately, in the same way that computers can be successful at chess without any direct connection to how humans play the game or airplanes can fly with only a tangential relationship to how birds fly, computer vision approaches can achieve high performance in visual tasks without mimicking neuronal circuits. Even though such algorithms can be useful in everyday tasks, they do not constitute a biophysically plausible model of primate vision.

    An advantage of paying attention to neural circuits and behavior is that we can take inspiration from biology to solve tasks that may be easy for humans and hard for machines. The insistence on biological plausibility should not be taken to imply that the operations or architectures in current networks are necessary, let alone sufficient, to understand visual computations. It is likely that we will have to make substantial changes to current neural networks, but the ultimate flavor of the implementation needs to be mapped onto biological hardware. Finding the correct level of detail when defining biophysical plausibility remains an interesting challenge (Sections 7.2 and 7.8).

8. *Restricted to the visual system.* The visual system is not isolated from the rest of the brain. There are plenty of connections between the visual cortex and other sensory cortices, memory systems in the medial temporal lobe, and frontal

cortex, among other brain regions. Even though we often operationalize multiple tasks to try to separate vision from other processes as much as possible, in the real world, the lines between vision and other computations are often blurred. Connections outside the visual system also play an important role in visual processing, predominantly through feedback signals that incorporate expectations (e.g., the probability that there is a lion in an office setting is minuscule), through prior knowledge (e.g., the object looks similar to another object that we are familiar with), and through cross-modal integration (e.g., the object is likely to be a musical instrument because of the sound). As an initial simplification, and as a strategy to tackle a difficult problem, we restrict the discussion to the visual system.

8.2 Common Themes in Modeling the Ventral Visual Stream

Several investigators have proposed computational models that aim to capture some of the essential principles behind the transformations along the primate ventral visual stream. Before discussing some of these models in more detail, we start by extracting common themes that are shared by many models.

The input to models of visual cortex is typically an image, defined by a matrix that encodes the color of each pixel. Typically, this is a three-dimensional matrix with the red, green, and blue (RGB) intensities for each pixel. Models can also work with unidimensional grayscale inputs, and it is also possible to extend the models to more than three input dimensions, for example, to consider species that can see beyond the visible portion of the spectrum for humans. Dynamic inputs can be incorporated as a sequence of frames. Because of the type of images and video available, and because of the computational resources required, most models deal with a cropped version of the entire visual field; for example, a famous computer vision study by Geoffrey Hinton's group used 224×224 pixel images as input.

Because the focus is often on the computational properties of ventral visual cortex, many investigators ignore the complexities of modeling the computations in the retina and LGN. The pixels are meant to coarsely represent the output of retinal ganglion cells or LGN cells. The map between pixels and degrees of visual angle is not always made explicit in the models. Most models use images with a uniform resolution as input, without considering the eccentricity-dependent sampling that is evident in the retina and throughout visual cortex (e.g., Figures 2.7 and 2.8). These assumptions, of course, are among the many oversimplifications in typical computation models; images go through several transformations before retinal ganglion cells convey information to the LGN and on to cortex (Chapter 2). Incorporating a better account of the retina and LGN circuitry will likely improve the performance and robustness of current vision models.

Most models have a hierarchical and deep structure that aims to mimic the approximately hierarchical architecture of the ventral visual cortex (Figure 1.5, Section 5.12). The properties of deep neural networks have received considerable attention in the computational world, even though the mathematics of learning in deep neural networks with nonlinear responses are far less understood than their shallow counterparts. Neocortex and computer modelers have adopted a *divide-and-conquer* strategy whereby a complex problem is divided into many simpler tasks (Section 5.10). Ascending through the hierarchical structure of the model, units in higher levels typically have larger receptive fields, respond to more complex visual features, and show an increased degree of tolerance to transformations of their preferred features.

Most computational models assume, explicitly or implicitly, that "cortex is cortex"; that is, that there exist canonical microcircuits and computations that are repeated over and over throughout the visual circuitry. Thus, visual processing can be approximated by a hierarchy of sequential computational steps, each one of which is quite simple and encompasses basic biophysically plausible operations such as computing dot products, applying a nonlinear transformation to the integrated activity in the neuronal soma, and normalizing the outputs (Section 7.2).

8.3   A Panoply of Models

The oldest idea for visual object recognition is template matching, whereby the model stores a certain number of templates, and any new image is compared at the pixel-by-pixel level with those templates. Straightforward template matching at the pixel level does not work well for pattern recognition. Even shifting a pattern by one pixel would pose significant challenges for an algorithm that merely compares the input with a stored pattern in a pixel-by-pixel fashion.

As noted at the beginning of this chapter, a key challenge in visual recognition is that an object can lead to an infinite number of retinal images. If all objects were always presented in a standardized position, scale, rotation, and illumination, recognition would be considerably easier. Based on this notion, several approaches are based on trying to transform an input image into a prototypical canonical format by shifting, scaling, and rotating objects. The type of transformations required is usually rather complex. While ingenious computational strategies can overcome some of these problems, it is not entirely clear how the brain would implement such complex rotations and inferences, nor is there any apparent link from this family of models to the neurophysiological responses observed along ventral visual cortex.

Multiple models are based on describing an object based on its parts and inter-actions among those parts. The idea behind this approach is that there could be a small dictionary of object parts and a small set of possible interactions that act as building blocks of all objects. This intuition can be traced back to the prominent work of David Marr (1945–1980), who proposed that the constituent parts are based on generalized cone shapes.

The artificial intelligence community has also embraced the notion of structural descriptions. In the same way that a well-behaved mathematical function can be decomposed into a sum over a certain basis set (e.g., polynomials or sine and cosine functions), the idea of thinking about objects as a sum over parts is attractive because it may be easier to detect these parts in a transformation-invariant manner. In the simplest instantiations, these models are based on merely detecting a conjunction of object parts, an approach that suffers from the fact that part rearrangements would not impair recognition by the model but, in reality, they should (e.g., a house with a garage on the roof and the chimney on the floor). More elaborate versions include interactions between object parts and relative positions of different object parts. This approach converts the problem of object recognition into the problem of object part recognition plus the problem of recognizing characteristic relations between such parts. It is not entirely evident that object part recognition should be easier than object recognition, nor is it obvious that *any* object can be uniquely and succinctly described by a universal and small dictionary of simpler parts. The distinction between objects and parts is not well defined either. There have been few computational implementations of these part-based structural descriptions. More importantly, it is not entirely apparent how these structural descriptions relate to the neurophysiology of the ventral visual cortex. Despite these caveats, the idea of decomposing an object into parts and the computational advantages of a compositional representation are appealing and worth studying further.

A series of computational algorithms, typically rooted in the neural network literature, attempt to build deep structures whose purpose is to reconstruct the inputs. One version of this type of model is called an *autoencoder*. In an extreme version of this type of network, there is no information loss along the deep hierarchy, and backward signals carry information capable of recreating arbitrary inputs in lower visual areas. There are interesting applications for such autoencoder deep networks – in particular, the possibility of performing dimensionality reduction. However, the purpose of the cortex is precisely the opposite of perfect input reconstruction; it is to lose information in biologically helpful ways (Sections 5.10 and 5.13). The data processing inequality stipulates that the information contained in a signal cannot be increased via any kind of processing, without adding external information. Consider an input image that is processed via a sequence of steps from A to B to C. The representation at the C level can contain less information about the original image than at the A level (as a trivial example, we can multiply the signal in B times 0). The representation at the C level can contain the same amount of information as at the A level (as a trivial example, we can copy the signal from A to B to C). However, the representation at the C level cannot contain more information about the original image than the original image itself; the processing steps cannot create new information. Ascending through the visual system, and without adding external information, information content has to either decrease or stay the same. It is not clear why one would build an entire network to copy the input (even if the copy requires fewer units). In other words, a key goal of the ventral visual cortex is to extract relevant information such as object identity despite changes in the input at the pixel level.

Not all information is lost due to processing along ventral cortex, not even if that information is orthogonal to a given task. For example, it is possible to read out object location from neurons in inferior temporal cortex despite their relative tolerance to position changes (Sections 6.5 and 6.7). However, whereas the retina has neurons with receptive field sizes spanning a few minutes of an arc (1 degree of visual angle = 60 minutes of arc), and which can follow temporal changes at a rate of 100 hertz, neurons in the inferior temporal cortex are coarser in space and time. Even though we do not have a complete understanding of what information is lost in the transformations along the ventral visual cortex and what is preserved, it is clear that some information is lost; the goal of cortical processing is *not* reconstruction with perfect fidelity.

Particularly within the neurophysiology community, there exist several "metric" modeling approaches where investigators attempt to parametrically define a space of shapes and then record the activity of neurons along the ventral visual stream in response to the predefined parameters. For example, in some cases, investigators start by presenting different shapes in search of a stimulus that elicits strong responses. Subsequently, they manipulate the "preferred" stimulus by removing different parts and evaluating how these transformations modify the neuronal responses. While interesting, these approaches suffer from the difficulties inherent in considering arbitrary shapes that may or may not constitute truly "preferred" stimuli. Additionally, in some cases, the transformations examined only reveal anthropomorphic biases about what features could be relevant. Another approach is to define shapes parametrically. For example, several exciting studies considered a family of simple geometric shapes parametrized by different types of curvatures, and modeled neuronal responses in a six-dimensional space defined by a sum of Gaussians with parameters given by the curvature, orientation, relative position, and absolute position of the contour elements in the display. This approach is appealing because it has the attractive property of allowing investigators to plot "tuning curves" similar to the ones used to represent the activity of units in earlier visual areas. However, this approach also makes strong assumptions about the type of shapes preferred by the units. These parametrized stimulus shape descriptors have not readily lent themselves to image-computable models applicable to any possible natural image.

The visual system does much more than recognition, and the development of the visual system involves partly unsupervised learning from the environment during navigation, social interactions, and playing. Nevertheless, many of the computational models of vision have been tested in visual object recognition tasks. An appealing feature of recognition tasks is that they can be readily evaluated at the behavioral, neurophysiological, and computational levels. Additionally, many recognition tasks can be directly used in non-human animals. Before we delve into state-of-the-art image-computable models, let us define the approaches to solve object recognition tasks.

8.4   A General Scheme for Object Recognition Tasks

Figure 8.1 illustrates a typical approach in computer vision approaches to solve visual recognition tasks. Consider a series of M labeled images (x_i, y_i) where $i = 1, \ldots, M$, x is a matrix representing the image, and y is a label (e.g., whether a face is present or not, or a categorical label applied to the image). A set of features f is extracted from the images: $f_i = g(x_i)$, where g is the computational model. Those features may include properties such as edges, principal components, and colors, among many others. How those features are chosen is one of the key aspects that separates different computer vision

Figure 8.1 General scheme for visual classification tasks. Features are extracted from an image (or video). Those features are used to train a classifier via supervised learning. The resulting boundary is used to assign labels to novel images (i.e., images different from the ones used during training).

algorithms. The function g that extracts features could be hard-coded, or it could have multiple parameters – we shall call them w – that require tuning for a specific recognition challenge.

We will consider how those parameters are learned in Section 8.6. For now, let us assume that the parameters w are known and fixed. After extracting an adequate set of features f, a supervised learning scheme is used to learn the map between those features and the labels y. For example, a support vector machine (SVM) classifier with a linear kernel may be used to learn the correspondence between the features and the labels. This process is analogous to the readout from a population of neurons described in Section 6.7, except that here we use computationally extracted features as opposed to the biologically extracted features encoded in the firing rates.

A cross-validation procedure is followed (Section 8.8), separating the data into a training set and a test set to ensure that the algorithm is evaluated on new data – that is, to ensure that merely memorizing every training data point does not lead to good performance. Some investigators like to separate data into a training set, a validation set, and a test set. In this case, investigators fine-tune hyperparameters of the model by considering the training and the validation set and then use the test set for the final performance evaluation. After training, the algorithm is evaluated with the images in the test set. By using different algorithms applied to the same data, the merits of alternative computational models can be quantitatively compared.

8.5   Bottom-Up Hierarchical Models of the Ventral Visual Stream

Let us revisit the type of hierarchical neural network models introduced in Sections 7.3 and 7.5. A hierarchical network model can be described by a series of layers $l = 0, 1, \ldots, N$ (Figure 7.4). Each layer contains $n_l \times n_l$ units arranged in a matrix (the matrix does not need to be square), each unit having a circumscribed receptive field and, therefore, being activated by a specific location in the image. Additionally, there may be multiple different filters K_l at each location (sometimes referred to as kernels), creating a collection of such matrices; for example, the input image ($l = 0$) may have $K_0 = 3$ colors. Such a collection of matrices in each layer is called a tensor. The activity of all units in each layer can be represented by the value $\mathbf{x}_l$ ($\mathbf{x}_l \in \mathbb{R}^{n_l \times n_l \times K_l}$). Each entry in **x** is typically represented by a scalar value, usually referred to as its activation, which can be coarsely interpreted as the firing rate of the unit. The image is the input to the initial layer; x_0 represents the pixel values in the image. A different image would lead to a different set of activations x_l (in the previous section, we used the subindex i to denote the activations, or features, for each individual image, which is dropped here for simplicity and should not be confounded with the subindex l used here to denote a given layer).

From one layer to the next, the matrices are transformed through various convolution operations (Section 7.7), nonlinearities like the ReLU operation (Figure 7.2), and pooling operations like max-pooling (Figure 7.6). In the most typical scenario, these operations take place between layer l and layer $l + 1$. All of these operations together are referred to as a *convolution block* – including the convolution operation itself, ReLU, and the pooling operation. In fact, a single biological neuron may implement all of these computations as schematically illustrated in Figure 7.1.

This formulation based on sequential processing assumes that the activity in a given layer depends exclusively on the activity pattern in the previous layer. This simplification implies that at least three types of connections are ignored (Figure 7.4): (i) connections that "skip" a layer in the hierarchy (e.g., synapses from V1 directly onto area V4, skipping area V2); (ii) top-down connections (e.g., synapses from V2 to V1), and (iii) connections within a layer (e.g., horizontal connections between neurons with similar preferences in V1). Some variations, like the so-called ResNet architecture, also include connections that bypass some of the layers (introduced in Section 7.4).

It is tacitly assumed in most models that there exist general rules, often summarized in the epithet "cortex is cortex," such that only a few types of transformations are allowed in the computations from one layer to the next. One of the early models that aimed to describe object recognition, inspired by the neurophysiological findings of Hubel and Wiesel (Section 5.4), was the *neocognitron*, developed by Japanese computer scientist Kunihiko Fukushima. This model had two possible operations: a linear tuning function (performed by "simple" cells) and a nonlinear OR operation (performed by "complex" cells, Section 5.5). These two operations were alternated and repeated through the multiple layers in the computational hierarchy. This model demonstrated that such linear/nonlinear cascades can achieve scale and position tolerance in a letter recognition task. The neocognitron architecture inspired several subsequent efforts.

One such effort to expand on the computational abilities of the neocognitron is the HMAX model developed by Max Riesenhuber, Thomas Serre, and Tomaso Poggio at MIT. This model is characterized by a purely feedforward and hierarchical architecture. An image, represented by grayscale values, is convolved with Gabor filters (Section 5.7) at multiple scales and positions to mimic the responses of simple cells in V1. Like other computational efforts, the model consists of a cascade of linear and nonlinear operations. These operations come in only two flavors in the model: a tuning operation and max-pooling operation. The HMAX and similar architectures have been submitted to several tests, including comparison with psychophysical measurements and neuro-physiological responses, which we will discuss later in this chapter.

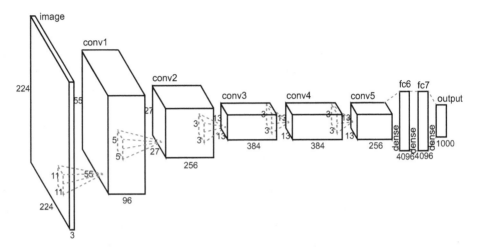

Figure 8.2 A deep convolutional neural network. Schematic architecture of the AlexNet deep convolutional neural network, consisting of the input layer, five convolutional layers (conv1 through conv5), two fully connected layers (fc6 and fc7), and the output layer. The numbers below each layer denote the size in pixels. The small elements inside each layer denote the size of the convolution filters. Modified from Krizhevsky et al. 2012

This family of models is referred to as *deep* neural networks, as opposed to *shallow* networks where the goal is to perform all computations in a single layer. Because these models are image computable, they can also be directly used to solve computer vision tasks. Indeed, in the last decade, these deep hierarchical models have gained appreciation and momentum in computer vision. One such model, often referred to as *AlexNet*, introduced by Alex Krizhevsky and Geoffrey Hinton in 2012 (Figure 8.2), caused an uproar in the computer vision world because it led to a considerable improvement in the ability to label objects in computer vision competitions. AlexNet subsequently inspired progress in many other pattern-recognition problems (Sections 9.2 and 9.4). A critical feature in AlexNet and many other neural networks is the ability to tune the parameters *w* to improve performance.

Historically, many computer vision efforts consisted of trying to develop better and better features to extract from the image. These features were then submitted to a suitable classifier. All the task-dependent learning happened at the level of the classifier. Various types of features were found to be generally useful for object classification tasks – including extraction of edges, colors, principal components, shift-invariant feature transformations (SIFT), corners, spatial frequency decomposition, and many others. A classifier, such as an SVM, was then in charge of learning the map between those features and the corresponding image labels, as in Figure 8.1. In the neocognitron, and in the initial implementation of the HMAX architecture, the weights between layers were handcrafted and fixed.

In stark contrast to these approaches, the bulk of the work nowadays consists of building end-to-end trainable systems, typically with a fixed architecture with randomly initialized weights, and where all the weights are plastic and can be modified to achieve the best-possible classification accuracy.

8.6   Learning the Weights

We have not yet described how the feature extraction parameters w are set. In general, we will consider neural network models (Section 7.3), where the main parameters are weights that dictate how activity in a given unit impacts activity in the postsynaptic target units, typically in the next layer. Let us now consider an example of a way of learning those weights that illustrates the interesting computations that can be performed by neural networks. The weights can be learned in a supervised manner (where we have labels for each image), or in an unsupervised manner (e.g., automatically extracting statistical regularities in the images in the environment). Here we will focus on supervised learning strategies, and we will come back to unsupervised tuning of weights in Section 8.17.

One of the earliest instantiations of a biologically inspired computational algorithm, a two-layer neural network called the *perceptron*, can be trained to perform interesting classification tasks. Imagine that we have some data that we want to classify into two possible groups. For example, there may be a collection of images of dogs or cats (each image contains only one animal), and we want to teach the algorithm to distinguish whether an image contains a dog or a cat. Each image, indexed by i, is a matrix of grayscale values that can be vectorized and represented by x_i. With each image, we have an associated label $y_i = +1$ (dog) or -1 (cat). We have a training set consisting of multiple such example images. In this type of exercise, it is always important to separate the data into a training set (used to fit parameters) and a test set (used to evaluate performance), a process referred to as *cross-validation* (Section 8.8; see further discussion in Section 9.12). In the two-layer perceptron network, we will consider the input to the output unit to be $w \bullet x$, where $\bullet$ represents a dot product. The output y will take the value $+1$ if $w \bullet x - \gamma > 0$, and -1 otherwise, where γ is a threshold value. The perceptron learning rule tells us how to choose the weights w to minimize the error in this classification task.

Instead of a binary classification task, we may be interested in approximating a given output function $h(s)$ (for example, $h(s)$ could represent the firing rate of a neuron in cortex in response to a stimulus s). For a given stimulus s, $h(s)$ is the target output for the neural network, and we define $\hat{h}(s)$ to be the actual output of the network. The error is the squared difference between the two: $E = \left(h(s) - \hat{h}(s)\right)^2$; this Euclidian distance is a typical way of evaluating the error, which has the nice property of being differentiable; this will become useful soon. Gradient descent refers to changing w to minimize the error in this task by making adjustments to w along the direction of greatest change in the error, $w \rightarrow w + \epsilon \nabla_w E$, where ϵ is a learning rate, and $\nabla_w E$ is the gradient of the error in the direction of w.

Classification problems need not be restricted to two classes, like cats versus dogs. In general, the goal is to take an image and assign a label to it. For example, the goal may be to detect whether the image contains a handwritten $0, 1, 2, \ldots,$ or 9, as in the MNIST dataset (Section 8.10), to distinguish cats versus dogs, or to identify a face.

The situation becomes more complex when we have multiple layers. Now, changing the weights in one layer will impact the next layer, which will, in turn, impact the next layer, and those changes are propagated all the way to the output. We need to take all of these interdependencies into account when tuning the weights in a deep neural network. One of the most successful ways of adjusting the weights via supervised learning in a deep neural network is *backpropagation*, where the difference between the target outputs and current outputs (that is, the error) is propagated back via gradient descent throughout the entire network. Backpropagation is an elegant example application of the chain rule from calculus.

Let us follow one simple example step by step to describe the concept of backpropagation. Consider the three-layer network shown in Figure 8.3A. The network consists of an input layer with two units whose activation values are represented by i_1, i_2; a hidden layer with two hidden units whose activation values are represented by h_1, h_2; and an output layer

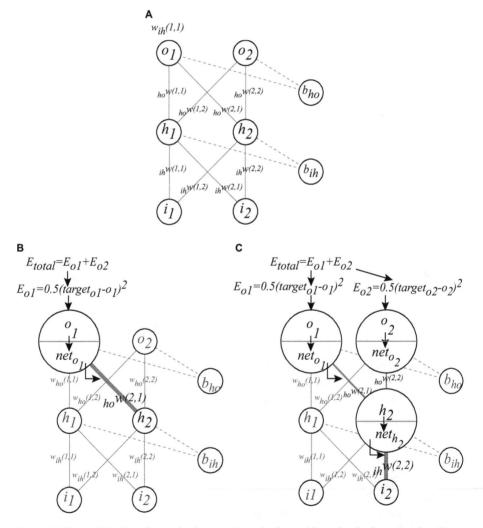

Figure 8.3 The weights in a deep neural network can be learned by using backpropagation. Deep convolutional neural networks take advantage of backpropagation, an efficient procedure to train the weights in a supervised learning fashion. (**A**) Example three-layer neural network. (**B**) To change the weight $w_{ho}(2,1)$ we calculate its effect on the total error by using the chain rule (see text for details). (**C**) Similarly, to change the weight $w_{ih}(2,2)$, we propagate the error throughout the network. (See text for details, adapted from Matt Mazur)

with two output units with activations o_1, o_2. The term "hidden unit" in a neural network is a somewhat strange nomenclature that refers to all the units that are neither the input or the output. Perhaps the term "intermediate unit" would be more reasonable, but the jargon of hidden units has stuck in the field. The weight from the input unit i to hidden unit h is $w_{ih}(i, h)$, and the weight from hidden unit h to output unit o is $w_{ho}(h,o)$. The bias for the hidden layer is b_{ih}, and the bias for the output layer is b_{ho}. The net input to each hidden unit is

$$net_{h_1} = i_1 * w_{ih}(1, 1) + i_2 * w_{ih}(2, 1) + b_{ih}.$$
$$net_{h_2} = i_1 * w_{ih}(1, 2) + i_2 * w_{ih}(2, 2) + b_{ih}. \tag{8.1}$$

Instead of the ReLU operation (Figure 7.2), here we calculate the output of each hidden unit by passing the net inputs through the nonlinear logistic function:

$$h_1 = \frac{1}{1 + e^{-net_{h1}}}$$
$$h_2 = \frac{1}{1 + e^{-net_{h2}}}. \tag{8.2}$$

The outputs of the hidden units are the inputs to the output units. The net input to each output unit is

$$net_{o_1} = h_1 * w_{ho}(1, 1) + h_2 * w_{ho}(2, 1) + b_{ho}$$
$$net_{o_2} = h_1 * w_{ho}(1, 1) + h_2 * w_{ho}(2, 2) + b_{ho}, \tag{8.3}$$

and those are passed through a logistic function as well:

$$o_1 = \frac{1}{1 + e^{-net_{o1}}}$$
$$o_2 = \frac{1}{1 + e^{-net_{o2}}}. \tag{8.4}$$

Now, given the inputs i_1, i_2 (we can think of these as the image that we are trying to classify), we obtain the outputs o_1, o_2. Our target values are the outputs $target_{o_1}$, $target_{o_2}$; we can think of these target values as the desired probabilities for class 1 and class 2 labels. For example, if we are classifying an image as a cat or a dog, the desired probabilities may be 0 and 1 for cats and 1 and 0 for dogs. The total error is

$$E_{total} = E_{o_1} + E_{o_2} = 0.5\left[\left(target_{o_1} - o_1\right)^2 + \left(target_{o_2} - o_2\right)^2\right]. \tag{8.5}$$

Now imagine that we change one of the weights – say, $w_{ho}(2,1)$ – what would we expect to happen to the total error (Figure 8.3B)? If we change $w_{ho}(2,1)$, that will cause a change in net_{o1} (but not in net_{o2}; see Equation (8.3)). Changing net_{o1} will, in turn, cause a change in o_1 (but not o_2). The change in o_1 will impact E_{total}. We can calculate how much we expect the total error to change by using the chain rule, and decomposing the gradient of E_{total} with respect to $w_{ho}(2,1)$ into each of these parts:

$$\frac{\partial E_{total}}{\partial w_{ho}(2, 1)} = \frac{\partial E_{total}}{\partial o_1} \frac{\partial o_1}{\partial net_{o1}} \frac{\partial net_{o1}}{\partial w_{ho}(2, 1)}. \tag{8.6}$$

Here is where the definition of the square error in Equation (8.5) comes in handy because it is easy to calculate derivatives. Each of these three factors can be readily computed by calculating the derivatives in Equations (8.3), (8.4), and (8.5), respectively:

$$\frac{\partial E_{total}}{\partial o_1} = 2 * 0.5 * \left(o_1 - target_{o_1} \right) \tag{8.7}$$

$$\frac{\partial o_1}{\partial net_{o1}} = o_1(1 - o_1) \tag{8.8}$$

$$\frac{\partial net_{o1}}{\partial w_{ho}(2, 1)} = h_2 \tag{8.9}$$

.   In order to make the total error smaller, we will change the weights according to

$$w_{ho}(2, 1) \rightarrow w_{ho}(2, 1) - \varepsilon \frac{\partial E_{total}}{\partial w_{ho}(2, 1)} \tag{8.10}$$

where ε is a learning rate that controls how big the changes in the weights are in each step.

We can follow the same procedure to change $w_{ho}(2,2)$, $w_{ho}(1,2)$, and $w_{ho}(1,2)$. In general, in a neural network, we want to change *all* the weights to make the output as close as possible to the target. How do we change the weights from the input units to the hidden units, such as $w_{ih}(2,2)$? We follow the same procedure (Figure 8.3C), back-propagating the error all the way from E_{total} down to the weight that we want to change. Going through multiple layers requires a few more maneuvers, but it follows the same ideas as before. The dependence of the total error on $w_{ih}(2,2)$ goes through hidden unit h_2 (and not h_1). Therefore, we can write

$$\frac{\partial E_{total}}{\partial w_{ih}(2, 2)} = \frac{\partial E_{total}}{\partial h_2} \frac{\partial h_2}{\partial net_{h2}} \frac{\partial net_{h2}}{\partial w_{ih}(2, 2)} \tag{8.11}$$

The last two factors are straightforward (in analogy to Equations (8.8) and (8.9)):

$$\frac{\partial h_2}{\partial net_{h2}} = h_2 * (1 - h_2)$$

$$\frac{\partial net_{h2}}{\partial w_{ih}(2, 2)} = i_2$$

The dependence of the total error on h_2 goes through both output units. Therefore, the first factor in Equation (8.11) becomes

$$\frac{\partial E_{total}}{\partial h_2} = \frac{\partial E_{o_1}}{\partial h_2} + \frac{\partial E_{o_2}}{\partial h_2} = \frac{\partial E_{o_1}}{\partial o_1} \frac{\partial o_1}{\partial net_{o1}} \frac{\partial net_{o1}}{\partial h_2} + \frac{\partial E_{o_2}}{\partial o_2} \frac{\partial o_2}{\partial net_{o2}} \frac{\partial net_{o2}}{\partial h_2}$$

$$\frac{\partial net_{o_1}}{h_2} = w_{ho}(2, 1)$$

$$\frac{\partial net_{o_2}}{h_2} = w_{ho}(2, 2)$$

According to Equation (8.8), we have $\frac{\partial o_1}{\partial net_{o_1}} = o_1 * (1 - o_1)$ and, similarly, $\frac{\partial o_2}{\partial net_{o_2}} = o_2 * (1 - o_2)$. According to Equation (8.7), we have $\frac{\partial E_{o_1}}{\partial o_1} = (o_1 - target_{o_1})$ and, similarly, $\frac{\partial E_{o_2}}{\partial o_2} = (o_2 - target_{o_2})$. We want to change the weight $w_{ih}(2,2)$ by the following amount:

$$w_{ih}(2, 2) \rightarrow w_{ih}(2, 2) - \varepsilon \frac{\partial E_{total}}{\partial w_{ih}(2, 2)}$$

The beauty of these steps is that we can go on applying the chain rule no matter how deep the network is. In fact, scientists and engineers routinely build neural networks that have more than a hundred layers and train them using essentially the same back-propagation procedure outlined here. In addition, iterating backward from the last layer avoids redundant calculations of intermediate terms in the chain rule such that all the previous terms from late layers can be reused for early layers.

Given an example with input values i_1, i_2, and target output values $target\ o_1$ and $target\ o_2$, we perform the steps outlined earlier to change all the weights in the network. In general, we have many examples consisting of input pairs and target output values (Section 8.4). In *stochastic gradient descent*, we go through those examples one by one, changing the weights after each iteration. A batch can also be introduced where the calculations are made for a few examples before actually changing the weights. The word stochastic refers to choosing the examples and order randomly.

Once we go through all the examples in the training set in a given iteration, we start a new iteration, readjusting the weights. This procedure goes on until convergence. The learning rate ε plays an important role. If the learning rate is too large, the procedure may diverge. If it is too small, convergence can be very slow, and the algorithm may also get stuck in local optima. Several heuristic approaches have been developed to adjust the learning rate, sometimes even changing it throughout learning (with faster learning at the beginning and slower learning toward the end). It is also possible to use distinct learning rates for different layers. There are multiple other variations that go beyond the scope of this chapter, and they can be found in computer vision and machine learning textbooks.

In general, the initial weight values are assigned randomly, but there has also been considerable empirical investigation of the virtues of different starting conditions. Biological brains probably do not start with entirely random connectivity weights. There is an inherent structure that subsequent plasticity rules act upon during learning. This initial structure could be the product of evolution and also activity-dependent developmental processes.

A particularly interesting starting condition arises when a network is "pre-trained" with a somewhat different problem than the one we are trying to solve. The application of weights trained in one problem to another problem is referred to as "transfer learning." For example, imagine that we want to build a network that recognizes handwritten letters. One might first train a network to recognize handwritten digits and use the weights from this pre-trained network as a starting condition for the letter recognition problem. Many of the computations needed to build a handwritten digit recognizer may be shared with those required to build a handwritten letter recognizer. Thus, starting with such a pre-trained network could accelerate training and may also lead to the same accuracy using fewer training examples. It is not immediately obvious what kind of problems would be suitable for this type of transfer learning approach. Intuitively, if the two tasks are very similar, then this approach may be advantageous, but if the two tasks are too different, then such pre-training might not provide any advantages.

As noted earlier, the chain rule enables the propagation of error through deep networks with many layers, and more layers typically mean more weights that need to be tuned. To adjust large numbers of weights, it is useful to have many example pairs of inputs and target outputs. In the case of image classification algorithms, these examples come in the form of images and labels.

8.7   Labeled Databases

There has been significant progress in a large number of image categorization tasks in the computer vision community. This progress has been fueled by a combination of increased computational resources, access to a large number of digital images (as well as videos), and exciting competitions in academic conferences.

The last decade has seen an explosion in the number of digital images available on the web. In 2019, users uploaded on the order of a few *billion* digital images every day (for instance, Facebook: ~300 million pictures per day; Instagram: ~100 million pictures per day). In addition, many users are inadvertently extremely helpful to the computer vision community by providing more and more content in the form of "tags," brief captions, "likes," and other commentaries. Every minute in 2019, humans took more digital photos than the total number of photographs available in the entire world a century ago. There has also been a rapid increase in the amount of video material being uploaded (for instance, YouTube: 0.5 million hours of video per day). In parallel to the availability of imagery, there are also now accessible platforms such as Amazon Mechanical Turk, where users can answer queries on images for a small fee. Investigators upload their images and pay subjects in Amazon Mechanical Turk to label them, leading to fascinating datasets with image content annotation and labels. Images, content, and the concomitant exponential growth in computational power have opened the doors to use networks with millions of tunable parameters for recognition tasks.

A typical example is the "ImageNet" large-scale visual recognition challenge. This dataset consists of color images downloaded from the web, each one associated with a label. In a typical instantiation of this competition, those labels include categories like "volcano," "hippopotamus," "dome," or "African elephant" (Figure 8.4). The 2014 version of ImageNet has been used extensively to compare different computer vision algorithms for object classification, and included 1,000 object classes, 1,281,413 images for training (732–1,300 images per class), and 100,000 images for testing (100 images per class).

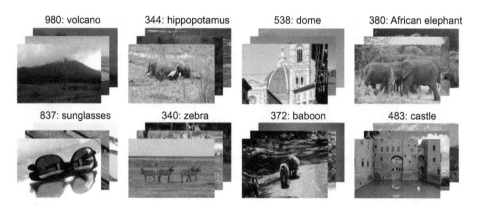

Figure 8.4 Example images from the ImageNet dataset. The availability of datasets consisting of millions of labeled images provided a significant boost to supervised learning algorithms for object categorization.

The fact that the images are downloaded from the web is a blessing and a curse: a blessing because the images encompass a wide diversity of properties where the object responsible for the image label can appear in multiple positions, at multiple scales, rotations, colors, illumination, degrees of occlusion, and other variations. To some coarse approximation, this may reflect the natural distribution of objects in the world. This approximation is not exactly accurate because those images are filtered through the lenses and biases of human photographers. For example, there are probably very few images of a hippopotamus in the middle of a rainy night. Images taken from the web are also a curse because of their uncontrolled nature and a large number of other somewhat miscellaneous contextual factors that contribute to classification. For example, in the three pictures of "domes" in Figure 8.4 (top row, third column), the pixels in the upper left are mostly blue. It seems likely that when people take pictures of domes, the pictures are set against the sky, and there is a higher propensity of blue at the top. In contrast, none of the "baboon" examples (bottom row, third column) contain blue at the top. Blue at the top is not a unique identifying feature of domes, though. Many other pictures also typically contain blue at the top (e.g., volcanos, elephants, zebras, and castles). There are also probably pictures of domes without blue at the top, and pictures of baboons with blue at the top. The point is that there are many complex correlations in the images that are only minimally related to the object labels themselves. Depending on the particular task and objective, these contextual correlations can represent a confounding factor or a useful property.

Another curious property of the ImageNet dataset is that several of the categories are quite intriguing. In fact, there are many category labels that I would have to look up in the dictionary (e.g., tench, junco). Additionally, many of those 1,000 classes correspond to specialized and refined groups of animals (how many humans can distinguish between the whiptail lizard, the alligator lizard, the green lizard, the komodo lizard, and the frilled lizard?). Nevertheless, computers are trained to recognize these categories from scratch, and the distinction between whiptail lizards and frilled lizards may be as crystal clear for a computer as the differences between sunglasses and domes are for humans. The point of these competitions was to quantitatively evaluate and compare computer vision algorithms, which can be readily done with whiptail and frilled lizards. We will return to discuss further aspects of training datasets in Section 9.12.

Computer vision algorithms that capitalize on supervised learning approaches with randomly initialized weights are typically data hungry. ImageNet contains on the order of 1,000 categories $\times$ 1,000 examples per category = 10^6 images. A database of this size was not available before circa 2012, and therefore, these images provided a nice playground to develop, refine, and build more complex deep convolutional neural networks. Given the huge amount of digital content, we should expect enormous growth in the size of vision datasets.

Another noteworthy aspect of ImageNet and similar datasets is that it empowered direct comparison and benchmarking of different algorithms. Comparing how algorithm X processes a dataset I_x to how an algorithm Y processes a different dataset I_y is challenging, a bit of an apples-versus-bananas comparison. Although this is a simple concept, benchmarks based on standard datasets are not common in other domains. For example, in neuroscience, almost every lab creates its own tasks, using their custom-made images, rendering results challenging to integrate and compare, and data sharing is still in its infancy.

8.8 Cross-Validation Is Essential

Armed with such a large dataset of labeled images, we prepare to train a computational algorithm to learn the map between the image features and their labels. Critically, we do not want to merely memorize every single image/label pair. Instead, we want to be able to infer correct labels for *novel* images that the algorithm has never seen before. To avoid sheer rote memorization camouflaged as high performance, it is critical to use *cross-validation* by separating the images within each label into a *training set* and a *test set*. All the model parameters can be modified ad libitum only while examining the training set, but we are not allowed to change any more parameters when evaluating the model on the test set.

In many cases, we use multiple random splits of the same dataset into non-overlapping training and test sets. The proportion of trials that go into the training set may not matter too much; the data can be split with 50 percent of the examples going into the training set, or 70 percent, or even leave-one-out where a single example is used for testing in each iteration. This procedure is repeated multiple times, and results are reported as the average performance over all random splits plus a measure of variation within the splits. As a control, it is useful to randomly shuffle the image labels, repeat the same procedure, and also report average and variation in performance for the case of shuffled labels.

In deep convolutional network models, the training step typically amounts to modifying the weights in a supervised fashion via backpropagation (Section 8.6). However, it may also be possible to explore other aspects of the model – including its architecture, number of layers, size of each layer, and computational motifs – as long as we limit ourselves to the training set. After training, the algorithm is tested with new images, and the fraction of images that are correctly labeled is reported.

In general, splitting the data into a training set and a test set is done randomly. To the extent that there are no duplicates in the dataset, no crops of the same images, and no other potential confounds, a random split should suffice to avoid deceiving ourselves via rote memorization, though we will have more to say about cross-validation in Section 9.10. Importantly, datasets should be carefully curated to avoid problems, such as duplicates or slightly modified versions of the same image, in order to properly assess performance. For example, consider an algorithm to recognize the faces of celebrities. People like to crop the same images of celebrities over and over again and upload them to their favorite social media. If a random split causes the training set to contain the same or essentially the same picture as in the test set, then we are not doing cross-validation properly, and we may be deluding ourselves into thinking that the algorithm is more impressive than it actually is.

8.9   A Cautionary Note: Lots of Parameters!

For modern neural networks with many layers, an intriguing aspect of the backpropagation procedure outlined in Section 8.6 to learn from examples is that adjusting the weights involves an enormous number of free parameters. Consider an image of 256×256 pixels with three colors: this amounts to 196,608 inputs. If there are 1,000 possible output category labels and, in the simplest scenario of mapping, the inputs directly onto the outputs, we would have about 200×10^6 parameters. The ImageNet dataset contains on the order of 10^6 images. In other words, the number of weights in a neural network (free parameters) can be orders of magnitude larger than the number of training examples.

More parameters than constraints can be problematic. As a simple example, let us go back to basic linear algebra and consider a system of linear equations with four unknowns. In general, if we have four "independent" equations, we are guaranteed to have a unique solution. However, if we only have two equations, the system is underdetermined; without any additional constraints, there are infinite possible solutions. The same problem arises when fitting a curve. If the curve has 10 free parameters, and we only have five data points, there are infinite solutions, and it is easy to overfit; that is, to fit the data with a fancy curve that may describe the data exactly, with zero error, but that does not extrapolate to new data. For example, consider a plot with the number of women versus the number of men in a given state, showing data from five states. We would probably not want to fit a polynomial of degree 10 to describe the data!

These classic examples of underdetermined systems and overfitting are well studied in high school math classes. What is surprising is that the most successful computer vision systems available today work precisely in this overfitting regime. As an illustration of the problem of hyperparametrization, we can randomly shuffle the labels in the training set in ImageNet: an elephant is labeled "chair," another elephant is labeled "tree," a car is labeled "sunglasses," and so on. A computer vision system can be trained to achieve high performance *on the training set* in this randomly shuffled set. In other words, a network with more parameters than training examples has a vast expressive power and can even memorize the entire data set. Of course, such a network would be at chance in the test set, further emphasizing the importance of cross-validation. There is currently significant interest in understanding how neural networks can still perform well on the test set and, thus, avoid overfitting, despite the enormous number of free parameters.

One way toward alleviating the potential problem of overfitting is to use more constraints for the same number of parameters. In many computer vision problems, one way to increase the number of constraints is to obtain more data. Getting labeled data can be a bottleneck in many practical applications, as well as in more biologically plausible learning mechanisms. Therefore, there is interest in ways to increase the amount of data without additional labeling, an idea generally referred to as "data augmentation." For example, consider a dataset like ImageNet. One could take each image and crop it, horizontally flip it, blur it, rotate it, add noise, and then use it as a separate training example with the same label.

8.10   A Famous Example: Digit Recognition in a Feedforward Network Trained by Gradient Descent

As an example application of these ideas, consider the task of learning to recognize handwritten digits from 0 to 9. In homage to Kernighan and Ritchie's introduction to coding in the C programming language, most programming courses start by learning how to print "hello world" to the screen. In machine learning, the equivalent to "hello world" is learning how to write code to identify handwritten versions of the digits 0–9. The MNIST (Modified National Institute of Standards and Technology) database consists of 60,000 training images and 10,000 test images.

In 1998, Yann LeCun and colleagues developed a feedforward network, trained by gradient descent, that could perform this task quite well, achieving an error rate of 7.6 percent, which was quite remarkable at the time (chance performance would be 90 percent error rate because there are 10 possible classes). A more recent computational model in 2019 achieves an error rate of 0.21 percent (that is, about one error in 500 images). This computational model includes a combination of multiple deep convolutional neural networks, a strategy that is common in computer vision systems: creating many expert systems and combining their predictions. Recognizing handwritten digits is an example task where computers have reached an accuracy that is comparable to, if not better than, human performance.

8.11   A Deep Convolutional Neural Network in Action

Next, we illustrate step by step how all the outputs of a deep convolutional neural network are generated. We want to show the activation of all the units. Because modern networks typically have a huge number of units, we will consider a simplified network for illustration purposes (Figure 8.5). This network takes as input a color image of size 56 × 56 pixels × 3 colors. The network has three convolutional layers, and it is trained to classify six categories of images from ImageNet (Figure 8.4): images of biological cells, Labradors, fire ants, sports cars, roses, and ice. These six categories were chosen randomly for illustration purposes. The output layer contains six values, one for each category. The network is trained by backpropagation (Section 8.6), using a randomly selected training set. After about 1,200 iterations, the network achieves an accuracy of 84 percent on the training set and an accuracy of 76 percent on the test set (where chance is one out of six, or 16.7 percent). As noted when discussing cross-validation (Section 8.8), the difference in performance between training accuracy and test accuracy typically reflects overfitting to the specific example images seen during training.

Figure 8.5 shows the activation of every unit in the network for one particular image of a sports car. To visualize every unit, activation values were normalized to remain between 0 and 1, and they are shown as a grayscale value (see color scale on the left of the figure). The image (top) consists of three channels: R, G, and B (which appear pretty similar in this example because the image is mostly gray). There are eight filters in the first step (conv1), each with a size of 3 × 3 pixels (like the filters shown in Figure 7.6). The number of filters in each layer is one of the many architecture decisions that we have to make when building a model; here, the number was arbitrarily set to eight for the first layer for illustration purposes. We can still see a semblance of the input image in the first layer activations, with each of the different filters accentuating certain features. The convolved image is passed through a batch normalization step, followed by the rectifying linear units (Figure 7.2). Batch normalization is a technique that improves the speed, performance, and stability of neural networks by normalizing the inputs to a given layer. Finally, the output is passed through a max-pooling step, which reduces the size from 56 × 56 to 28 × 28. The conv1 layer consists of 56 × 56 × 8 = 25,088 units, and the max pool 1 layer consists of 28 × 28 × 8 = 6,272 units.

The second and third layers go through the same steps with 16 and 32 filters, respectively, all of size 3 × 3 pixels. The activations are shown as an "image" in each square in Figure 8.5 by putting together all the units at a given step and for a given filter. As we go through the calculations from conv1 to relu3, the resulting "images" look less and less like the original one. The entire purpose of the network is *not* to produce an image that looks like the original one but rather to extract adequate features that can solve the classification task.

The relu3 values are passed onto a fully connected (fc) layer consisting of six outputs, reflecting the probability that the image label corresponds to each of the six possible categories. For the image in this example, unit 4 in this fc layer shows the maximum activation, which corresponds to sports car. However, other units in this layer still show non-zero probabilities. The resulting values, $z_1, \ldots, z_6$, are passed through a *softmax* function, $\sigma(z) = \frac{e^{z_i}}{\sum_{j=1}^{6} e^{z_j}}$, an operation that converts the values into probabilities that add up to 1, and then through a threshold to create the final winner-take-all value. These final activation values indicate the most likely label. In this case, the network correctly infers that the label for the image is a "sports car."

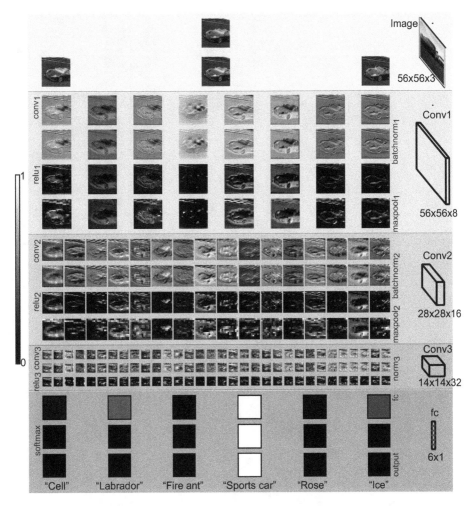

Figure 8.5 Example outputs from a deep convolutional neural network. A neural network where the input image is passed through three convolutional layers and produces six output probability values (see text for details). fc stands for fully connected layer, batchnorm stands for batch normalization, maxpool stands for max pooling, relu corresponds to a ReLU operation. The size of each convolutional filter is shown on the right. The network is trained to classify images from the six groups shown at the bottom. This figure shows the activation of every unit in the network in response to the image of a sports car shown at the top (see scale bar on the left). Of the six output units (bottom), the "sports car" unit shows the maximum activation; therefore, the network correctly infers the label for this example.

The activation of the fc units after the softmax function can thus be interpreted as the probabilities for each of the six labels. It is difficult to visualize the activation patterns in response to each of the ~8,000 images in this six-dimensional space. To represent the 8,000 × 6 matrix of activations, there are many dimensionality reduction techniques – including principal component analysis, independent component analysis, multidimensional scaling, and others. In Figure 8.6A, we used a dimensionality reduction technique

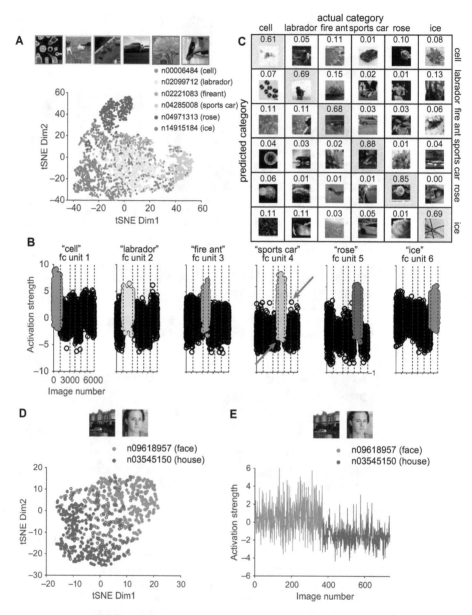

Figure 8.6 Examining the activity of the output layer in a deep convolutional neural network. (**A**) Rendering of the activity of the six fc units from the model shown in Figure 8.5 in response to every image, after reducing the dimensionality to two axes using a technique called tSNE (see text). Each color connotes a different object category. **B**. Activation of each of the six fully connected (fc) units in response to every image. Vertical dashed lines separate object categories; the color accentuates the images from the category that the fc unit is meant to classify. (**C**) Confusion matrix showing the proportion of images whose actual category label is the one shown in each column and where the model predicted the category shown in each row. (**D**)–(**E**) Even though this network was never trained to recognize human faces or houses, we can still find units that respond differentially to faces versus houses, and we can still use the same network to detect faces or houses. Modified from Kreiman 2018

with the fancy name of *t-distributed stochastic network embedding*, or tSNE for short. It is beyond the scope of this chapter to describe the mathematics of this technique (see the work of van der Maaten and Hinton, and, of course, there is also a Wikipedia page for it). With tSNE, like other dimensionality reduction techniques, similar images (in the sense of their distance in the six-dimensional fc space) are represented by nearby points, and different images are represented by points that are farther away. Each point represents one image, and the points are colored according to the actual labels (the coloring is not part of tSNE, which is an entirely unsupervised procedure and does not use any labels). Images with the same label (same color) tend to cluster together. Ultimately, classification accuracy depends on the comparison between the output layer (Figure 8.5) and the ground truth labels, but the separation in this two-dimensional tSNE space provides an intuitive hint that it is possible to adequately separate images with different labels.

Notably, this neural network used here for illustration purposes is relatively simple, in order to show the activation of all the units. A state-of-the-art network would achieve higher accuracy, and the clusters would be much better separated.

One could also use the same dimensionality reduction technique to render the activation of units in each of the other layers. What is particularly interesting about the fc layer is that its activation values are directly correlated with the network's output. In other words, in terms of the behavior of this network, we could refer to the fc unit number four as a "sports car" unit. We can also plot the activation of each of the six fc units for every image (Figure 8.6B). As expected, on average, the "sports car" unit (fc unit 4) shows higher activation for the images with a ground truth label of "sports car" (highlighted in cyan in Figure 8.6B). However, there are some images containing sports cars that elicit low activation in this unit (for example, the gray arrow on the bottom), and there are images that do not contain sports cars but still elicit high activation in this unit (for example, the gray arrow on the top). In other words, the "sports car" fc unit may fail to be activated by many images of sports cars, and it may show high activation by other images that do not contain a sports car. In Section 9.9, we will introduce techniques that can be used to describe what types of images elicit high activation for a unit in a network and also for neurons in the brain.

The network's output depends on the maximum fc value across all six units. If the ground truth label for a given image is "sports car" but the activation in the sports car fc4 unit is lower than the activation in another fc unit, then the network will make a mistake by selecting a different label. Conversely, if the ground truth for a given image is not "sports car" but the fc4 unit shows the maximum activation, then the image will be erroneously labeled sports car. Figure 8.6C shows how often these mistakes happen in the form of a confusion matrix. Columns indicate the actual category labels, and the rows indicate the predicted category labels. All of the entries along the diagonal are correct responses. For example, 88 percent of the time, when the image contained a sports car, the network correctly labeled it sports car (row 4, column 4 in the matrix). Sometimes, the image contained a sports car, and yet the network labeled it as "ice"; this happened for 5 percent of the sports car images in the test set (row 6, column 4 in the matrix). Other times, the image depicted ice, but the network labeled it as "sports car"; this happened for 4 percent of the ice images (row 4, column 6 in the matrix).

The six object categories used in Figures 8.5 and 8.6 were chosen randomly. The fc units are also activated by images that the network has *not* been trained on. One of the advantages of working with image-computable models is that we can directly quantify the response of the network to *any* image. For example, we can ask whether the same fc units, in the same network, would be activated by images of houses or human faces. Importantly, we are not retraining the network with these new images. The weights are fixed, and we merely monitor the activation of the fc units. The network has never seen a house or a face before; however, the units in the network are still activated by those images (in the same way that neurons in our visual cortex would be activated if we were shown a unicorn, even if we have never seen one before).

Again, we use tSNE to render the activation of all six fc units to all the images of houses and faces (Figure 8.6D). Even though the network was never trained with those images, it can still separate them quite well: the network achieved an accuracy of 86 percent in distinguishing faces from houses (where chance is 50 percent). The fc unit that showed the most distinct separation between faces and houses was the "sports car" unit (fc unit 4, Figure 8.6E). This unit showed a stronger activation to faces (0.47 ± 1.72), compared to houses (-1.54 ± 1.18). If an investigator were to conduct a study with this network and only were to show images of faces and houses, the investigator would probably call this unit a "face" unit. Yet, the activation of this fc unit to sports cars was 4.59 ± 2.27. Thus, merely showing a set of random images is not sufficient to interpret the activation of units in a network (see also the discussion in Section 6.4 and Section 9.9).

The exercise of evaluating the activity of the network for images that it was never exposed to before also helps us make another point. Without retraining, the network can solve visual classification problems that it was not trained on. The dictionary of features and computations learned by the network while trying to separate six arbitrary random object classes is sufficiently rich to be able to distinguish other image categories. One could even go on and, starting with the network pre-trained to distinguish among these six categories, retrain the network for a new task. Such retraining is another example of transfer learning, introduced in Section 8.6: training in one task first and then using the pre-trained network as an initial condition to learn a new task.

8.12   To Err Is Human and Algorithmic

In the type of visual classification problems that we have been discussing, the ground truth is set by humans. Let us go back to the MNIST dataset of handwritten digits; those digits have labels assigned by humans. Only by comparison to human behavior, we can define whether a computational model of vision makes mistakes or not.

In Figure 8.6B and C, we showed how computational models make mistakes, again by referring to labels provided by humans. Similarly, Figure 8.7 shows a confusion matrix comparing the outputs of a two-layer neural network and humans for MNIST.

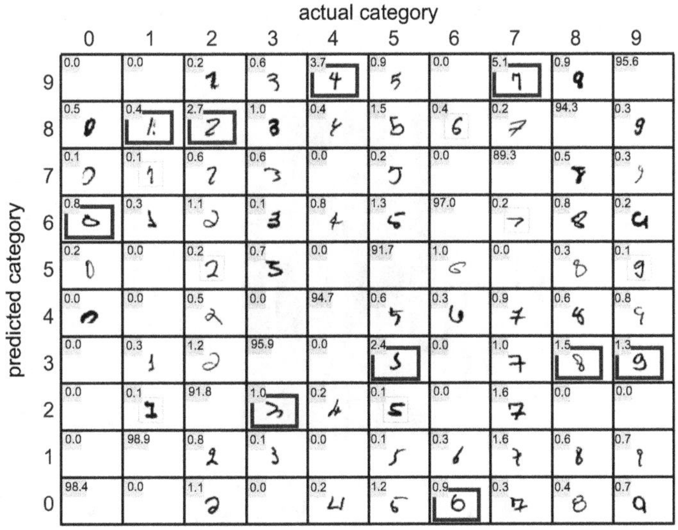

predicted \ actual	0	1	2	3	4	5	6	7	8	9
9	0.0	0.0	0.2	0.6	3.7	0.9	0.0	5.1	0.9	95.6
8	0.5	0.4	2.7	1.0	0.4	1.5	0.4	0.2	94.3	0.3
7	0.1	0.1	0.6	0.6	0.0	0.2	0.0	89.3	0.5	0.3
6	0.8	0.3	1.1	0.1	0.8	1.3	97.0	0.2	0.8	0.2
5	0.2	0.0	0.2	0.7	0.0	91.7	1.0	0.0	0.3	0.1
4	0.0	0.0	0.5	0.0	94.7	0.6	0.3	0.9	0.6	0.8
3	0.0	0.3	1.2	95.9	0.0	2.4	0.0	1.0	1.5	1.3
2	0.0	0.1	91.8	1.0	0.2	0.1	0.0	1.6	0.0	0.0
1	0.0	98.9	0.8	0.1	0.0	0.1	0.3	1.6	0.6	0.7
0	98.4	0.0	1.1	0.0	0.2	1.2	0.9	0.3	0.4	0.7

Figure 8.7 Confusion matrix for the MNIST dataset. The values highlighted in gray in entry (i,j) indicate the percentage of MNIST test images that belong to category label j and were classified as category label i by a two-layer neural network. The diagonal entries correspond to correct classifications, and off-diagonal entries are mistakes. Examples of mistakes are shown for each possible combination. The boxes highlight the most likely type of mistake for each number.

The overall performance of this network was 95 percent. Better algorithms certainly abound, but here we deliberately use this two-layer network to illustrate the mistakes made by an algorithm. All of the percentages along the diagonal correspond to cases where the neural network correctly classified the images. Not all digits were equally well classified. The accuracy for number 7 was 89.3 percent, that is, it was easier to confuse number seven with other numbers, perhaps reflecting the heterogeneity in how people draw 7s. Number 1 had the highest accuracy at 98.9 percent. In the test set of 10,000 images used in Figure 8.7, some mistakes never happened; for example, the network never mistook a 1 for a 0 or a 0 for a 1. The most confusable digits in every column are highlighted in red. The worst case was number 7 being confused with number 9, which happened 5.1 percent of the cases when a 7 was presented.

Staring at some of the example mistakes in Figure 8.7, it is perhaps intuitive to appreciate how the model may have misinterpreted some of those digits. For example, number 6 in the bottom row does look like a 0. To err is not only algorithmic but human as well. What would it mean in this context for humans to make mistakes? We could consider a behavioral experiment where a set of subjects is asked to classify those images. Of course, this set of subjects should be independent of the original set of subjects who established the ground truth labels in the first place. In this manner, we can assess the degree of between-subject variability in visual recognition. In the same fashion, we can also compare performance between humans and other species. For example, a monkey can be trained to behaviorally discriminate a set of images, and then we can directly compare the human and monkey labels on an image by image basis.

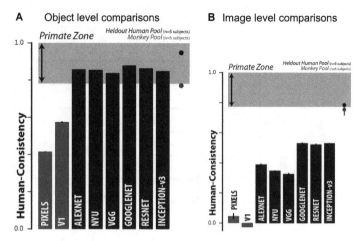

Figure 8.8 Of humans, monkeys, and computers. Comparison of classification performance between different computational models (dark gray) and humans, and between monkeys (gray dot) and humans. The degree of consistency (y-axis) shows the correlation in performance at the level of object categories (**A**) or individual images (**B**); see text for details. Modified from Rajmalingham et al. 2018

Rajmalingham and colleagues followed this path to compare visual recognition performance between monkeys, humans, and computational models (Figure 8.8). The authors considered 24 objects – including "elephant," "shorts," "wrench," and others. Rotated and scaled photographs of these objects were pasted onto natural images. Human or monkey subjects were shown a test image for 100 milliseconds, followed by a choice screen containing a canonical rendering of the test object and a canonical rendering of one of the other 23 objects. Subjects had to indicate which of the two matched the test image. Based on these behavioral measurements, the authors computed the discriminability of each object versus every other object (object-level comparisons, Figure 8.8A), averaging across all images (all rotations and backgrounds). They also computed the discriminability of every image against every other image where an image is a particular combination of an object, rotation, and background (image-level comparisons, Figure 8.8B). Human subjects were quite consistent with each other, as evaluated by excluding some of them and comparing their performance with the rest (black dot in Figure 8.8A, consistency > 0.9). There is more variability at the level of individual images, as demonstrated by the ~0.8 degree of consistency between human subjects in Figure 8.8B. Monkeys also thrived in this task and showed ~0.8 consistency with humans in both Figure 8.8A and 8.8B (gray dots).

Next, the authors considered several computational models tested on precisely the same images. They considered six deep convolutional neural networks: AlexNet, NYU, VGG, GoogleNet, ResNet, and Inception-v3. Computer vision scientists have incorporated the fervor of biologists about naming their models. The names in Figure 8.8 correspond to several popular computer vision models, and we will not get into the details of their different architectures (all of these architectures are expansions and variations of the one shown in Figure 8.2). Suffice to say that all of these models contain anywhere from seven layers (AlexNet) to more than 150 layers (ResNet), that they were trained on the ImageNet dataset (Figure 8.4), and that they have been successful in computer vision recognition challenges. The authors also considered a model that used only pixel-level information and a model that aimed to mimic the computations performed in primary visual cortex (V1). Showing perform-ance metrics for pixels is always a simple low-level benchmark to include in these comparisons: after all, if one can solve a given problem using the pixel values, why bother with more complex models?

At the object level (Figure 8.8A), all the deep convolutional neural network models (but not the pixel and V1 models) showed a remarkable degree of consistency with human behavior. These models were slightly more similar to humans than monkeys were and slightly less similar than accounted for by between-subject variability. In contrast, for the image-level comparisons (Figure 8.8B), even though all of the deep models better accounted for human behavior than pixel-based or V1-based models, they all fell short in accounting for human behavior. Both humans and models can perform quite well, but not perfectly, in this task. The pattern of mistakes of humans and models is still distinct when considering each image separately. When considering all the variability in object positions, sizes, and rotations, there was still more consistency between different human subjects, or between monkeys and humans, than between any of the models and humans.

8.13   Predicting Eye Movements

We can further constrain computational models by going beyond assessing whether we can match the pattern of mistakes in image classification tasks. One prominent aspect of human visual behavior is the rapid sequence of eye movements that takes place about three times per second under normal viewing conditions (Section 2.4). The types of deep neural network models that we have described so far do not have anything akin to eye movements, yet we can modify the models to predict what aspects of an image are salient and may drive eye movements.

One of the most salient aspects of an image is sudden motion changes. If a person in our field of view starts running, our eyes will be drawn to that person. While such temporal changes provide strong saliency cues, spatial changes in the image – including contrast, color changes, and texture changes – also attract shifts in spatial attention via eye movements. For example, if we are looking at an image where everything is gray except for a yellow car, that car will be very salient. These notions of saliency have been extensively studied in the psychophysics literature. In many cases, these principles were rediscovered by people making movies and also in the advertisement industry.

Task goals also influence eye movements. For example, if we are looking for our car in the parking lot, our eyes may be drawn to locations where there are cars as opposed to buildings or the sky, especially to other cars that share the same color and shape. We may even disregard other strong saliency cues like movement (in all likelihood, our car is not moving). The target features take over and have a prominent role in dictating our spatiotemporal sequence of eye movements.

Let us consider an example visual search task (Figure 8.9A). Subjects are presented with a target image containing an object to look for (in this example, a horse). Next, subjects are presented with a search image containing six objects presented around the fixation point. One of these six objects is a horse, and the other five are distractors. In principle, one could solve the search problem by simple template matching, by exhaustively moving a template of the same size as the target object throughout the entire image until a perfect match is found. To avoid this solution, the objects in the search image are shown at a different scale, and they are also randomly rotated. Furthermore, the target horse is actually a different exemplar from the same object category (that is, a different horse in this case).

We are interested in a visual search algorithm that can find the target object efficiently (that is, without exhaustively scanning the entire image); selectively (to differentiate the target object from the distractors); and in an invariant fashion with respect to changes in the target object's scale, rotation, and even different exemplars. Furthermore, we also want to test whether the algorithm can capture fundamental aspects of how humans move their eyes to solve the search problem.

Figure 8.9B shows a schematic of such a computational model. At the heart of the model is a deep convolutional neural network that extracts visual features from the target and search images, allegorically referred to here as "ventral visual cortex." In this case, the authors used the "VGG" neural network, which is one of the networks also tested in Figure 8.8. This convolutional neural network was pre-trained using ImageNet (Figure 8.4) so that it would have an extensive dictionary of visual features from natural images.

The model needs to keep in memory the information about the target object to be able to look for it in the search image. We also need to decide what aspects of the target image the model should keep in memory. Should the model store all the features in every layer of the network? Keeping all the features would correspond to an entire multi-level representation of the target object in terms of the layer 1 responses, the layer 2 responses, and so on. Alternatively, we could keep only layer 1 responses. The problem with keeping exclusively layer 1 features is that those low-level features are too sensitive to the metric properties of the image and are not ideal for searching for objects that have been scaled and rotated. At the other extreme, we could keep only the top layer responses; this is the approach illustrated in Figure 8.9B. As a simplification, the model perfectly and indefinitely stores all the features in the top layer of the ventral visual cortex model. In reality, this type of memory, often referred to as working memory, decays rapidly over a few seconds. This part of the model is referred to as "prefrontal cortex" because investigators have found neurons in prefrontal cortex that play an important role in storing task-dependent information in working memory tasks.

Information about the target object is used to modulate the activations of the model in response to the search image. This *top-down* modulation takes place in parallel throughout the entire image. The result is an activation map that essentially describes

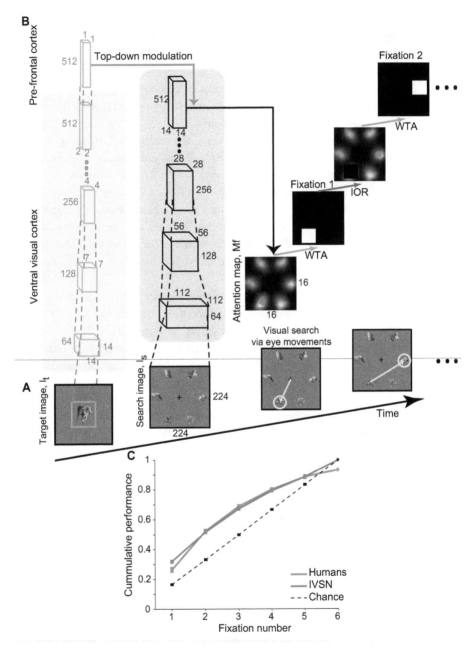

Figure 8.9 A neural network that predicts eye movements during visual search. (**A**) Visual search task where subjects or the model needs to move their eyes to find a target object (left) in an image. (**B**) Schematic illustration of the Invariant Visual Search Network (IVSN) model (see text for details). (**C**) Cumulative performance of humans (red) and IVSN (blue) in the task (dashed line indicates chance). Adapted from Zhang et al. 2018

how similar each part of the image is to the target, where similarity is defined by the high-level features stored in prefrontal cortex, and where the spatial resolution depends on which level of the hierarchy is modulated. This activation pattern is referred to as an *attentional map*. In this example, this map has a resolution of 16×16 regions. A winner-take-all (WTA) mechanism selects the maximum of the attentional map. This location corresponding to the maximum in the attentional map becomes the position of the model's first "fixation."

If the target is found at this location, the search ends. If the target is not found, the model goes back to the attentional map. Because the model is deterministic, if we select the maximum again, the model would always keep fixating on the same location. To avoid this problem, the model uses an infinite inhibition of return (IOR) mechanism, meaning that it never goes back to fixate on a location that it has already selected before. The winner-take-all mechanism selects the next maximum in the attentional map for fixation. Thus, by adding a few computational steps, we can use a deep convolutional neural network to make a sequence of eye movements and detect the location of target objects in a search image.

Does this work? First, let us examine human behavior in this task (Figure 8.9C). Because there are six objects (one target and five distractors), by chance, there is a probability of 1/6 of finding the target in the first fixation, 2/6 of finding the target by the second fixation, and so on. Humans do much better than chance. They are not able to find the target in just one fixation, but they can do so with a probability of approximately 1/3. These numbers are not too critical; the exact probabilities likely depend on multiple factors such as how large the objects are, how far they are from the fixation point, how similar the distractors are to the target, how many distractors there are, and how different the target in the search image is from the one in the target image. Regardless of the quantitative numbers, humans can efficiently find the target objects. Intriguingly, humans are slightly below 100 percent performance, which is below chance, at six fixations because humans do not have infinite inhibition of return, as the model assumes. Humans are stubborn creatures, and sometimes they move their eyes back to the same location even when that location does not contain the target.

Next, let us examine the model depicted in Figure 8.9, tested on the same images and task used in the human psychophysics experiment. The model does surprisingly well: it can localize target objects more efficiently than sequentially or randomly scanning the entire image. Both humans and the model can find the target in a manner that shows invariance to some target features given the experimental design choice of using different exemplars from the same categories and scaling and rotating the objects. Of note, this model had never seen these specific objects before, and therefore, it was able to find objects even without any kind of object-specific training. The strong similarity between human and model behavior is partly coincidental. Experiments with other images, including searching for objects in natural images or the famous example of searching for Waldo, show that the model does not entirely account for human eye movement behavior. It should be noted that the model was not trained to match human behavior; i.e., there is no data fitting in this procedure. A model that was trained for object classification can be adapted for the task of visual search and explain human eye movements, without tuning any parameters.

8.14   Predicting Neuronal Firing Rates

The previous two sections demonstrate that deep convolutional neural network models that are trained for object classification tasks can provide a reasonable first-order approximation to human and monkey visual behavior, both in terms of tasks like object categorization and also in terms of other tasks such as making eye movements during visual search. Nonetheless, current models do not provide a perfect description of human behavior. We pointed out earlier several cases where models may qualitatively capture certain aspects of visual behavior (e.g., object-level classification performance, eye movements during visual search in object array images). However, in other aspects, there is ample room for improvement (e.g., image-level object classification performance, eye movements during visual search in natural images). We will come back to several astonishing failures of current models in Sections 9.11 and 9.12.

We now turn our attention to what happens inside the brain, and we ask whether current models can capture the internal mechanisms of visual function. Even if we had a model that explained visual behavior exceptionally well, this would not necessarily imply that the inner workings of brains and the model are the same. Brains and models could be solving the same problem in entirely different ways. Understanding the differences between brain mechanisms and computational mechanisms can inspire the development of better models.

The question of whether the inner workings of a brain and the model are similar or not requires further specification. If we go down to the level of individual molecules, the hardware is very different. To assess whether a model captures aspects of neural circuit function – and, therefore, whether a model can help us better decipher neural mechanisms – we need to define which aspects of neural function we want to explain. A natural question is to try to explain the firing rate properties of neurons. As discussed in Chapters 2, 5, and 6, neuronal spikes constitute the gold standard to study neural function and represent the main mechanism by which neurons can send signals over long distances. We therefore consider whether a model can predict the number of spikes emitted by a neuron in response to a given image.

An example of this type of analysis is shown in Figure 8.10. Investigators presented an extensive collection of images to a monkey while recording the activity of neurons in the inferior temporal cortex (ITC). Similar to the study described in Figure 8.8, the monkeys were presented with images of animals, boats, faces, and five other object categories. The objects were pasted in front of natural backgrounds (example images are shown in Figure 8.10A). As described in Section 6.2, ITC neurons showed selective responses to different types of images. For example, the recording site in Figure 8.10A1/B1 (black trace) demonstrates generally higher responses to images containing chairs and, to a lesser degree, planes (where "responses" are defined here

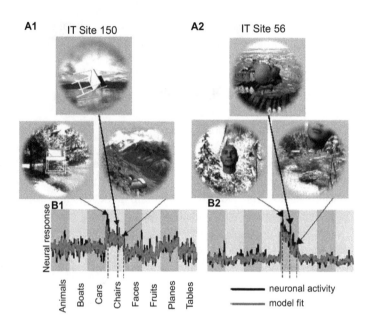

Figure 8.10 Computational models can approximate neuronal firing rates. (**A**) Example images shown to a monkey while recording the activity from two different sites (site 150 and site 56) in the inferior temporal cortex (ITC). (**B**) Neuronal responses (black) versus predicted responses from a deep convolutional neural network model (red). Each entry along the x-axis corresponds to one out of 1,600 different images divided into eight object categories (animals, boats, and others). Modified from Yamins et al. 2014

as the total number of spikes in a fixed window from 70 to 170 milliseconds after stimulus onset). As discussed in Chapters 2 and 5, neuronal responses can be variable upon repeated presentation of the same stimulus; the neuronal responses shown in Figure 8.10B represent averages over tens of repetitions of the same stimulus.

The same images can be passed to a deep convolutional neural network, extracting the activation values in each layer, as shown in Figure 8.5. Next, we can compare those model activations to the neuronal responses. One way to make this comparison is to take the activation values in a given layer and build a linear map onto the responses of a given neuron. This linear fitting procedure has one free parameter per unit in the neural network, and the number of equations is the number of images. Some of the images are used to fit the linear map, and the rest are used to test how well the model can approximate neuronal responses to novel images (Figure 8.10B1/B2 red trace). The correlation between the predicted responses and the actual neuronal responses is better when using model activations from higher layers than in the early layers of deep convolutional networks, suggesting that more complex features may be required to explain the activity of neurons in ITC. These models can typically account for more than 50 percent of the variance in the neuronal responses. Thus, despite the fact that neural network models constitute a far cry from the intricate complexities of biological tissue, the unit activations provide a good initial approximation to predict neuronal responses.

8.15   All Models Are Wrong; Some Are Useful

State-of-the-art deep convolutional neural networks are appealing because they fulfill many of the desiderata articulated in Section 8.1. Furthermore, we will show in Section 9.5 that these models have been successful in a wide range of visual processing problems in the real world. As discussed in the previous three sections, these models also provide an imperfect but reasonable first-order approximation to visual behavior and visual neurophysiology.

It is intriguing that deep convolutional neural networks can capture aspects of behavior and physiology, given that they abstract away so much of the underlying neuronal circuitry. As discussed in Sections 7.3 and 7.4, an educated guess about the right level of abstraction in modeling neural circuits is essential for progress. Biologists examining a deep convolutional neural network are appalled at the lack of a myriad of actual elements present in nervous tissue. To mention only a few, from larger scales down to smaller scales, the visual system is characterized by a mesmerizingly complex array of interconnections (Figure 1.5), most of which are not present in current models. We also know that there are many different neuronal types – including at least tens, if not hundreds, of different types of interneurons in the brain – whereas current models have essentially only one or a handful of different types of computational units, depending on how we count. Neurons are characterized by complex geometries, and the spatiotemporal distribution of inputs to different dendrites can have a significant impact on the biophysics of single-neuron computations. Biochemists may even wonder about the intricate expression patterns of the approximately 20,000 genes in the human genome in different types of neurons.

While biologists worry about abstracting away these and many other aspects of the neural circuitry, at the other end of the scientific spectrum, psychologists worry that there is too little abstraction in current models. Psychologists are appalled at the lack of a myriad of conceptual structures. To mention only a few in increasingly more ethereal levels, these models do not have a clear sense of semantic knowledge (see discussion in Section 6.8), beyond what is imposed by the labels used during training. Additionally, common-sense intuitions about the visual world, including the notion of "objectness" or the notion of agents that interact with each other, are not explicitly incorporated into these models. Psychologists argue based on introspection that these concepts are critical to interpreting the visual world. Some psychologists further argue that we cannot understand visual processing isolated from how we interact with the world and that vision cannot be dissociated from language.

The discussion of the biological and psychological components that are missing in current models can be approximately mapped onto Tomaso Poggio and David Marr's three levels of analysis (Section 1.9). Psychologists tend to think about the high-level computations that the system may want to implement, and biologists tend to think about the hardware required to perform all of these computations. An essential goal of models is to bridge these levels of analysis by building algorithms that can implement those computations and by linking those algorithms to the actual biological hardware.

Inputs from both biologists and psychologists will be invaluable in further improving current computational models.

8.16   Horizontal and Top-Down Signals in Visual Recognition

One of the several simplifications in deep convolutional neural networks that deserves further scrutiny is the lack of horizontal and top-down signals. We know that there are abundant horizontal and back projections throughout the neocortex. The functions of top-down connections have been less studied at the neurophysiological level, but there is no shortage of computational models illustrating the rich array of computations that could emerge with such connectivity.

Essentially all computational models consider that top-down signals play a critical role during learning. In fact, the procedure of backpropagation described in Section 8.6 requires a top-down propagation of errors throughout the network. However, purely bottom-up models do not capitalize on top-down signals after learning and *during* visual processing.

Several models have used top-down connections to guide attention to specific locations or features within the image (Section 5.17, Section 8.13). The allocation of attention to specific parts of an image can significantly enhance recognition performance by alleviating the problems associated with image segmentation and clutter. The model introduced in Figure 8.9 uses top-down signals to guide eye movements – that is, overt attention – toward specific locations that may contain the sought object.

Horizontal and top-down signals can also play an important role in recognition of occluded objects. When only partial object information is available, the visual system must be able to perform pattern completion and interpret the image based on prior knowledge (Section 3.5). Attractor-based recurrent networks can retrieve the identity of stored memories from partial information (Section 7.6). Similarly, computational models have combined bottom-up architectures with attractor networks at the top of the hierarchy. The attractor-based recurrent dynamics can help make inferences from partial information and thus recognize heavily occluded objects. In addition to horizontal connections, top-down signals could also play an important role during pattern completion by providing prior stored information that influences the bottom-up sensory responses.

The idea that top-down signals can carry task-relevant prior information has been embraced by several proposals formulating visual recognition as a Bayesian inference problem. Considering three layers of the visual cascade (e.g., LGN, V1, and higher areas like V2) and denoting activity in those three layers as x_0, x_1, and x_h, respectively, the probability of obtaining a given response pattern in V1 (x_1) depends both on the sensory input and feedback from higher areas:

$$P(\mathbf{x_1}|\mathbf{x}_0) = \frac{P(\mathbf{x}_0|\mathbf{x}_1)P(\mathbf{x}_1|\mathbf{x}_h)}{P(\mathbf{x}_0|\mathbf{x}_h)} \qquad (8.12)$$

where $P(\mathbf{x}_1|\mathbf{x}_h)$ represents the feedback biases conveying prior information.

8.17   Predictive Coding

An interesting version of how top-down signals could be used during visual recognition was proposed by Rajesh Rao and Dana Ballard, who argued that feedback connections provide *predictive* signals, whereas bottom-up signals convey the difference between sensory inputs and the top-down predictions. For example, consider the phenomenon of surround suppression (Section 5.5): if we present an optimally oriented sinusoidal grating within the receptive field of a V1 neuron, the firing rate increases with the size of the stimulus up to a certain point; when the stimulus size exceeds the receptive field size, the firing starts to diminish with increasing size. According to the predictive coding model, neurons in higher areas with larger receptive field sizes (e.g., V2) send a feedback signal that can predict the responses, and the V1 neuron subtracts those predictions from the sensory inputs, thereby leading to a smaller response for large stimulus sizes. Indeed, silencing activity of V2 neurons leads to a reduced surround suppression effect – that is, stronger responses in V1 to larger stimuli.

Predictions can take place not only in the spatial domain but also in the temporal domain. A constant visual stimulus (in the absence of any external changes or any internal changes like head or eye movements) can be predicted. According to the predictive coding model, the feedback signals lead to a reduction of the initial transient response. Indeed, transient responses to constant stimuli are the norm throughout the visual system (Section 2.9).

Such predictive coding ideas can be extended to a multilayer network. The model architecture shown in Figure 8.11A consists of multiple layers (only two of which are shown in the schematic); each layer is composed of four types of units: input units (blue, A_l), recurrent representation units (green, R_l), error representation units (red, E_l), and prediction units (blue, $\hat{A}_l$). If we remove, or silence, the recurrent units, then the pathway from A_l to E_l to A_{l+1} to E_{l+1} is a standard deep convolutional neural network. The recurrent units provide top-down signals. If we go from the higher layers down to the lower layers, we generate a progressively larger representation, which can be thought of as a generative deconvolutional network, similar to other algorithms to generate images which are discussed in the next chapter (Sections 9.8 and 9.9). The investigators refer to this network as *PredNet*.

In this network, the error units pass the difference between the predictions and the inputs to the next layer. The recurrent units take as input both the error in the current layer and the top-down activity from the next layer. In contrast to standard deep convolutional neural networks like the one in Figure 8.2, here the network shows rich dynamics: the activation of every unit evolves over time.

Let x_t represent the input frame at time t. For the first layer, $A_l^t = x_t$. For the next layers, the input units compute a convolution (plus rectification and pooling) over the activation of the error units in the previous layer:

$$A_l^t = \text{MAXPOOL}\left(\text{ReLU}\left(\text{CONV}\left(E_{l-1}^t\right)\right)\right) \qquad (8.13)$$

The recurrent units combine the top-down signals from the recurrent units in the upper layer and the propagated errors in the current layer. The inputs from the upper

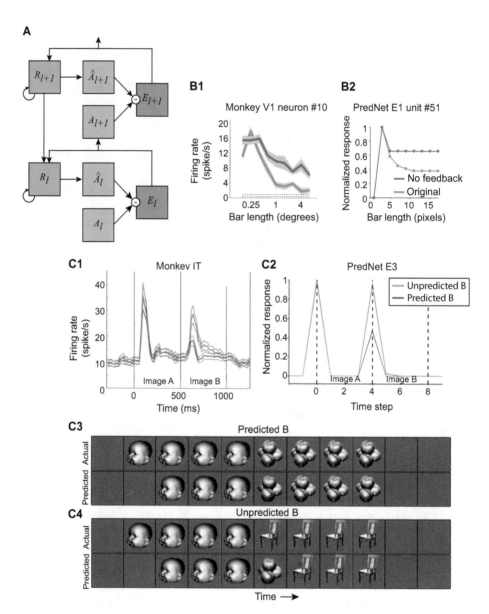

Figure 8.11 PredNet, a deep predictive coding architecture. (**A**) Schematic illustration of two layers of the PredNet architecture. *R* units send predictive feedback signals to the previous layer. The bottom-up inputs pass a difference between the predicted signals and the signals from the previous step (see text for details). (**B**) Surround suppression in a monkey V1 neuron (**B1**) and a PredNet layer 1 unit (**B2**). Responses to an optimal bar of increasing lengths in the original conditions (red) or in the absence of feedback (blue). (**C**) Sequence prediction by monkey IT neurons (**C1**) or PredNet layer 3 unit (**C2**) when the second stimulus is predictable (blue) or unpredictable (red) (**C3**). Modified from Lotter et al. 2018

layer need to be upsampled because of the pooling operation from one layer to the next. The recurrent computations within the layer imply that there are horizontal connections that link the R_l units. We discussed a model with such horizontal connections, the Hopfield network, in Section 7.6. Many current models use a different implementation of a recurrent network known as a long short-term memory (LSTM) module, a special type of recurrent module that is well suited to learn long-term dependencies in the data. We can schematically describe the activation of recurrent units as

$$R_l^t = \text{CONVLSTM}\left(E_l^{t-1}, R_l^{t-1}, \text{UPSAMPLE}\left(R_{l+1}^t,\right)\right). \tag{8.14}$$

The predictions are directly computed from the recurrent unit activations:

$$\widehat{A}_l^t = \text{ReLU}\left(\text{CONV}\left(R_l^t\right)\right). \tag{8.15}$$

The error units signal the difference between inputs and predictions, with both possible signs:

$$E_l^t = \left[\text{RELU}\left(A_l^t - \widehat{A}_l^t\right), \text{RELU}\left(\widehat{A}_l^t - A_l^t\right)\right]. \tag{8.16}$$

This network can be trained in an end-to-end fashion. The deep convolutional neural network architecture discussed in Figure 8.5 was trained to perform object recognition. In contrast, the PredNet model in Figure 8.11 was trained to predict the next frame in video sequences. The investigators trained the network using videos extracted from a camera mounted on a car and tuned the network to predict the next frame. The loss function was based on minimizing the difference between a predicted frame in the video and the actual frame. The loss function could be based on consecutive frames or a short interval between the two frames. Of note, the training procedure is similar to the backpropagation formalism described in Section 8.6, even though the type of loss function is different.

Whereas in the previous examples, the loss function was given by a difference between a target label and a predicted label for an image, here the network is *not* trained using any explicit labels, or even any explicit notion of objects. The type of training procedure where there is a loss function that is directly embedded in the input sequence without any need for external annotation is referred to as *self-supervised learning*. Some people also refer to this scenario as *unsupervised learning*, but it is preferable to use the term unsupervised in a situation where there is no loss function for every image, video, or trial – such as when clustering data, when applying tSNE, Hebbian learning, spike-timing dependent plasticity, or similar mechanisms.

What can a network like PredNet do? To begin with, the model can predict the next frame in video sequences. After all, this is what the model was trained for. The model can achieve these video predictions even in other videos that are different from the ones that it was trained on. Furthermore, the unit activations can be used to classify objects. Even though the network is not explicitly trained for object classification, it develops a sufficiently rich set of features that relate to natural images, and a linear classifier can be used to assign labels to objects using this feature set.

We can therefore evaluate the network by using all the same tests described earlier for bottom-up neural networks, including object classification performance, but also by comparing their output with behavioral and neural data. For example, units in the network show surround suppression (Figure 8.11B, red curve). Like monkey V1 neurons (Figure 8.11B), units in the first layer show larger activation for longer bars up to a point, and then the activation decreases with longer bars. In large part, surround suppression is due to top-down signals, as demonstrated by silencing the R units in the network (Figure 8.11B, blue curve).

Surround suppression can be thought of as a form of spatial prediction. The model can also make temporal predictions, such as inferring the next frame in a video sequence. One type of paradigm that has been used extensively in neuroscience is a sequence learning task where animals learn that a given stimulus B typically follows a stimulus A (Figure 8.11C). Monkeys can be trained to learn this type of temporal contingency, and neurons in ITC show a lower response to a predictable second stimulus compared to a new, surprising, second stimulus (Figure 8.11C, cf. response to the predicted B (blue) versus the unpredicted B (red)). Error units in layer 3 in PredNet also show this type of novelty detection and display a lower activation when the second stimulus is expected (Figure 8.11C).

Even though the PredNet model was never trained to label objects, or to show surround suppression, or perform novelty detection, these and other biological properties emerge in this type of network when it is trained to make predictions in video sequences. This emergence of unrelated properties is particularly exciting because it suggests that fundamental aspects of the visual system architecture can develop through experience with the natural statistics of the world, without the need to train the model with millions of labeled examples in a supervised fashion. In sum, it is possible to build biologically plausible neural architectures that learn to extract fundamental structure in the world in a self-supervised manner. Several biological properties emerge naturally in these networks by training them with basic principles like predictive coding.

8.18   Summary

- Biologically plausible computational models of visual processing should be image computable, should be based on neural network architectures, and should display the fundamental properties of selectivity, invariance, speed, and generalization.
- State-of-the-art vision models are based on a divide-and-conquer hierarchical architecture composed of layers that sequentially process information.
- Ascending through the hierarchy, units show larger receptive field sizes, display preferences for more complex features, and show increasingly more tolerance to metric transformations of those features.
- Deep convolutional neural networks are trained end to end so that all weights in the network are modified according to a predefined loss function and without the need for manual tuning of model parameters.

- One of the main ways of learning the weights in deep convolutional neural networks is by using gradient descent implemented by the backpropagation algorithm.
- Large datasets such as ImageNet have allowed extensive training of deep convolutional neural networks via supervised learning.
- Modern networks have an enormous number of tunable parameters, raising the question of how they can generalize and avoid overfitting.
- Cross-validation is an essential step to avoid obtaining inflated performance values that do not extrapolate to novel data.
- Once trained, the responses of units in the network to any arbitrary image can be readily computed. These responses can be directly compared to behavioral and neurophysiological measurements.
- Deep convolutional neural networks provide a first-order approximation to primate behavioral performance, and the networks can also approximate the pattern of mistakes in visual recognition tasks and the pattern of eye movements during visual search.
- The activation of units in the network can also be used to approximately predict the responses of biological neurons throughout the ventral visual cortex upon presentation of visual stimuli.
- Current models lack many low-level biological mechanisms and also many high-level psychological intuitions.
- Top-down signals are essential to bridge sensory inputs to memories and previous knowledge about the world.
- Top-down signals are essential during learning (an example of which is backpropagation).
- Top-down signals also play an important role during visual processing by merging bottom-up sensory signals with predictive signals based on higher knowledge.

Further Reading

See more references at http://bit.ly/36RxOGX

- Krizhevsky, A.; Sutskever, I.; and Hinton, G. (2012). ImageNet Classification with Deep Convolutional Neural Networks. Presented at Neural Information Processing Systems, Montreal.
- Rao, R. P., and Ballard, D. H. (1999). Predictive coding in the visual cortex: a functional interpretation of some extra-classical receptive-field effects. *Nature Neuroscience* 2:79–87.
- Riesenhuber, M., and Poggio, T. (1999). Hierarchical models of object recognition in cortex. *Nature Neuroscience* 2:1019–1025.
- Serre, T. (2019). Deep learning: the good, the bad and the ugly. *Annual Review of Vision* 5: 399–426.
- Yamins, D. L.; Hong, H.; Cadieu, C.F.; Solomon, E. A.; Seibert, D., and DiCarlo, J. J. (2014). Performance-optimized hierarchical models predict neural responses in higher visual cortex. *Proceedings of the National Academy of Sciences of the United States of America* 111:8619–8624.

9 Toward a World with Intelligent Machines That Can Interpret the Visual World

Supplementary content at http://bit.ly/2t53QRd

In the previous chapter, we introduced the idea of directly comparing computational models versus human behavior in visual tasks. For example, we assess how models classify an image versus how humans classify the same image. In some tasks, the types of errors made by computational models can be similar to human mistakes. Here we will dig deeper into what current computer vision algorithms can and cannot do. We will highlight the enormous power of current computational models, while at the same time emphasizing some of their limitations and the exciting work ahead of us to build better models.

There are many visual problems where computers are already significantly better than humans. A simple example is the ability to read bar codes, such as the ones used in a supermarket to label each product. Even if humans could, in principle, go through enormous training to read bar codes, it would be extremely challenging to achieve machine-level performance in this task. In most supermarkets, there is still a need for a human to turn the product, locate the bar code, and position the bar code in such a way that the scanner can process it. This level of human intervention will probably vanish soon, yet in some sense, it is interesting to note that localizing the bar code and adequately positioning it is still easier for humans than machines.

There is a double dissociation here in terms of which tasks humans find easy (locating a bar code and positioning the product the right way) and which tasks are easy for machines (deciphering the bar code). The task may seem somewhat limited: it all comes down to measuring bar widths and distances. The human solves the challenging invariance problem (recognition of an image at different scales, positions, and angles, as in Figure 3.6) by positioning the object in the right place. A similar case can be made for reading quick response (QR) codes. As we will discuss soon, there are many other visual tasks where computers already match or outperform humans. There are also many visual tasks where machines still have a long way to go to reach human performance levels. Hans Moravec, Rodney Brooks, and Marvin Minsky articulated this dissociation between machine and human performance in Moravec's paradox. The paradox states that it is relatively easy to endow computers with adult-level performance on traditional intelligence tests and incredibly challenging to give machines the skills of a one-year-old in terms of perception and mobility.

What would it mean for computational algorithms to match or outperform humans in every possible visual task? Imagine a world where machines can truly see and interpret the visual world around us – a world where machines can pass the *Turing test for vision.*

9.1   The Turing Test for Vision

Alan Turing (1912–1954) was one of the great minds of the twentieth century and pioneered the development of the theory of computer science. In his seminal 1950 paper, he proposed the "Imitation Game," whereby a series of questions is posed both to a human and to a computer. Turing proposed that if we cannot distinguish which answers came from the human and which ones came from the computer, then we should call that computer intelligent.

The term intelligence is ill defined and used in many different ways. Furthermore, the notion of machine intelligence is often a moving target: once computers can solve a given task (such as beating world champions at the game of chess or Go), then critics invariably argue that such a feat is *not* an actual demonstration of intelligence (even though the same experts claimed otherwise before computers beat humans). Those people often have in mind a useless definition of intelligence: intelligence is whatever computers cannot do! To avoid such tautologies, the Turing test has become the standard goal to assess intelligence.

We can define a specialized version of the Turing test for visual intelligence (Figure 9.1). Suppose that we present a human or computer with an image (or a video without sound). It is important that there are no restrictions on the image: it can be a frame extracted from a Disney movie, a Kandinsky, or a photograph like the one in Figure 9.1. We are allowed to ask *any* question about the image. For example, we can ask whether it contains a tree, how many cars there are, whether any person is wearing a

Figure 9.1 Turing test for vision. Given an arbitrary image and any question about the image, if we cannot distinguish whether the answers come from a human or a computational algorithm, we say that the algorithm has passed the Turing test for vision.

hat, whether the person wearing a hat is closer to the viewer than the tree, whether our friend John is in the picture, whether John looks happy in that picture, whether the picture is funny or sad, how many people are riding a bicycle, and so on. If we cannot distinguish whether the answers come from the human or the computer, we can claim victory. We claim that, from a behavioral standpoint, humans interpret images in the same way as the computer vision algorithm.

A few clarifications and further specifications are pertinent here. If someone asked me questions about an image, and the questions were posed in Chinese, I would not be able to answer the questions. This is not a failure of my visual system; this merely shows that I cannot speak Chinese. I would pass the Turing test for vision, but I would not pass a Turing test for Chinese! Therefore, the definition of the Turing test for vision assumes that we have some way of encoding the questions and answers in a format that the computer understands. For example, if we ask whether John appears to be happy or not, the computer needs to be able to interpret what "happy" means. We seek to circumscribe the Turing test strictly to visual processing and dissociate it from language understanding.

Language is, of course, another fascinating aspect of cognition, and we want computers to be able to use language too. One could even extend the Turing test to include both vision and language. For example, we will briefly discuss later in this chapter the task of image captioning – that is, coming up with a short description for an image. However, the main concern in this chapter is to pass the test of visual processing. Therefore, we define the Turing test strictly in the domain of vision. We still want the computer to be able to answer *any* question, but we are not going to be concerned with whether the computer knows the words and the grammar in the question or not.

For a computer to answer whether John appears to be happy or not, one would need to train the computer with pictures rendering happy people and pictures rendering people who do not look happy. Alternatively, we could figure out some other ways to educate the computer about what happy people look like. This training to interpret the task holds for all other questions as well. If we want to know whether a woman is riding a blue bicycle, the computer needs to understand what woman, riding, blue, and bicycle mean. Of course, the same holds for human vision, even though we tend to take this for granted and underestimate this obvious point. In the same way that I would fail in answering questions in Chinese, if we ask a human whether there is a *beldam* in the picture, the person will not be able to answer unless they understand what the word beldam means (beldam is an archaic noun meaning an old woman).

It is important in this definition that the number of questions remains infinite. For example, one could build a computational model that excels at recognizing whether our friend John is in the picture or not; that is, a perfect John detector that can recognize John even better than we do. Such a computational model would be quite nice, but it would not pass the Turing test for vision. Similarly, one could build a model that can label every pixel in the image (this pixel is part of a tree; this pixel is part of a red car; this pixel is part of John). Such a model would be even more impressive, but it would not be able to answer any arbitrary question about the image, such as whether John is happy or not, and therefore, the model would not pass the Turing test for vision either.

While the Turing test, as defined thus far, focuses on *human* vision, we can also define a Turing test for rat vision, meaning an algorithm that is indistinguishable from a rat's behavior in visual tasks. We can also define a Turing test for visual processing of a one-year-old infant, meaning an algorithm that is indistinguishable from the behavior of a one-year-old human infant. Similarly, some people may possess rather specialized knowledge, like a bird watcher who can classify different types of birds or a doctor who can diagnose certain conditions based on clinical images. One could define restricted versions of the Turing test for those cases, such as a machine that cannot be distinguished from a world expert bird watcher in terms of classifying birds from images.

9.2 Computer Vision Everywhere

Despite enormous progress in computational modeling of visual processing, we are still far from being able to build algorithms that can pass the Turing test for vision. Most computer vision studies focus on specific sets of questions or tasks en route toward building systems that can pass the general Turing test. Many exciting algorithms have been developed to address several interrelated problems in computer vision (Figure 9.2).

One of the most common tasks is *object classification* (Figure 9.2A): the computer is presented with an image, and it has to produce one of a fixed number of possible labels. For example, does the image contain a tree [yes | no]? Which of the following objects is in the image: [people | tree | building | flower]? Another instance of object classification is the task of clinical diagnosis based on images; for example, does the mammogram image

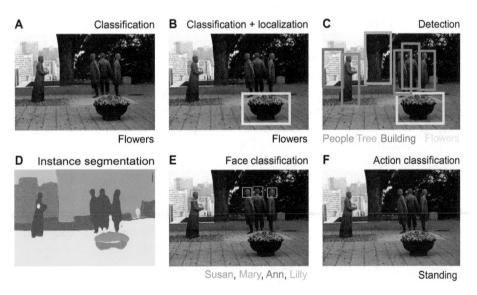

Figure 9.2 Typical computer vision tasks. (**A**) Object classification. (**B**) Object classification and localization. (**C**) Object detection. (**D**) Instance segmentation. (**E**) Face classification. (**F**) Action classification.

contain a tumor [yes | no]? Yet another instance of object classification is the task of face recognition (Figure 9.2E); for example, is [Susan | Mary | Ann | Lilly] in this image?

When assigning a label to an image, those labels could be nested into structures and hierarchies. For example, some psychologists refer to object *categorization* (does the image contain a car or a face?), as distinct from object *identification* (which particular car is it, which particular face is it?). From a computational standpoint, these are essentially the same problem, and it is possible to design hierarchical algorithms that will answer these questions sequentially or in parallel.

An intriguing and ubiquitous aspect of human language is the definition of categorical distinctions that transcend the exact visual features in the image; the notion of semantic categories was discussed in Section 6.8 (Figure 6.5). For example, we can put together images of ants, snakes, lions, birds, and dolphins and categorize them as animals. If we train a computer vision that excels at recognizing ants and snakes, *exclusively* ants and snakes, the algorithm may not be able to understand that a bird is another type of animal. This failure to extrapolate to another animal may seem like a significant problem for computer vision: of course, essentially any human can tell that a bird is an animal. However, it is unclear whether humans could succeed in this same task, with the same type of training that the computers were subject to. Imagine a person who is an expert in ants and snakes but has never seen *any* other animal. Given a picture of a bird (without movement, without contextual information, or any other cue; remember that we want to match the human task to the computer task as closely as possible; otherwise, humans have an unfair advantage), would the person be able to understand that the bird is another type of animal? One may think that the answer is yes. However, it is difficult to imagine what his or her understanding of "animalness" would be if their entire visual expertise were restricted exclusively to static pictures of ants and snakes. We often tend to underestimate the amount of visual experience that we have.

Another version of object classification is the problem of *object verification*: given two (or more) images, the task is to determine whether the images correspond to the same object or not. For example, the airport security officer may examine a passport and the person in front of him or her, and assess whether the person matches the picture or not. Yet another related problem is that of image retrieval; given an image, retrieve all instances of similar images from a dataset. For example, one may want to retrieve all the images on the web that are visually similar to a given picture.

Extending the task of object classification, algorithms have been developed for *object detection* or *object localization* (Figure 9.2B and C). In these tasks, the goal is to place a bounding box around the object of interest in an image. For example, "locate all the pedestrians in the image." Progress in object localization rapidly accelerated with the development of the MSCOCO dataset, which contains detailed tracing contours around objects from 80 common categories. One example of object detection is the ability to put a box around a face in an image (face detection), which is routinely used nowadays for digital cameras to focus on faces. Current algorithms can detect and place bounding boxes around multiple objects in an image. This type of effort has provided a tremendous boost to the possibility of developing self-driving cars, which are equipped with sensors to detect other cars, pedestrians, car lanes, and many other objects of interest.

Related to the problem of object detection is the question of *object segmentation,* where the goal is to trace the contour of a given object (Figure 9.2D). An initial map of segmented objects in an image can be extracted by adequately detecting edges. However, more complex problems often involve a deeper understanding of the interrelationships among different object parts. An example of a challenging problem for object segmentation is the case of a zebra: the algorithm should separate the zebra as a whole, rather than marking every stripe as a separate object. Another typical challenge in segmentation arises when there is occlusion. For example, consider the rotated B letters in Figure 3.8: the object segmentation algorithm should isolate every letter rather than merely mark each letter fragment as a separate object. Investigators may be interested in algorithms to segment all the objects in an image rather than localizing every single object of a specific class. *Semantic edge detection* refers to drawing the outlines of objects in an image without labeling edges that do not separate objects.

There has been extensive discussion in the literature about the chicken-and-egg problem of whether segmentation comes before recognition or whether recognition comes first. When there are depth boundaries defined by stereo and motion discontinuities, segmentation may occur early, prior to recognition. However, when the only cues are based on luminance, there is no clear biological evidence for segmentation taking place prior to recognition or vice versa. It is likely that both computations happen in parallel. In many practical applications, object classification, detection, and segmentation are often combined.

An example application combining all three tasks involves analyzing microscopy images in cellular biology. Biologists are interested in an algorithm that can automatically detect cells with a given shape, mark them with a given color, and count them. A particularly difficult and exciting challenge along these lines was advanced by a community of researchers working toward mapping connectivity in the nervous system based on electron microscopy images (Figure 9.3). These images consist of section after section of high-resolution rendering of the inner structure of nervous tissue; the goal is to automatically trace the connectivity of every neuron from these images. *Instance segmentation* refers to separating and labeling every pixel in an image. For example, we want to label every neuronal dendrite, soma, axon, glial cell, and other cell types in the electron microscopy images. We especially want to follow dendrites and axons across multiple sections to map where they originate and where they synapse onto another neuron.

Action recognition refers to the ability to identify actions in an image or video (Figure 9.2F, Figure 9.4). Is a person playing soccer [yes | no]? Which of these actions is the person performing [playing cello | brushing teeth | bowling | soccer juggling]? Action recognition can be based on individual images, but it has also triggered the development of databases based on videos. In sports, people are interested in building computer vision systems that can automatically analyze the game in excruciating detail, including detecting individual players, tracking them, and identifying what they are doing (e.g., running with the ball, passing the ball, dodging the opponent, or shooting).

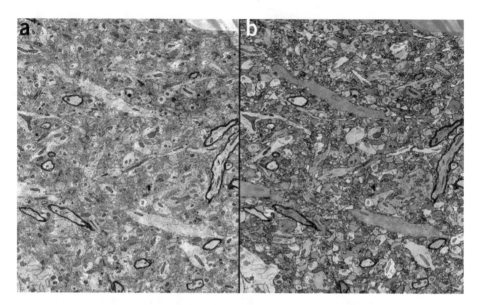

Figure 9.3 Image segmentation algorithms can help map neuronal connections. (**A**) Electron micrograph from a $40 \times 20\mu m$ section of mouse cerebral cortex. (**B**) Automatic computer segmentation, where each cellular object is shown as a separate color overlaid on the original image. Reproduced from Lichtman et al. 2014

Action recognition and tracking are examples where many of the computer vision tasks defined earlier are intertwined and need to be combined. Action recognition applications have also become widespread among biologists studying animal behavior. Traditionally, quantifying animal behavior has been a tedious and time-consuming task: a graduate student interested in mouse behavior may easily mount a camera to record hours and hours of behavioral data. Analyzing those data typically involved long hours of scrutinizing those videos and subjectively describing the animal's behavior. Nowadays, some systems can objectively and reliably perform these types of annotations: computer vision approaches can automatically analyze the videos, quantify the amount of time spent in different behaviors, and describe the sequence of different types of movements. Yet another widespread application for action recognition systems is surveillance. One may be interested in detecting "anomalous" behavior near a house, at an airport, or at a crowded concert. Computer vision scientists refer to this problem as *anomaly detection*.

Action recognition is a good example to illustrate how experimental design and databases can make tasks easy or hard. Distinguishing whether someone is playing the cello or juggling a soccer ball based on the types of images shown in Figure 9.4A can be easy. However, determining whether a person is reading or not based on the types of images shown in Figure 9.4C can be substantially harder. We will discuss this point again in Section 9.10.

The list of computer vision applications is so extensive and grows so rapidly that it is likely that by the time the reader has access to these lines, there will already be a plethora of impressive new feats.

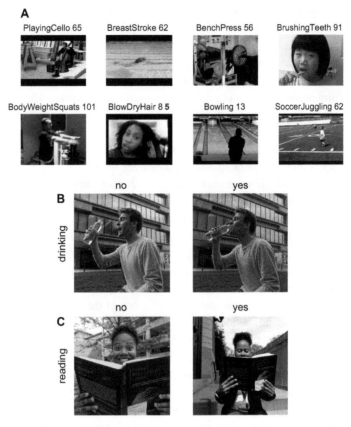

Figure 9.4 Dataset design can make problems easy or hard in action recognition. (**A**) UCF-101 dataset of videos with labeled actions (Soomro et al. 2012). The first frame in eight examples out of the 101 action categories are shown here. Titles indicate the category number and description. (**B**)–(**C**) A challenging dataset for action recognition where subjects need to indicate in a binary fashion whether a subject is drinking or not (**B**), or reading or not (**C**).

9.3   Incorporating Temporal Information Using Videos

Historically, many computer vision studies have been restricted to analyzing static images. In part, work has focused on static images because both humans and machines can recognize objects in images quite well. The focus on static images is also partly a historical accident: it was easier to create databases with static images, images occupy less hard drive space, and they require fewer computational resources to process. These practical restrictions are less relevant today.

Under natural viewing conditions, there are several cues that depend on integrating information over time. These dynamic cues can significantly enhance object classification. A paradigmatic case where temporal integration can be essential is action recognition. Although it is possible to recognize actions purely from static images (e.g., Figure 9.4), it is generally significantly easier to do so using videos both for computers and for humans. For example, it can be difficult to discern whether a person is talking or not using only a static image. Modern models for action recognition from spatiotemporal input based on deep convolutional neural network architectures can be partitioned into three groups: (i) networks with three-dimensional convolutional filters, where spatial and temporal features are processed together via three-dimensional convolutions; (ii) two-stream networks where one stream processes spatial information and another stream obtains optical flow from consecutive frames, and the two streams are merged at a late stage for classification; (iii) networks that feed onto a recurrent architecture such as a long short-term memory (LSTM) (Section 8.17) that integrates spatial features over time.

Temporal information is relevant for many other tasks beyond action recognition. Object segmentation generally becomes significantly easier with video data. The importance of temporal change for segmentation has been exploited by the ubiquitous use of camouflage in the animal world. In the absence of movement, matching colors, contrast, and textures can help animals avoid predators, or at least buy sufficient time to escape. It is particularly challenging to segment objects in the visual periphery, yet neurons with receptive fields located at large eccentricities remain highly sensitive to visual motion. Furthermore, motion is one of the most robust bottom-up saliency cues.

Temporal information can also play a critical role in visual learning. In an elegant experiment, cats were reared under stroboscopic lighting conditions – that is, with flashes of lights turning on and off like those used at a disco, which prevent seeing continuous motion. The development of the primary visual cortex in those cats was abnormal in terms of orientation selectivity, binocular integration, motion detection, and receptive field sizes. These results further corroborate the discussion in Section 2.2 about natural stimulus statistics governing the tuning properties of neurons in the visual system.

Additionally, because objects do not just simply vanish instantaneously, using video data can naturally help humans and models learn to recognize objects from multiple viewpoints. Video sequences automatically provide a biologically plausible way to perform "data augmentation" by getting many similar images of an object from a single label (Section 8.9). Another example of how temporal information can be used for visual learning is the case of self-supervised learning to predict future events, discussed in the PredNet algorithm in Section 8.17 (Figure 8.11).

9.4   Major Milestones in Object Classification

In Section 8.7, we introduced several image databases, such as ImageNet, which have played an essential role in the development of computational models of visual recognition (Figure 8.4). These databases were created for large-scale visual recognition challenges where investigators compete to get low classification errors.

A good way to report performance in these competitions is to cite top-1 classification accuracy where the model produces a single label per image, and the result is either right or wrong. Many computer vision applications have reported a more lenient and more confusing metric: top-5 classification accuracy, where the model is allowed to produce five different labels for each image, and the result is considered to be correct if any of these labels is correct. One excuse for considering the top-5 metric is that some natural images extracted from the web contain multiple objects. An image may contain both a dog *and* a tree; the association between that image and a label of tree is therefore arbitrary. The same image could have easily been labeled dog as well. While this makes sense, reporting top-5 accuracies exaggerates the accuracy of the algorithms and makes it more difficult to directly compare against human performance. For example, consider an image from the ImageNet dataset (where there are 1,000 possible labels) showing exclusively a tree in the street. The image label is "tree." A computational algorithm may provide the following five labels, sorted in decreasing probability order given by the numbers in parenthesis: elephant (probability = 0.62), refrigerator (0.31), car (0.02), tree (0.02), ice (0.01). These probabilities add up to 0.98 and not 1 because the remaining 1,000 − 5 = 995 categories add up to 0.02. These five labels would be considered a correct answer according to the top-5 accuracy measure, yet they are somewhat strange. Humans would not say that the image has 0.62 probability of containing an elephant and 0.31 probability of containing a refrigerator! Other databases like MSCOCO label multiple objects per image, and therefore, it is possible to check the accuracy of multiple labels.

Figure 9.5 shows top-1 performance in ImageNet for several computational models, many of which have won object classification competitions over the last decade, and some of which were already mentioned in Chapter 8. Current top-1 performance is slightly greater than 80 percent, and current top-5 performance is almost 95 percent. These metrics are quite impressive, considering that there are 1,000 classes and, hence, chance level is 0.1 percent. It is not easy to directly compare these performance metrics with humans, particularly top-5 measures, given the arguments in the previous paragraph. Humans are not very good at 1,000-way classification: it is hard to remember those 1,000 labels, and

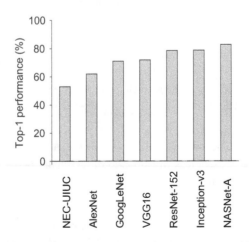

Figure 9.5 Evolution of performance on the ImageNet dataset. Top-1 classification performance in object classification based on the ImageNet dataset. Each column refers to a different computational algorithm. Chance = 0.1 percent.

humans may have lots of biases toward remembering and using some labels more than others. Additionally, as we discussed in Section 8.7, some of the image categories in ImageNet are somewhat esoteric (how many times have you seen an isopod, a jetty, or a cuirass?). Humans could potentially be trained in the same way that the algorithms in Figure 9.5 have been trained to become experts at distinguishing an isopod, a jetty, a cuirass, or any of the other 997 labels. Regardless of these considerations, informal measures of human performance in this dataset yield accuracy rates that are between 90 and 95 percent. Hence, even with all their limitations, current algorithms can perform object classification on ImageNet images as well as or even better than humans.

It should be noted that top-1 performance is not always a great metric. For example, in the next section, we will consider the problem of analyzing clinical images. Consider a particular disease that is present in one out of 10,000 people. Suppose that we train an algorithm, and the algorithm achieves 99.99 percent performance. At first glance, this performance seems quite impressive. However, it is easy to achieve 99.99 percent performance by simply indicating that all the images do not show evidence for the disease! Trivially, such an algorithm would not be useful at all. The algorithm would have 9,999 true negatives, 0 true positives, 1 false negative, and 0 false positives. Particularly in situations where there is a difference between the number of images with each label (an imbalanced classification problem), it is useful to define two metrics, precision and recall:

$$\text{recall} = \text{true positives}/(\text{true positives} + \text{false negatives})$$

$$\text{precision} = \text{true positives}/(\text{true positives} + \text{false positives})$$

.   An algorithm stating that none of the images show the disease has zero recall and zero precision, even though it reached 99.99 percent accuracy. Conversely, consider another algorithm that is also *not* useful, which labels all the images as showing evidence for the disease. This algorithm would have 0 true negatives, 1 true positive, 0 false negatives, and 9,999 false positives. The recall would be 1 – which may seem quite nice, except that the precision would be very low, despite the high recall. The same ideas are often discussed in statistics classes as Type I error (false positives) and Type II error (false negatives). For the aficionados, some investigators also use another metric called the F_1 score, which is the harmonic mean of the precision and recall:

$$F_1 = 2\frac{precision \cdot recall}{precision + recall} = \frac{TruePositives}{TruePositives + 0.5(FalsePositives + FalseNegatives)}.$$

Depending on the nature of the problem and the consequences of errors, false positives could be much worse than false negatives, or vice versa. It is possible to assign weights in loss functions to differentially penalize the different types of errors. For example, if recall is considered to be β times as important as precision, one can define $F_\beta = (1 + \beta^2)\frac{precision \cdot recall}{(\beta^2 \cdot precision + recall)}$ (which is equivalent to F_1 when $\beta = 1$).

Independently of the specific metrics, it is clear that there has been notable progress in object classification tasks (Figure 9.5). AlexNet itself showed a substantial boost with respect to all its predecessors, giving rise to a rapid exploration of deeper and more complex architectures that have boosted performance by more than 20 percent in less than a decade. This notable improvement in academic competitions attracted the attention of many people looking to solve pattern-recognition applications.

9.5 Real-World Applications of Computer Vision Algorithms for Object Classification

Success in image labeling competitions inspired a large number of efforts in image classification across many domains. One of the earliest real-world applications was optical character recognition (OCR), which rapidly became mainstream in sorting mail based on the handwritten zip codes. Now, there are even neat applications that can translate handwritten traces into mathematical formulae. On the one hand, some mathematical symbols are relatively simple; on the other hand, mathematical symbols are probably less stereotyped, and there is less training data than in other OCR applications. Computer vision algorithms have already made rapid progress in a wide array of exciting applications; we discuss next only a few examples.

A field that is rapidly being transformed by computer vision is clinical image analysis. Clinical diagnosis based on images can *sometimes* be simplified into a visual pattern-recognition problem. Clinicians may combine information from image-based diagnosis with a wealth of other information – including medical history, genetic information, symptoms, and more. How to combine these different sources of information into automatic diagnosis methods is an interesting problem in and of itself, but this is beyond the scope of our current discussion. Here we restrict the problem of diagnosis strictly to image analysis. For example, a radiologist can examine a mammogram to determine whether it contains a breast tumor or not (Figure 9.6). A database consisting of many mammogram images annotated by experts can be readily used to train computer vision algorithms. The American Cancer Society recommends obtaining a mammogram, generally consisting of two X-ray images of each breast, to all women

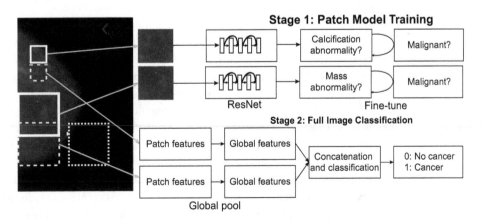

Figure 9.6 Computer vision can help clinical diagnosis based on images. Example algorithm to detect cancer in breast mammograms. Modified from Lotter 2018

once or twice a year, depending on age. This number of mammograms leads to a lot of images (about 40 million images a year in the United States alone). The problem is important because early diagnosis can have a critical impact on deciding the course of action. It is estimated that radiologists read on the order of 10,000 cases per year; a radiologist with three decades of experience may have seen 300,000 cases. Nowadays, a computer vision algorithm can be trained with many more examples than a human clinician can see in his/her lifetime.

Computer vision algorithms have thrived in a wide variety of image diagnosis efforts. To train and test these computer vision algorithms, ground truth labels provided by clinicians are needed. It should be noted that humans are capricious creatures. Clinicians do not always agree with each other on the diagnosis of a given image (between-expert variability). Furthermore, clinicians sometimes do not even agree with themselves when repeatedly tested on the same images (within-expert variability)! In the case of breast tumor detection, computational algorithms are now on par or even better than human clinicians. In other words, the differences between a state-of-the-art computer vision algorithm and a human expert are the same as the within-expert and between-expert variability. Future generations may regard humans trying to diagnose images in the same way that we now regard a human trying to interpret a bar code in the supermarket or trying to compute the square root of 17 by hand.

While the presence or absence of a tumor is the central question of interest in the vast majority of breast exams, occasionally, there may be other relevant questions clinicians may want to ask about an image. For example, sometimes there are incidental findings where a person is scanned to diagnose a given condition X (e.g., breast cancer), the scan does not reveal any finding regarding X, but the radiologist detects other anomalies that lead to a different diagnosis Y. Such incidental findings may be challenging for current computer vision algorithms because they may be extremely infrequent. The algorithms are ultra-specialized and outperform radiologists in detecting condition X but were never trained in detecting the rare condition Y. One possible compromise as an initial solution for this challenge would be for computer vision systems to flag such images as anomalous and route them back to a human for further inspection.

Incidental findings represent one arena where humans may still surpass machines in clinical image diagnosis, where humans can find patterns that computers miss. The reverse is also true: machines may be able to discover novel patterns that were not previously found by humans in clinical images. An intriguing example of this phenomenon arose when investigators were developing computer vision approaches examining retinal fundus photographs to diagnose a condition known as diabetic retinopathy (Figure 9.7). Diabetic retinopathy is a condition that may arise in diabetic patients when high blood sugar levels cause blood vessels in the retina to swell and leak. These blood vessels can be examined in fundus photographs, which are images of the back of the eye, used by ophthalmologists to diagnose the disease. After collecting hundreds of thousands of labeled images, a deep learning computer vision algorithm quickly learned to match clinicians in diagnosis, a feat that comes as no surprise at this stage.

The diagnosis label is only one of the questions that one can pose about those images. The investigators decided to turn their machine learning algorithms to other questions

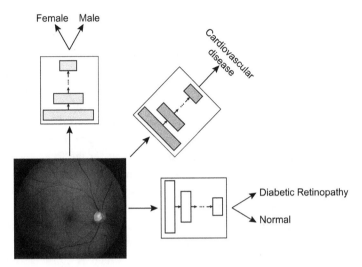

Figure 9.7 Computational algorithms can make new observations. Example clinical application of computer vision, taking a photograph of the back of the eye (fundus photograph) and using a deep convolutional network to diagnose diabetic retinopathy (Poplin et al. 2018). In addition, computer vision algorithms can be trained to ask other questions from the same image, including predicting the subject's gender or even the risk of cardiovascular disease.

on the same images. In a surprising twist, computer scientists asked whether they could extract other types of information from the fundus photographs. For example, instead of learning yes/no labels for diabetic retinopathy, they trained the same algorithms to predict the subject's age. The algorithms were able to predict age quite accurately, with an absolute error of less than 3.5 years. Next, the investigators assessed whether they could predict the subject's gender. Surprisingly, they were able to do so exceptionally well, with an area under the receiver operating characteristic (ROC) curve of 0.97. The ROC curve is a plot of the probability of correct detection versus the probability of false alarm. It is trivial to achieve high detection rates at the expense of high false alarm rates (by claiming that every image shows disease; see previous section) or low false alarm rates without any correct detection (by claiming that no image shows disease). A good algorithm will have a low false alarm rate and high probability of detection. The best that an algorithm could achieve is an area of 1.0; chance levels would yield an area of 0.5. Trained ophthalmologists had never been able to estimate somebody's gender or age from fundus photographs. Perhaps they never cared to ask that question; after all, the clinicians will have the subjects and their records right in front of them. However, even after telling clinicians that the gender and age information was present in these images and asking doctors to infer the gender or age, they were unable to do so. It is not entirely clear what exact image features the algorithm uses to discriminate gender or age. One could hypothesize that perhaps doctors, both male and female, might position the apparatus to take fundus photographs slightly closer to female patients than to male patients, on average, when acquiring these images. The algorithms could well capture such a slight unconscious bias. Alternatively, perhaps there exist real subtle differences between female and male blood vessels in the retina. Regardless of whether this explanation holds, this example shows that computer vision can discover image features that are not apparent even to experts in the field.

Estimating a subject's age and gender from fundus photographs is perhaps not particularly exciting from a practical standpoint. The most enigmatic finding emerged when the investigators decided to ask an even more daring question: would it be possible to predict the risk of cardiovascular disease from fundus photographs? Computer scientists discovered that they were able to predict cardiovascular disease from the fundus photographs with an area under the ROC curve of 0.7. This result is quite remarkable because this is a question that ophthalmologists had not thought about, it is a question that is extremely relevant from a clinical standpoint, and the computational analyses constitute additional information that comes for free from the fundus photograph without any additional clinical testing. What is perhaps even more remarkable is that the computer vision algorithm was able to predict cardiovascular disease better than the Framingham Risk Score, which is considered to be one of the best indicators of cardiovascular risk based on decades of clinical work. Computer vision algorithms can not only learn to diagnose images like doctors, but they can also teach us novel things about those images.

There are several situations where there is an enormous number of images (or videos) that needs to be classified. Automatic image classification has found applications well beyond clinical diagnosis. For example, computer vision has shed light on the gargantuan task of classifying galaxies and exoplanets from telescope images. There are vast amounts of imagery to help us understand the shape of galaxies and characterize planets outside the solar system, but we do not have enough astrophysicists to classify all those images. Astrophysicists turned to crowd-sourcing by engaging the public in looking at images and learning to categorize galaxies. This is an ideal setting to apply pattern-recognition techniques from computer vision: the last few years have seen many exciting discoveries made by machine learning algorithms. A conceptually similar example is the categorization of plants and animals. Computer vision has been used to classify flora and fauna, quickly surpassing any naïve observer and becoming the envy of expert biologists.

Another image classification problem that has been radically transformed by computer vision is face identification. There is a wide variety of applications for automatic face-recognition algorithms. Many smartphones have algorithms that use faces to log in, which used to be the domain of science fiction movies not too long ago. Facebook can now search for photos that include a particular person when that person is not tagged. Quantitative studies of face identification have shown that computer vision systems are better than forensic experts and also better than so-called superrecognizers, people with an extraordinary capacity to recognize and remember faces. There is also a growing industry of security applications based on facial recognition capabilities. Security applications in the near future may also rely on action recognition classification algorithms. Concomitant with advances in face recognition, there are vigorous and timely discussions about issues of privacy. It is quite likely that, very soon, it will be rather challenging to walk down the street without being recognized.

George Orwell's Big Brother scenario with cameras that can recognize people is now technically feasible.

The exciting progress in self-driving cars has also been fueled by progress in computer vision – with tasks such as localizing pedestrians, cars, brake lights, traffic lights, other signs, lanes, the sidewalk, and even animals, bicycles, or anomalous objects on the road. While the majority of computer vision applications rely on video or camera feeds from regular cameras, images do not have to be restricted to such sensors. For example, self-driving cars can simultaneously use information from multiple cameras and many other sensors. There has been so much progress in terms of computer vision that most engineers trying to build self-driving cars think that the main challenges ahead transcend vision and involve decision making, legal issues, and vulnerability.

Other applications of computer vision algorithms are still under development but will be ready quite soon. For example, there is much interest in intelligent content-based image or video search (referred to as image retrieval in the computer vision literature). Searching the web by content (as opposed to searching for the word "dog" and using the label to search for text or images with a dog tag) opens the doors to a whole set of applications. Initial prototypes of these types of searches are already in place.

The previous section introduced advances in face identification. These algorithms will allow searching for people from photographs, which may have a lot of exciting applications such as searching for missing people or finding a friend from long ago. Progress in face identification may soon lead to ATMs that can recognize customers. Cars and houses may also soon recognize their owners from their faces. Progress in person recognition and action recognition may radically transform security screening in crowded environments, including airports, stadiums, and perhaps every street in large cities. Efforts in computer vision applications for security screening, and perhaps other purposes, are already ongoing in several major cities.

9.6   Computer Vision to Help People with Visual Disabilities

A particularly exciting application of computer vision systems is to help people with visual deficits, particularly the blind (Figure 9.8). In the United States alone, there are approximately one million people who are legally blind and about 3.25 million people with visual impairment. Combined with high-quality and relatively inexpensive cameras, computer vision algorithms can help digest the output of digital cameras to convey information to the blind. Most phones these days can determine a person's location by using GPS coordinates, yet one may soon be able to get even more precise information by pointing the phone and having it determine the direction of certain shops, bus stops, or landmarks. Phones can also help read signs and restaurant menus. However, blind people need and deserve much more.

An interesting application of computer vision would be to restore visual functionality to people with severe visual impairment. By restoring "visual functionality," we do not necessarily mean getting a blind person to *see* in the same way that a sighted

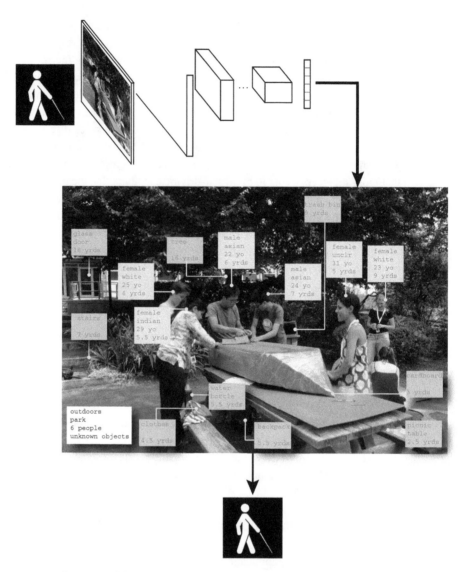

Figure 9.8 Computer vision could help visually impaired people. Example potential approach to use computer vision to help people with visual impairment. A blind person may carry a camera that connects to a computer vision algorithm and that can interpret the surrounding scene. The computer vision algorithm can deliver information about people, objects, distances, and relative locations in real time.

person does. Instead, visual functionality refers to the ability to rapidly and accurately convey information that blind people can use. A blind person could easily wear a camera on their forehead, or in a pendant. Imagine an algorithm that can label every object in an image (instance segmentation). How can we convey such rich information to a blind person? An image is worth a thousand words. In a glimpse, we get a rich representation of our surroundings, which is quite different from labeling every object.

This representation highlights certain aspects of the image while ignoring other, less relevant information. For example, we may not be interested in the shape of every branch in a nearby tree, though we could access that information by attending to it if we wanted to. Instead, we may be more interested in whether a bicycle is coming toward us at full speed. In a glimpse, we can discern distances, relationships between objects, and even actions and intentions. Even if we could accurately label all the objects in an image, there is much more to visual understanding, a theme that we will come back to at the end of this chapter. The main challenge in helping the blind is to provide *relevant* information in real time.

As a side note, we could easily extend these ideas to enhancing the visual capabilities of sighted people as well. It would be easy to wear a camera that would give us immediate access to a 360-degree view of the world, or grant us access to other parts of the light spectrum that our eyes are not sensitive to, such as infrared. We are all "blind" in the infrared and ultraviolet frequency bands, or behind our heads, but we have instruments that can detect those signals. Computer vision systems could help us parse and interpret those images. Of note, the basic operations of convolution, normalization, pooling, and rectification (Section 8.5) do not depend on whether the signals come from the visible part of the spectrum or infrared, ultraviolet, or other sources. In sum, computer vision could help restore, and perhaps even augment, human vision.

9.7   Deep Convolutional Neural Networks Work Outside of Vision Too

The same mathematical operations used to analyze images taken from photographs can be extended to non-visible parts of the spectrum. Furthermore, there is no reason to restrict ourselves to light patterns. Although our focus is the discussion of computer vision systems, it is interesting to point out that the same mathematics, the same types of architectures, and the same types of training algorithms have extended well beyond vision.

Vision has led the way to success in a wide variety of other problems. For example, systems for speech recognition; systems that suggest automatic replies to emails; systems to predict the weather, the stock market, or consumer behavior; and many other questions have now been revolutionized by deep convolutional neural networks originally developed to label images. Each of these domains requires training with different types of data, changing the inputs, and, in some cases, also making adjustments to the architectures themselves. However, at the heart of these domains outside of vision is a similar mathematical problem: training a neural network to learn to extract adequate features from the data and then classifying the resulting features. What changes is the input: instead of using pixels in RGB space, in the case of speech recognition, one can use a spectrogram of the frequencies of sound as a function of time to process sounds. However, the subsequent processing steps and the procedure to train those algorithms are remarkably similar, if not exactly the same, in many applications.

In neuroscience, the idea that similar computational principles can be used for different problems is sometimes phrased as "cortex is cortex" (Section 8.2), alluding to the conjecture that the same basic architectural principles are followed in the visual, auditory, and tactile systems. Without a doubt, there are important differences across modalities, and engineers will also fine-tune their algorithms for each application. However, as a first approximation, some of the primary ingredients seem to hold across multiple seemingly distinct tasks.

9.8   Image Generators and GANs

The basic paradigm in most of the computer vision applications that we have discussed thus far follows the structure shown in Figure 8.2. An image is processed through a neural network that learns to extract features for the task at hand. Another remarkable development from deep convolutional neural networks has been the idea of turning this process in reverse and using features to *generate* images. The computational models discussed so far are discriminative algorithms that assign descriptive labels to images or parts thereof. In contrast, the goal of generative algorithms is not to assign a label but rather to create a new sample from a given distribution. In the context of vision, this typically amounts to creating novel images or videos. A particularly successful approach to generating images is the use of generative adversarial networks (GANs, Figure 9.9).

GANs consist of two main components: an image generator, and an image discriminator. The image generator can be thought of as an inverted deep convolutional neural network. In a typical deep convolutional neural network, the input is an image, and the output is a series of features. In an image generator, the input is a series of features, and the output is an image. For example, using random initial inputs, the goal may be to create images of realistic faces. The image discriminator takes as input both real images and images created by the generator; the task of the discriminator is to ascertain whether

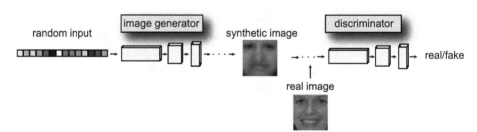

Figure 9.9 Generative adversarial networks (GAN) play police-versus-thief games. A generative adversarial network is an algorithm that creates new samples from a given distribution – for example, generating new images. The algorithm consists of two main components: an image generator and an image discriminator. The generator can be thought of as an inverted deep convolutional neural network, using features as inputs and creating images as output. The discriminator takes samples from the generator and real images and determines whether the generated images are real or fake.

an image is real or fake. The two components are jointly trained – the generator trying to fool the discriminator and the discriminator trying to catch the impostor generator.

Such image generators have found fun applications in several domains. One of these domains is style transfer. One can take an arbitrary picture and re-render it according to the style of a famous painting. One can use a GAN to merge different faces, to make a face look like a celebrity, or to visualize how a given person might look like when he or she gets older. Another application is to create graphic art. Recently, an image generated by a GAN, *The Portrait of Edmond Belamy*, was sold by Christie's for the sizable prize of $432,500.

Other GANs have focused on trying to create realistic-looking photographs. In fact, to the naïve eye, it can be difficult to distinguish a fake from a real photograph. Beyond Hollywood, these algorithms raise a lot of interesting questions. The notion that "seeing is believing" may require some serious revision in the era of sophisticated digital fakes.

9.9   DeepDream and XDream: Elucidating the Tuning Properties of Computational Units and Biological Neurons

A particularly exciting use of image generators is to help address the curse of dimensionality when studying the tuning properties of neurons in visual cortex (Figure 5.10). A family of techniques initially referred to under the poetic name of *DeepDream* was introduced by computer scientists to visualize the types of images preferred by units in deep convolutional neural networks. When considering these neural networks, we know the architecture and all the weights; in other words, we can mathematically define perfectly well the activation of every unit. Under these conditions, we can reverse the process to ask what types of images will yield high activation for a given unit. Here the "loss function" is the unit activation (which is to be maximized), and we can still apply the gradient descent algorithm introduced in Section 8.6, except that we calculate derivatives with respect to the image itself instead of changing the network weights.

Now imagine that we want to generate images that will maximally activate a neuron in the brain rather than a unit in a neural network. The situation is far more complicated when it comes to the neural networks in biological brains, where we do not know the architecture, let alone the weights. To circumvent these challenges, Will Xiao and colleagues developed the XDream algorithm (e**X**tending **D**eepDream with **r**eal-time **e**volution for **a**ctivation **m**aximization, Figure 9.10), which was briefly introduced in Section 6.4. The algorithm consists of three components: (i) an image generator, (ii) a mechanism to assess the fitness of each image, and (iii) a search method to create the next set of images (Figure 9.10A). The image generator is an inverted deep convolutional neural network along the lines of the algorithms introduced in the previous section. The image generator takes a set of features as input and creates a color image. The initial conditions are random images. Next, the algorithm evaluates the images created by the generator and rank orders them according to a fitness function defined by what we want to maximize. For example, the algorithm may maximize the activation of

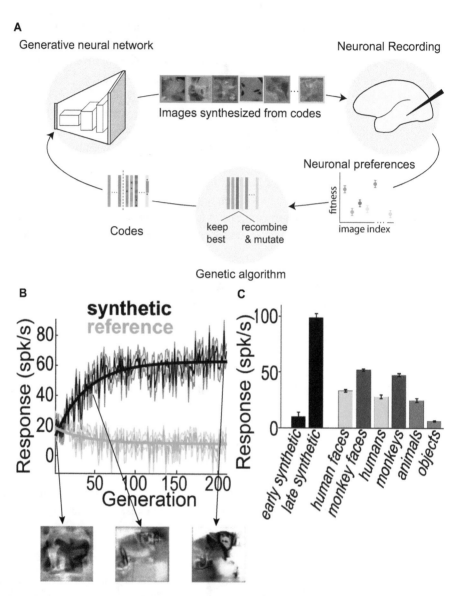

Figure 9.10 Image generators can help probe neuronal tuning in an unbiased manner.
(**A**) A promising recent application of image generators is the development of closed-loop algorithms to investigate neuronal tuning. Schematic of the XDream algorithm consisting of an image generator, neuronal recordings, and a genetic algorithm. (**B**) The firing rate of an inferior temporal cortex neuron increases with each iteration of the XDream algorithm (synthetic images, black), creating images that are better than reference natural images. (**C**) While the average responses of this neuron to natural images may lead some investigators to infer tuning for faces, the synthetic images trigger even higher firing rates.

a particular unit in the network, the average activity of all units in a given layer, or the standard deviation of the activity of units within a layer. In neuroscience, the fitness function could be the firing rate of a given neuron in response to the images (as shown in multiple examples in Chapters 5 and 6). After ranking the images based on the fitness function, XDream uses a genetic search algorithm to select, delete, and recombine the initial set of features to create a new round of images. Importantly, XDream does not make any a priori assumptions about neuronal tuning, nor does it require any knowledge about the architecture or weights in the neural network or brain; the algorithm only requires a way to evaluate fitness values for each image.

XDream can visualize the features preferred by units in neural networks. It can discover images that trigger high activation – extrapolating across different layers, different architectures, and even different training regimes. Remarkably, XDream is also very effective in discovering images that trigger high activation in real biological neurons (Section 6.4). Without any assumption about cortical connectivity or preconceptions about neuronal preferences, and within the constraints introduced by biological recordings, the algorithm generates images that trigger high firing rates (Figure 9.10B). These synthetic images turn out to be as effective as – or, in several cases, more effective than – the types of random natural images that have been used in neuroscience for decades (Figure 9.10C).

9.10   Reflections on Cross-Validation and Extrapolation

In this chapter, we have highlighted some of the remarkable achievements of computer vision algorithms. We shift gears now to emphasize some of the critical challenges for current algorithms and some of the exciting opportunities ahead. Let us start with the critical question of generalization. In Section 8.8, we introduced the concept of crossvalidation. To reduce the risk of overfitting and deluding ourselves into thinking our algorithms are better than they actually are, it is critical to separate the data into a training set and an independent test set.

What is not well defined in most computer vision applications is how different the test set should be from the training set. In most typical scenarios, we have a large dataset, and we randomly select some images for training and the rest for testing. How excited we should be about the results depends critically on how distinct the test set really is. In a trivial example, we alluded earlier to the potential problem of duplicate images in datasets (Section 8.8). Suppose that image 5,000 and image 8,000 are actually identical, and suppose that the random selection assigns image 5,000 to the training set and image 8,000 to the test set. Of course, this is not real cross-validation, and correctly classifying image 8,000 should not be considered to be an achievement of the algorithm. In a barely more complex example, suppose now that image 8,000 is identical to image 5,000 except for one pixel, or that image 8,000 is a slightly cropped version of image 5,000. Although we can follow all the rules of cross-validation and adequately separate images into an independent test set, adequately assessing performance is problematic if the test images are very similar to those in the training set.

There are more subtle and pernicious versions of this problem. Many databases are based on pictures from the web. There may be strong biases and spurious correlations in the types of pictures that people upload on the web. For example, imagine that we want to build an algorithm to recognize the Tower of Pisa in Italy. Tourists who visit the Leaning Tower of Pisa tend to take pictures of the famous tower and upload those pictures on the web. There are only so many positions from which one can take a picture of the Tower of Pisa, and there are many, many tourists (about 10^6 tourists every year). There may be many biases in the locations from which people take those pictures. For example, people may tend to approach the tower from certain streets, there may be specific locations where people tend to sit, and few people use drones to take aerial pictures. There may be biases also in terms of what exactly the pictures show (for example, most people photograph the entire tower as opposed to parts of it; most pictures may contain much of the surrounding grass area around the tower). There may even be general biases in the color of the sky surrounding the tower (for example, there may be many more pictures on a sunny day and very few pictures during a thunderstorm). Collecting all the Leaning Tower of Pisa pictures and performing adequate cross-validation to ensure that the test images are not too similar to those in the training set is difficult. Unless cross-validation is done extremely carefully, an algorithm might achieve high accuracy in recognizing the Tower of Pisa yet fail miserably with an unusual picture taken from a drone on a rainy day. In other words, it is easy for the algorithm to overfit to the training data, despite our best intentions and best efforts to separate the training and test datasets.

This problem is not restricted to famous landmarks. For example, many people are fond of showing off the food that they prepared by uploading pictures to social media. Consider all the pictures of omelets on the web. Are they mostly taken from the same angle? Are the omelets typically on a plate? Is the plate white in many pictures? Are most of the pictures taken with more or less uniform kitchen illumination? Do some of them also contain forks and knives? How many pictures of an omelet hanging from a tree branch in the park on a rainy day are there on the web?

Yet another example of this family of problems can be gleaned from the action recognition task illustrated in Figure 9.4. The frames in Figure 9.4A are taken from a well-known video database for action recognition, UCF101. Without any sophisticated processing, using only single frames and pixel-level information, one can infer that if the image contains many blue pixels, it is likely to correspond to "breaststroke," whereas if the image contains many green pixels, it is likely to correspond to "soccer juggling." Other actions also contain a lot of blue or green, but it is nonetheless possible to get well above chance performance in this task without any acute understanding of the images, let alone any comprehension of what the action labels mean. In contrast, the controlled datasets shown in Figure 9.4B are significantly harder: here, the task is to determine whether the person is drinking or not. There are lots of different ways of drinking (from a cup, from a bottle, using a straw, using hands as a vessel, from a drinking fountain). A true action classifier capable of discriminating pictures showing drinking should be able to generalize to all of these conditions. We cannot get significantly above chance performance in the task in Figure 9.4B by merely considering the number of blue pixels. Above chance performance in pixel-level classification is a good indication that the task is too easy, that there are strong similarities between training and test images, and that there could be a significant degree of overfitting.

Because of these types of correlations in the images within a dataset, contextual information tends to play a prominent role in computer vision algorithms. Algorithms can adequately infer the right label even if the object itself is completely occluded, purely based on the statistics of contextual information. For example, pictures of traffic lights tend to be in a street environment, and the traffic light tends to be positioned in the upper part of the picture. While this may be seen as favorable capitalization on image statistics, the converse is also true: neural networks can misclassify an object placed out of context. Contextual information can help humans too (Section 3.7); however, humans tend to be more immune to image manipulations like placing objects out of context.

Not all real-world applications depend on generalization. For example, if Facebook wishes to automatically tag the Tower of Pisa in pictures uploaded by its users, Facebook may be satisfied with achieving 99 percent accuracy and miss those few instances of an aerial picture during a thunderstorm. Other applications may critically require preparing for the unexpected. We want self-driving cars to be able to detect a cow crossing the highway, even if this is a rare circumstance.

The problem of cross-validation is related to the question of bias in training datasets (referred to as dataset bias in the computer vision community). For example, suppose that we build an algorithm to detect breast tumors using mammograms from white women between 50 and 60 years old who live in California. Will the algorithm work with similarly aged white women from Massachusetts? And from Europe? Would the algorithm work with African American or Asian women? Would the algorithm work with women in their thirties or their eighties? The issue of biases in training data has recently been highlighted in the news for the task of face identification systems that performed better for certain ethnic groups than for others.

Of note, the problem of biases is not unique to computer vision. Visual recognition biases are prevalent in human vision too. Radiologists trained to recognize breast tumors in mammograms from white women in their fifties may also fail when tested with mammograms from other groups of women. In the case of face identification, there are well-known human biases based on where people grow up and the amount of exposure they have had to faces from different ethnic groups.

Generalization is an essential and desirable property for computational algorithms. The ability to generalize from cross-validated data is not well defined and depends on how distinct the test set is. One way to attempt to quantify this problem is to distinguish between interpolation (within-distribution generalization) and extrapolation (out-of-distribution generalization). Again, precisely what is meant by distribution is not well defined, but at least this provides a way to begin to quantify the ability of algorithms to extrapolate beyond their training set.

9.11 Adversarial Images

We have highlighted some of the exciting advances in how computational algorithms process images and how machine vision can match or even surpass human performance in many applications. However, caution should be exercised before thinking that machines might be about to pass the general Turing test for vision. There are still many visual tasks that machines cannot solve. Furthermore, it is relatively easy to fool machines in visual tasks (e.g., Figure 9.4).

One example of perplexing behavior by deep convolutional neural networks is the case of *adversarial images*, whereby minimal changes to an image drastically change the predicted class (Figure 9.11). Adversarial images appear similar, almost identical, to humans, yet they receive different labels by a computer vision system. For example, the two images in Figure 9.11 are virtually indistinguishable to human observers, yet a deep convolutional network correctly classified the one on the left as "corn," and incorrectly labeled the one on the right as "snorkel." Given an algorithm that is forced to assign a binary label to an image, A versus B, it is inevitable that there will be a boundary where we can move from A to B with small image changes. The separation between two labels in image space is akin to standing in the often-arbitrary border between two states or trying to define precisely where the rain starts when it is raining in location A and not B.

These adversarial images are typically created by using knowledge about the categorical boundaries and astutely changing a few pixels to push the image into the opposite side of the label. As in the DeepDream algorithm introduced in Section 9.10, the process of creating adversarial images involves gradient descent on the pixels of the image itself.

What is intriguing about the adversarial examples is the profound difference between machine and human perception. In many real-world applications, seeing the world the way humans do may be quite relevant. In fact, there has been a whole industry of

988: corn   801: snorkel

Figure 9.11 Adversarial examples are misclassified by computational algorithms, yet they seem indistinguishable to the human brain. The two images appear to be indistinguishable to humans. However, state-of-the-art computer algorithms classify the one on the left as "corn" and the one on the right as "snorkel." The image on the right was created by introducing small amounts of noise to the image on the left, along specific directions.

investigators designing "adversarial attacks" to confuse computer vision systems, together with a similarly vigorous community of defenses against such adversarial attacks. For example, one may ask whether the image on the right in Figure 9.11 would revert back to corn upon scaling it, changing its color, using different versions of the same network (e.g., starting from different random initial conditions), or using different architectures. These examples clearly illustrate that, even when current algorithms can correctly label many images, state-of-the-art deep convolutional neural networks do not necessarily see the world the way humans do.

Adversarial examples are not unique to the field of computer vision. Humans also suffer from such adversarial examples; it is just much harder to generate such examples for humans because we cannot compute gradients on biological networks as we do with artificial neural networks. Even without such gradients, psychologists have discovered many images that confuse humans. Humans are fallible in many visual illusions that deceive us into seeing things that do not exist (Chapter 3).

In sum, humans and state-of-the-art computer vision systems make similar mistakes in object classification tasks (Section 8.12). However, many images can trick computer vision systems and not humans, and vice versa. These results show that even our best computer vision systems still do not fully account for human visual recognition capabilities. Because it is possible to find such double dissociations between machine and human vision, these results also show that current deep convolutional neural networks still cannot pass the Turing test. We can easily tell a machine from a human by showing the image on the right in Figure 9.11.

9.12   Deceptively Simple Tasks That Challenge Computer Vision Algorithms

Adversarial examples are especially constructed to fool computational algorithms. It is also possible to challenge computational algorithms in basic visual tasks that are not designed with the specific purpose of moving images across categorical boundaries. While there are many visual questions where computers outperform humans, such as bar code reading, there are also many common visual questions where it is easy to trick computers (Figure 9.11).

Many visual questions that are simple for humans represent a formidable challenge for current architectures. Consider the examples in Figure 9.12, taken from a set of 23 visual reasoning tasks introduced by Don Geman's group. Given a set of positive (top row) and negative (bottom row) examples, we need to figure out what the rule is to be able to classify novel images. Humans quickly realize that the rule is "same or different" except for translation for the two shapes in Figure 9.12A, "inside or outside" in Figure 9.12B, and whether the largest of the three shapes is in between the other two or not in Figure 9.12C. Even if humans have never seen these particular examples and tasks before, they can quickly infer what the rules are. Humans can then use those rules to reason about new examples. Thomas Serre's group has shown that current computer vision models struggle with these tasks despite extensive training with up to a million examples.

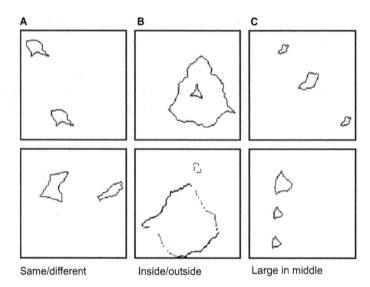

Same/different   Inside/outside   Large in middle

Figure 9.12 Some apparently simple tasks pose a challenge to current algorithms. The task involves learning to classify images into two groups according to certain fixed but unknown rules. Here are shown three types of rules: (**A**) same or different, (**B**) inside/outside, (**C**) large object in the middle. Positive examples are shown on the top row and negative examples on the bottom row. Reproduced from Fleuret et al. 2011

A related example is the CLEVR dataset consisting of images containing multiple geometrical shapes like spheres, cubes, and cylinders of varying sizes, colors, and material properties. The task involves answering questions such as whether the red cylinder to the left of the blue cube is larger than the red cylinder to the right of the blue cube or whether the number of large objects is the same as the number of metallic objects. Current networks appear to adequately learn to answer these questions when trained and tested on the same combinations of shapes and color properties. However, when tested on novel combinations of shapes and colors (e.g., when the network has never encountered a blue cylinder during training even though it has seen lots of blue cubes and lots of red cylinders), the networks failed to generalize.

9.13   Challenges Ahead

There has been significant progress in teaching computers how to see. We are already surrounded by machines that can successfully use automatic vision algorithms in real-world applications. The exhilarating progress in computer vision may lead us to think that we have almost solved the problem of vision. Indeed, prominent newspapers proposed headlines with statements hinting that vision has almost been solved. However, I would argue that we are still extremely far from passing the general Turing test for vision and that the best is yet to come.

In addition to some of the challenges discussed in the previous sections (adversarial images, generalization, visual reasoning in simple tasks), an area that is advancing rapidly and highlights progress and challenges is image captioning (also related to question-answering systems on images). Given an image, the goal is to provide a brief and "relevant" description. In contrast to categorization tasks, it is more challenging to quantitatively evaluate the results. Furthermore, these tasks may confound vision and language, as articulated at the beginning of this chapter. However, captioning algorithms provide a good summary to close this chapter while highlighting the exciting challenges ahead of us in the field.

An example of the state-of-the-art in image captioning is shown in Figure 9.13, which is based on results obtained using a caption bot (www.captionbot.ai, circa November 2018). It is important to emphasize the date because I suspect that we will see a major improvement in the years to come. The captions provided by this algorithm are quite

Figure 9.13 Successes and challenges in image captioning. Four example results from the www .captionbot.ai image captioning system

impressive. The system is good at detecting people, even quantifying whether the image contains one person (Figure 9.13A) or multiple people (Figure 9.13D). The system can also detect the gender in Figure 9.13A, and it makes a reasonable guess about whether people are happy in Figure 9.13D (I am in that picture, and I can attest that I was very happy; I suspect that most people visiting the Tower of Pisa are). The system also correctly infers that the person is sitting in Figure 9.13A and standing in Figure 9.13D. Furthermore, the system also detects other aspects of the scene, including the presence of a table in Figure 9.13A, water in Figure 9.13B, and a building in Figure 9.13D. Many other objects are not described, which is perhaps reasonable, given that the goal is to caption and not to mention every single object. Another caveat of using image captioning as a test-bed for vision is that we do not know whether particular objects are not mentioned because they were not detected or because the algorithm deemed those objects not to be too relevant.

It is a bit surprising that the system does not describe the Tower of Pisa in Figure 9.13D, given that such monuments have an exorbitant amount of training data. Perhaps even more surprisingly, there is a rather salient spoon in Figure 9.13A that was not described. It also seems likely that many humans would describe the bride in Figure 9.13B. The system is not able to deal with line drawings (Figure 9.13C), but it is nice that the algorithm was able to realize its limitations and admit that it cannot describe line drawings. Differentiating line drawings from photographs is perhaps not too difficult, particularly if the image has a considerable number of white pixels, a few black pixels, and essentially no textures. It is relatively easy for humans to recognize that there are three people in the drawing in Figure 9.13C, though it is not clear exactly how this deduction happens. Current algorithms such as the image captioning one illustrated here probably have minimal, if any, training with drawings. In contrast, most humans have had exposure to the underlying symbolism behind line drawings.

One easy way to break these captioning systems is to scramble the image. For example, we can divide the image into four quadrants and rearrange the quadrants randomly. The image mostly loses its meaning, yet the caption remains largely unchanged. If we present the fundus photograph from Figure 9.7 (only the fundus photograph, without the rest of the figure), the system responds with "I can't really describe the picture but I do see light, sitting, lamp." It is commendable that the system realizes that it cannot quite describe the image – that the system realizes that the image is different from its training set. There is indeed a light in the image. The system probably saw many examples where the word "light" correlated with the word "lamp," throwing it into the description.

It is a bit harder to deduce where the word "sitting" comes from in this example. The challenge in explaining where the labels come from is a characteristic of deep neural networks that many people have criticized. Given the large number of parameters in the system, it is not always easy to put into words why the system produces a given output. Humans can come up with post hoc explanations, but it is not always easy to evaluate those explanations. Radiologists do not tend to explain much about how they make their diagnoses, and they certainly are not required to come up with an explanation at the level of what neurons in their brains do. Humans would struggle to provide a mechanistic explanation of why they think that they see a tree in Figure 8.1.

Of note, the same type of architectures used in image captioning can be trained to outperform doctors in interpreting the same fundus photographs. The same architectures can be trained to detect the Tower of Pisa. Each one of these questions requires separate training steps. In contrast, a doctor can evaluate fundus photographs *and* also understand what is happening in Figure 9.13, whereas many current deep convolutional networks are ultra-specialized for specific tasks, and it is not easy to train the neural networks to perform multiple tasks.

Passing the Turing test requires being able to answer *any* question about an image, not just being trained to answer a single type of question. It is clear that one can ask many questions about the images in Figure 9.13. As impressive as those captions are, they do not come even close to solving the Turing test for vision. The captions completely fail to grasp fundamental aspects of the scene, what is happening, and who is doing what to whom and why. Humans can look at these images and understand the relationships between the different objects, their relative positions, and why they are where they are and even make inferences about what happened before or what may happen next.

Even more intriguingly, all these images are meant to be somewhat curious or funny. To end on a light note, I would like to highlight an example problem that I consider to be extremely challenging: understanding the human sense of humor based on images. Of course, even though the concept of funny is subjective and depends on age, gender, and cultural background, there are still strong correlations between different humans in what is funny or not.

Let us consider Figure 9.13C as an example. What is funny about this image? To grasp what is happening in the image, we need to incorporate not merely pixel-level information, not just labels of specific objects, but also their symbolism and relative interactions. The scale, together with the few traces that represent the attire of the person in the center, plus his relative position with respect to the other people, leads us to think that he is a judge. Note that it is the combination of many of these labels and their interactions that lead us to this understanding. Each one piece of information on its own would not necessarily be sufficient. The person sitting below the judge is probably the accused (or, less likely, a witness). This inference is partly based on the person's shirt with horizontal stripes but mostly based on his relative position and an understanding of the arrangement of the judge and the accused in a court of law. We can infer that the third person is a policeman, which is consistent with his outfit but also with the fact that he is standing and that he is behind the accused.

After deciphering that the person in the center is a judge, we realize that he is holding a gavel, he is shouting, and he is hitting the table with his gavel. The accused is also angry, making eye contact with the judge. Curiously, the accused also seems to be holding a gavel. This observation strikes us as unusual: the accused is not supposed to hold a gavel, let alone use it. The deviation from the norm is the essence of why the image is funny: it portrays an unexpected scenario. If we take out the few pixels that represent the accused's gavel, the image immediately becomes less appealing. Of course, humor is subjective and may vary from human to human.

Even if people do not find Figure 9.13C to be funny, they may still understand all the symbolism, the actions, who the people are, and how they relate to each other. Regardless of whether a particular image is funny or not, humans can interpret what is happening in Figure 9.13C the first time they see this image. Humans do not need extensive training with black-and-white drawings of people in a court of law to understand this image. There is a substantial amount of world knowledge that we need to have to be able to understand and interpret Figure 9.13C. Predicting whether an image is funny or not is further complicated by the fact that, even if we trained an algorithm to understand all the symbolism in Figure 9.13C, that would be of no help whatsoever to understand why Figure 9.13A is intriguing, nor to deduce what probably happened in Figure 9.13B.

There are trivial, brute-force, and ultimately uninteresting solutions that could yield above-chance performance in a funny versus not-funny discrimination task. Throwing lots of images like the ones in Figure 9.13 into a deep convolutional network trained via supervised learning could lead to some ability to decipher funny or not more than 50 percent of the time. For example, a lot of funny images are cartoons or drawings. A system could quickly learn to differentiate drawings from real photographs. If drawings are correlated with more "funny" labels, then the system might appear to perform quite well. However, in reality, the model would know absolutely nothing about humor. Removing the gavel from the accused in Figure 9.13C would not change the label for this type of model, even though this simple manipulation radically changes how funny the image is. This image manipulation is but another example of the problems with overfitting and biases elaborated upon in Section 9.11. A well-controlled visual task should ensure that the labels are not correlated with any other properties beyond the ones under study.

Determining whether an image is funny or not illustrates current challenges to incorporate additional knowledge into visual processing. However, it is worth pointing out that there is no physical limit to what computers can do. If we can do it, a computer can do it too. Significant progress has been made over the last decade in teaching computers to perform multiple tasks that were traditionally thought to be exclusively the domain of humans. Any desktop computer can play chess competitively, and the best computers can beat the world's chess champions. IBM's Watson has thrived in the trivia-like game of Jeopardy. Even more, while imperfect, Siri and related systems are making enormous strides in becoming the world's best assistants. In the domain of vision, computational algorithms are already able to perform certain tasks such as recognizing digits in a fully automatic fashion at the level of human performance, separating images from the web into 1,000 different categories, detecting faces to take pictures, recognizing faces to log in to a smartphone, or analyzing clinical images, galaxies, and much more. While humans still outperform the most sophisticated current algorithms in the majority of visual tasks, the gap between machines and human vision tasks is closing rapidly.

Significant progress has been made toward describing visual object recognition in a principled and theoretically sound fashion. However, the lacunas in our understanding of the functional and computational architecture of the ventral visual cortex are not small. The preliminary steps have distilled important principles of neocortical computation, including deep networks that can divide and conquer complex tasks and bottom-up circuits that perform rapid computations through gradual increases in selectivity and tolerance to object transformations. In stark contrast with the pathway from the retina to the primary visual cortex, we do not have a quantitative description of the feature preferences of neurons along the ventral visual pathway. Furthermore, several computational models do not make clear, concrete, and testable predictions toward systematically characterizing the ventral visual cortex at the physiological level. Computational models can perform several complex recognition tasks. However, for the vast majority of recognition tasks, machine vision still falls significantly below human performance. The next several years are likely to bring many new surprises in the field. We will be able to characterize the visual cortex circuitry at an unprecedented resolution at the experimental level, and we will be able to evaluate sophisticated and computationally intensive theories in realistic times. In the same way that the younger generations are not surprised by machines that can play chess competitively, the next generation may not be surprised by intelligent devices that can see the world as we do.

9.14 Summary

- A machine would pass the Turing test for vision if we cannot distinguish its answers from human answers in response to any arbitrary question about any image.
- Computer vision has shown remarkable success in a variety of tasks – including object classification, object detection, segmenting objects in an image, and action classification.
- Success in visual tasks has given rise to a plethora of real-world applications – including face recognition, visual interpretation of a scene for self-driving cars, analyses of clinical images, classification of galaxies from astronomy images, and many more.
- Inverting convolutional networks opened the doors to algorithms that generate synthetic images. One of the applications of image generators is to systematically study the tuning properties of neurons along ventral visual cortex.
- Despite rapid progress, computer vision applications remain fragile. Algorithms can be fooled relatively easily, and there are many tasks that are simple for humans yet very challenging for machines, such as determining whether a shape is inside or outside of another one.
- Due to the large number of parameters, it is often unclear how well current computer vision algorithms can extrapolate to novel scenarios as opposed to merely interpolating between training samples. Generalization is an essential requirement for future computational algorithms in vision.
- Many exciting challenges remain to teach computers to see and interpret the world the way humans do. As an example of a formidable challenge, training computer vision systems to determine whether an image is funny or not seems to be well beyond the capabilities of current systems.

Further Reading

See more references at http://bit.ly/2t53QRd

- Lotter, W.; Kreiman, G.; and Cox, D. (2020). A neural network trained for prediction mimics diverse features of biological neurons and perception. *Nature Machine Learning*. 2:210–219.
- Poplin, R.; Varadarajan, A.; Blumer, K.; et al. (2018). Prediction of cardiovascular risk factors from retinal fundus photographs via deep learning. *Nature Biomedical Engineering* 2:158–164.
- Russakovsky, O.; Deng, J.; Su, H., et al. (2014). ImageNet Large Scale Visual Recognition Challenge. In: CVPR: 1409.0575.
- Szegedy, C.; Zaremba, W.; Sutskever, I.; et al. (2014). Intriguing properties of neural networks. In: International Conference on Learning Representations.
- Turing, A. (1950). Computing machinery and intelligence. *Mind* LIX:433–460.

10 Visual Consciousness

Supplementary content at http://bit.ly/2FHXycS

As discussed in the last two chapters, there has been significant progress in computer vision. Machines are becoming quite proficient at a wide variety of visual tasks. Teenagers are not surprised by a phone that can recognize their faces. Self-driving cars are a matter of daily real-world discussions. Having cameras in the house that can detect a person's mood is probably not too far off. Now imagine a world where we have machines that can visually interpret the world the way we do. To be more precise, imagine a world where we have machines that can flexibly answer a seemingly infinite number of questions on a given image. Let us assume that we cannot distinguish the answers given by the machine from the answers that a human would give; that is, assume that machines can pass the Turing test for vision, as defined in Section 9.1. Would we claim that such a machine can *see*? Would such a machine have *visual consciousness*?

Most laypeople would still answer "no" to this question. They would argue that such a machine is nothing more, and nothing less, than a very sophisticated algorithm capable of extracting a relevant answer from a collection of pixels. They would claim that machines can beat the world champion in chess or Go, but they do not "understand" the game. They would point out that humans are different. Humans can *experience* the image, have *feelings* about the image, laugh at the image, or be scared by its contents; the image evokes sensations and specific quality. Humans have a sense of *qualia* about the image.

Qualia is an intriguing term introduced by philosophers; the dictionary defines qualia as "the internal and subjective component of sense perceptions, arising from stimulation of the senses by phenomena." This definition does not seem to be particularly helpful in discerning whether our extraordinary visual machine, which can pass the Turing test for vision, does or does not have consciousness. Nevertheless, this vague definition will have to suffice for now, until we have better ones that are directly based on a rigorous understanding of how qualia can be mapped to neuronal circuit function. The Turing test is defined strictly in terms of questions and answers – that is, in terms of behavior. Such observable behaviors do not necessarily reflect what humans or machines experience when exposed to a given image. It would be useful to have an operational definition, with a Turing test analogous to the one introduced in the previous chapter, for visual consciousness. Having such a Turing test may help us discern whether a machine can display consciousness or not, and can also help define which animal species are conscious.

To make progress toward a definition of consciousness and qualia, it is time to go back into the brain. We have accompanied and witnessed the adventures of information processing along the ventral visual stream, starting with photons impinging on the retina all the way to the remarkable responses of neurons in the inferior temporal cortex. Throughout this cascade of processes, we found neurons that respond when illumination changes in specific locations within the visual field; we marveled at neurons that are selectively activated by different types of shapes; we discussed how tolerant neurons are for changes in the stimulus properties; we were intrigued by neurons that can respond to imagined things that do not directly reflect what is in the outside world such as illusory contours; we discovered neurons that respond in the absence of a visual stimulus in a correlate of the mysterious process of visual imagery. Ascending through the visual hierarchy, there is an increasing degree of similarity between neuronal response properties and behavioral recognition capabilities. Along the way, we have perhaps forgotten about a profound aspect of our visual experience – namely, the subjective feeling of seeing and experiencing the visual world. How does neuronal activity give rise to those subjective feelings? What are the biological mechanisms responsible for qualia?

Coming up with concrete definitions in the arena of consciousness might be a bit premature. Several investigators have attempted to draw distinctions between consciousness, awareness, qualia, and subjective percepts. For example, the philosopher David Chalmers has proposed to reserve the term awareness to denote the reportable and accessible contents of consciousness while the other terms are linked to direct experience irrespective of reports. Here I will use all of these terms interchangeably. Likely, mixing these terms is not a wise idea, and future work will help us sharpen our understanding of the nuances of conscious perception. For the moment, rather than attempting a precise definition, we will examine concrete experiments that aim to elucidate the biological mechanisms that correlate with conscious perception. Within the context of those experiments, the questions are well defined by mapping percepts to behavioral reports. There are also "no-report" parallels of those experiments where we imagine that the percepts are identical except for the behavioral motor outputs.

The question of subjective awareness in the context of visual perception is part of the grander theme of consciousness. Visual consciousness is but one example of the type of sensations that our brain has to represent. Visual consciousness may be particularly dominant with respect to other sensations for primate species, but there are still other aspects of conscious experience that do not depend on vision. Other sensations include auditory consciousness, the feeling of pain, love, volition, and hunger. The age-old question of how a physical system can give rise to consciousness has been debated by philosophers, clinicians, and scientists for millennia. Over the last two decades, there has been increased interest in using modern neuroscience techniques to further our understanding of the circuits and mechanisms by which neurons represent and distinguish conscious content. Here we focus on those experiments and theories within the framework of visual processing.

10.1   A Non-exhaustive List of Possible Answers

A mechanistic explanation of visual consciousness should ultimately be expressed in terms of the fundamental physical structures that support qualia – that is, neurons and their interactions. However, it is perplexing to imagine how physical systems can have subjective awareness. It makes sense to assume that individual atoms do not possess or give rise to qualia. Connecting physical realism to the world of experience is perhaps one of the hardest questions of all time. There does not seem to be any chapter in our physics textbooks for anything closely resembling consciousness. Physics textbooks do not have a chapter about genetics either, but we can trace a path from atoms to molecules, to the rich chemistry of carbon molecules, to the structure of DNA, and onto genetics. We lack even a sketch of such a path in the case of consciousness.

Multiple answers have been proposed over the years in an attempt to explain how a physical system can give rise to consciousness. We will not be able to do justice or discuss all of those proposals in detail here. Instead, we coarsely classify those ideas and list some of the main answers that scholars have proposed through the ages.

1.   "Religious", "dualistic", and "nonphysical" answers. These are nonscientific explanations that often invoke the need for a soul, a homunculus, an engine, or some form of communication between physical systems and other nonphysical entities. Often, a distinction is made between the brain, a physical substrate, and the "mind," an ethereal concept that may or may not connect with the brain, depending on whom you ask. Several variants of these explanations abound, including passages in the Bible and the writings of Plato, Aristotle, Thomas Aquinas, Rene Descartes, Karl Popper, Sigmund Freud, and even top-notch neuroscientists such as John Eccles. For simplicity, I am taking the liberty of lumping every form of dualism into the same cluster, which I refer to as "religious"/"dualistic" answers. However, it should be noted that there are important differences among these different thinkers; certainly, not all of them embraced dualism because of religious reasons. To make matters more complicated, some religious people do *not* support dualism. I am merely pointing out that any explanation that is not based on physics – and, by extension, on brain science – necessitates some extra "magic juice." This magic juice has been called a soul, a mind, or a homunculus.

       The dualism between the brain and the "mind" pervades our vocabulary. We speak of "minding the gap," "keeping an open mind," or "changing your mind." Furthermore, even top-notch neuroscientists who do not necessarily embrace dualism still use strange dualistic descriptions, as in "the brain knows our decisions before we do" or "Our brain doesn't tell us everything it knows. And sometimes it goes further and actively misleads us." It is hard to eradicate the long and dark shadow of a Cartesian dichotomy between the mind and the brain.

2.   The "mysterian" answer. Proponents of this idea, including giants of the caliber of Thomas Nagel, Frank Jackson, and David Chalmers, argue that science simply cannot fully explain consciousness. There are several variations of this idea,

including statements such as "a system cannot understand itself," or "the answer is just too complex for our simple brains to grasp," or "science relies on objective measurements and consciousness requires a subjective aspect." This defeatist approach does not seem to be particularly useful. In the absence of any compelling proof that science cannot solve the problem, it seems better to try and fail rather than to not try at all. Even more problematic is the fact that this answer is not easily falsifiable without first solving the problem of consciousness, thereby making it a circular proposition.

3.   Consciousness as an illusion. Some philosophers like Daniel Dennett have argued that there is no such thing as consciousness. Therefore, there is nothing that warrants an explanation in terms of brain circuits. According to this view, consciousness is not a real phenomenon; the feeling of consciousness is just an illusion. But what an extraordinary illusion it is! We have made extraordinary progress in understanding the neural basis for multiple visual illusions. For example, when we perceive illusory contours, we know that there is no magic; there are actual neurons that respond vigorously to those contours and explicitly represent the lines that we see (Section 5.15). We even have computational models that suggest how the neuronal responses to illusory contours may come about through the integration via horizontal connections of signals from other neurons responding to real contours. It would be particularly exciting to be able to provide a similar mechanistic explanation for the neural basis of conscious sensations, regardless of whether these sensations are called illusions or not.

4.   Consciousness as an epiphenomenon. A related version of consciousness as an illusion is the notion that consciousness is an epiphenomenon. This proposal maintains that consciousness has no causal power – that is, that consciousness cannot cause any changes in the physical state of the system. As soon as multiple neurons and complex networks are connected, the feeling of consciousness arises. According to this viewpoint, this feeling does not serve any purpose. An analogy that is often used to illustrate this proposal is the following: a computer may heat up while it is doing its job, but this heat does not serve any purpose in and of itself; it is merely a side consequence of the machinery used to perform the actual computations. However, in this case, we also understand quite well where this heat comes from in terms of physical laws. It would be equally exciting to provide a mechanistic explanation for the neural basis of the "conscious heat," regardless of whether it serves a purpose or not.

5.   Consciousness and new laws of physics. Others, like the brilliant mathematician and physicist Roger Penrose, argue that we need new, as yet undiscovered laws of physics to explain consciousness. The argument is that current laws are insufficient in some way. This proposition may very well end up being true. However, at least historically, new laws have been discovered by trying to describe experimental results with existing laws and failing to do so. Even better is actually showing that existing laws lead to wrong predictions that are inconsistent with empirical findings. Stating a priori that new laws are necessary seems to skip an essential step in scientific inquiry. There are interesting philosophical and

practical questions about when enough evidence accumulates to suggest that the current paradigm is wrong. The field has been thinking about how to explain consciousness based on the activity of neural circuits for about two decades now; this does not seem to be enough time to declare that current laws of physics fail to explain the phenomenon. Penrose and others might be right, but we respectfully ask them to give us more time to try to solve the problem using nothing more and nothing less than the powerful artillery of current physics.

In stark contrast with the preceding approaches, several neuroscientists have become interested in the arguably more straightforward notion that consciousness arises from specific interactions within neuronal circuits that are defined by known neurobiological principles. Consciousness is a real observation intrinsic to an organism; like any other observation, consciousness deserves a mechanistic explanation. There is no need to invoke magic juice or to impose new laws of physics. Consciousness might well be considered to be an illusion in the sense that all of our percepts are constructs fabricated by the brain. Moreover, it seems premature to question whether consciousness has causal power or not, given that we are still taking the first preliminary steps toward defining consciousness in terms of brain science principles. According to this framework, we already have the key ingredients toward explaining consciousness. Which circuits, when, and how neuronal activity orchestrates consciousness remain to be determined through scientific investigation without invoking new laws or nonphysical engines. We assume that consciousness can and should be explained in neurobiological terms and that there is no limit to our capability of arriving at the answer. We still do not understand many aspects of brain function. In fact, I would argue that we still do not understand *most* aspects of brain function. If I had to guess and place the history of neuroscience in comparison with the history of research in physics, I would argue that neuroscience is still in a pre-Newtonian state. However, this delightful level of ignorance does not imply that we should give up and invoke the previously discussed explanations for all the observations related to brain function that we still cannot grasp.

The neuroscientific approach to studying consciousness involves several working assumptions:

1. We *are* conscious. Consciousness is not an epiphenomenon. There is a sensation produced by visual inputs, which is reliable, reproducible, and even mostly universal across humans. Therefore, consciousness deserves an explanation like any other empirical observation, like the tides, the position of the moon, the firing patterns of retinal ganglion cells, or the perception of illusory contours.

2. Other animals are also conscious. This assumption enables us to probe consciousness in non-human animals. It seems too early to draw the line and unequivocally dictate which animals do show consciousness and which ones do not. It seems prudent to assume that bacteria do not have any form of visual consciousness, even those that can capture light to perform photosynthesis. Beyond bacteria, it is hard to tell for other species. Plants can also capture light and perform photosynthesis, along with many other exciting processes; however, the working assumption of an explanation based on neural circuits would also rule them out of the

consciousness discussion. Once we understand the neuronal mechanisms that constitute consciousness, we might figure out that some species – say, the fruit fly, as an example – may show all the ingredients required for visual consciousness. Alternatively, we may come to understand that the fruit fly's visually triggered behaviors are purely automatic reflexes that involve no conscious sensation at all. Right now, it is too early to tell, and we should keep our brains open (not our minds open because that would be dualistic!), and we should be willing to be surprised by the scientific answers.

3.   We focus on visual consciousness in this chapter. There are several advantages to studying visual consciousness: we know more about the neuroanatomy and neurophysiology of the visual system than about other domains (Chapters 2, 5, and 6), we have image-computable models (Chapters 7–9), and we can rigorously control stimulus timing and content while measuring behavior (Chapter 3). Other investigators have begun studying consciousness in other domains outside of visual processing as well. We expect that we will be able to generalize what we learn from vision to other sensations (e.g., pain, smell, self-awareness). The study of visual computations in the brain has inspired progress in many other domains of neuroscience – including other sensory modalities, but also research on learning, memories, decision making, and other processes. Therefore, we hope that once we make progress toward elucidating the neuronal mechanisms that represent visual consciousness, the results might transfer to other aspects of consciousness as well.

The focus on visual consciousness leaves out many fascinating aspects of consciousness. Some of these topics include dreams, lucid dreaming, out-of-body experiences, hallucinations, meditation, sleepwalking, hypnosis, the notion of qualia, and feelings. We do not mean to imply these are uninteresting or irrelevant topics. Many courageous scientists are investigating some of these other aspects of consciousness as well.

4.   We need an explicit and mechanistic representation. Only a restricted set of brain parts will correlate with the contents of consciousness. It is not sufficient to state that consciousness is in the brain. We would like to have quantitative models of visual consciousness, similar in spirit and perhaps even similar in format and architecture to the types of models discussed in Chapters 7–9. We hope that these models will enable us to predict how conscious sensations impact neuronal activity and to read out conscious perception from neuronal activity.

10.2   The Search for the NCC: The Neuronal Correlates of Consciousness

The NCC (neuronal correlates of consciousness, Figure 10.1) is defined as a *minimal* set of neuronal events and mechanisms that are jointly *sufficient* for a *specific conscious percept*. The NCC is defined as a *minimal* set. A solution such as "the whole healthy human brain can experience consciousness" is not very informative. The neural mechanisms should be *sufficient*, not just necessary, to represent a conscious percept.

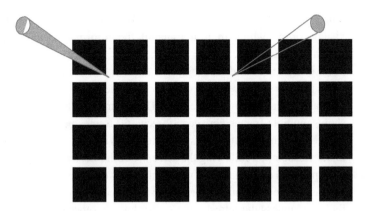

Figure 10.1 The neural correlates of consciousness (NCC). Any percept must be associated with a minimal and explicit representation. For example, if we were to record the activity of neurons that have a receptive field located at the intersections of the squares in this famous illusion, we would expect the NCC to be active if and only if the subject perceives a black spot at that intersection at any given time.

This clause leaves out so-called enabling factors, such as the heart or the cholinergic systems arising in the brainstem. We are seeking the correlates for the specific content of conscious percepts such as seeing a face, as opposed to generic aspects such as being conscious/unconscious.

It is quite clear that not all brain activity is directly linked to conscious perception at any given point in time. To clarify, this does not mean that those brain processes are not necessary or interesting. For example, significant resources and neurons are devoted to controlling breathing, posture, and walking. With some exceptions, most of the time, we are not aware of such processes.

A particularly striking documentation of sophisticated brain processing that does not reach awareness is given by a patient studied by Melvyn Goodale and David Milner, described in Section 4.6. This patient had severe damage along the ventral visual stream, while the dorsal stream was relatively unimpaired. The patient could not recognize shapes and had no awareness about shapes, but could still act on those shapes with relatively sophisticated precision. For example, the patient could not report the orientation of a slit but could place an envelope in the slit rather accurately. The search for the NCC concerns elucidating which neuronal processes correlate with conscious content and which ones do not.

10.3   The Representation of Conscious Content Must Be Explicit

Upon seeing an object, neurons in the retinae are activated. In fact, stimulating each of the retinae's photoreceptors in precisely the same pattern and magnitude evoked by a given object should elicit a percept of that object. Does this imply that the retinal photoreceptors constitute the desired NCC? Not quite. Those neurons in the retinae activate neurons in the LGN, which in turn activate neurons in the primary visual cortex, which in turn transmit the information to higher areas within the ventral visual cortex.

Several lines of evidence suggest that the activity in early visual areas from the retina to the primary visual cortex is unlikely to be the locus of the NCC. One striking example is what happens when we watch TV. The TV monitor has a certain refresh rate; that is, it shows multiple frames per second – say, 60 frames per second. Retinal ganglion cells and neurons in the primary visual cortex fire vigorously because of those rapid changes in the visual input, following the screen refresh rate, transiently increasing the firing rate in response to every flash of a new frame. However, our perception is virtually oblivious to this frame-by-frame information; we perceive continuous motion without any flickering unless the refresh rate is very low. In other words, there are RGC responses that do not reach conscious perception. Conversely, the contents of perception may include signals that are not directly reflected by RGCs. A striking example is the blind spot (Section 2.5). Covering one eye, there is a region of the visual field for which there are simply no photoreceptors in the eye. However, we do not see an empty or black scotoma in that region. Brains fill in the scene despite the absence of information coming from the retina in the blind spot. We are also rarely aware of blinks, even though the whole world becomes dark momentarily for the RGCs.

A critical aspect of the NCC is that the representation of visual information must be "explicit." If there are neurons representing information that we are not aware of at a given time, then those neurons cannot be part of the NCC at that moment in time. As noted earlier, some neurons control our breathing and how we walk, yet we are typically not aware of their activity. In the same fashion, our percepts do not directly correlate with neuronal activity in the retina.

What exactly is an *explicit representation,* and how would we ever know if we find one? After all, information from RGCs is obviously required for vision. What makes their representation implicit as opposed to explicit? One way to define an explicit representation is that it should be possible to decode the information via a one-layer neural network (Sections 6.7 and 7.7). In the simplest case, a perceptron should be able to decode the information: if we have a population of neurons with activities $x_1, x_2, \ldots, x_n$ then the perceptron classifier can be expressed as $g(w_1x_1 + w_2x_2 + \ldots + w_nx_n)$ where g is a nonlinear function like a threshold. An explicit representation may still depend on joint activity within a population of neurons, the emphasis being on whether it is readily decodable, as opposed to the type of implicit information as present in the retina.

If we see a chair, then that chair is represented by the activity of RGCs, but we cannot read out the presence or absence of a chair from the retina using a single-layer network. Analogously, a computer may hold a representation of the information for the chair in a digital photograph. However, as we have discussed in the previous chapters, decoding such information requires a cascade of multiple computations. Information about objects is not explicitly represented in the pixels of the digital photograph. Similarly, the retina does not hold an explicit representation of our percepts.

An explicit representation of the visual perception contents at any given time should not follow the refresh rate of the monitor, should be able to fill in the missing information in the blind spot, and should be subject to visual illusions in the same way that perception dictates. For example, consider the Kanizsa triangle (Section 3.1): the perception of an edge when there is none suggests that there should be neurons that represent that subjective edge. Neurons in the retina do not respond to such illusory contours, but neurons in cortical area V2 do (Section 5.15).

10.4   Experimental Approaches to Study Visual Consciousness

The Kanizsa triangle example and other visual illusions suggest a promising path to investigate the neuronal correlates of visual consciousness by determining which neuronal processes coincide with subjective perception. A particularly fruitful experimental approach has been to focus on situations where the same visual stimulus can lead to visual awareness only sometimes, but not always (Figure 10.2).

One example is to consider perception near discrimination thresholds. For example, a stimulus may be rendered hard to detect by decreasing its contrast. If the contrast is high enough, then subjects can detect the stimulus most of the time. If the contrast is too low, then subjects fail to detect the stimulus most of the time. There is an intermediate regime near threshold where subjects can sometimes see the stimulus, and other times they cannot, as assessed by behavioral measurements. The same physical stimulus sometimes leads to perception, but sometimes it does not. Let us assume that we can ensure that we are presenting the exact same stimulus, also that the eyes are fixating on the same location, and that there are no other changes. Under these conditions, it seems safe to assume that the neuronal responses in the retina would be similar in those trials when the stimulus is perceived and when it is not. However, something must change somewhere in the brain to lead subjects to report that they see the stimulus in some trials. We can investigate where, when, and how neuronal responses along the visual cortex correlate with the subjective percept.

A similar situation can be reached in backward-masking experiments where a stimulus is flashed for a brief amount of time, followed by a rapid noise mask (Figure 10.2D, Section 3.6). If the duration is too long, then subjects can easily see the stimulus. If the duration is too short, then subjects never see the stimulus. There is an intermediate regime, with durations on the order of 25 milliseconds, where subjects report seeing the stimuli only in some but not all trials.

Another example is the interpretation of images that are hard to recognize, like Mooney images. These images are black-and-white impoverished renderings that are difficult to interpret at first glance. A famous example is the Dalmatian dog illusion. A few more examples are shown in Figure 10.2B. Consider the example on the top left in Figure 10.2B. At first glance, the image appears to contain multiple arbitrarily shaped black spots randomly scattered throughout. Yet the image contains a rhino in a natural scene. If someone traces the rhino's contour, or upon observing the grayscale counterpart to this image (bottom left in Figure 10.2B), observers can readily recognize the rhino and also interpret the rest of the scene. The same image, and assuming the same fixation location, can lead to interpreting it as noise or a rhino. We conjecture

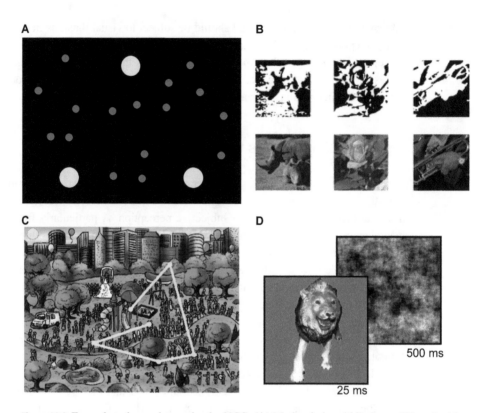

Figure 10.2 Example tasks used to probe the NCC. (**A**) Motion-induced blindness. When the blue dots move about, the yellow circles intermittently disappear from perception. (**B**) Mooney images. It is generally difficult to interpret the images in the top row. Exposure to the grayscale counterparts (bottom row) immediately renders the Mooney images interpretable. (**C**) During visual search, subjects will often fixate on the target object and continue searching without realizing it. (**D**) Backward masking can render a stimulus invisible.

that the neural representation of the image at the level of the retina would be indistinguishable between the noise and rhino interpretations. However, there must be a representation of the rhino, perhaps in the inferior temporal cortex neurons (Section 6.2), and this representation should be activated if and only if the observer can correctly interpret the image.

A daily example takes place during visual search. Imagine that we are looking for our car keys on top of a cluttered desk or looking for Waldo in Figure 10.2C. The eyes scan the desk for several seconds through multiple saccades. Sometimes we will directly fixate on the car keys, yet we will not be aware that our eyes landed on the keys, and we will continue searching. Eventually, our eyes fixate on the keys, *and* we become aware that we found them. Here is a case of two fixations, let us assume for the sake of simplicity in the same location, with the same visual stimulus, one with and one without awareness.

A similar situation arises during the phenomena of *inattentional blindness* and *change blindness*. During inattentional blindness, observers fail to notice a fully visible object, presumably because attention is engaged elsewhere. A notable demonstration of this phenomenon is the well-known video where there are two teams, a black and a white team, passing around two basketballs. Subjects are asked to count the number of passes between members of one team. Unbeknown to the subjects (and I apologize beforehand if I am spoiling the effect for the reader), a man disguised as a gorilla slowly walks through the middle of the scene. Remarkably, about half of the subjects utterly fail to notice the gorilla. Without a doubt, the information about the gorilla reaches the retinal ganglion cells, and probably also up to the primary visual cortex, maybe even higher areas within the visual cortex as well. However, many subjects are utterly oblivious to the presence of the gorilla. In the related case of change blindness, subjects fail to notice that something has been altered in a display. One instantiation involves flashing an image repeatedly with a brief blank interval in between. In alternate flashes, there is a substantial change in the image; for example, the color of the trousers of one person may change. Even though subjects can freely move their eyes to scrutinize the display, it is often quite tricky and frustrating to spot the change, which may require tens of seconds to detect.

A particular type of visual illusion that has been influential in the study of visual consciousness is bistable percepts. A famous example of a bistable percept is the Necker cube. The same visual input can be seen in two different configurations. In the case of the Necker cube, it is possible to voluntarily switch between the two possible interpretations of the same input.

Such volitional control is not possible in the case of a phenomenon known as *binocular rivalry* (Figure 10.3). Under normal circumstances, the information that the right and left eyes convey is highly correlated. What the right eye and left eye see is not identical: the small differences between the input from the right and left eye provide strong cues to obtain three-dimensional information. What would happen if we show two completely different stimuli to the right and left eyes? Under these conditions, observers perceive either one stimulus *or* the other one, alternating between the two in a seemingly random fashion, a rivalry between the inputs from the two eyes.

Extensive psychophysical investigations have provided a wealth of information about the conditions that lead to perceptual dominance of one or the other visual stimulus, what can or cannot be done with the information that is being suppressed, and the dynamics underlying perceptual alterations. What is particularly interesting about this phenomenon is that, to a reasonably good first approximation, the visual input is constant and yet subjective perception alternates between two possible interpretations of the visual world.

A simple demonstration of binocular rivalry can be elicited by rolling a piece of paper and looking through it with one eye. With both eyes open and holding the piece of paper with one hand, it is possible for one eye to be focusing on objects far away and for the other eye to focus on the hand in front of you. The percept mysteriously alternates between the hand, and those objects far away seen through an apparent hole in your hand.

The duration of dominance for each of the two stimuli follows a gamma distribution, and percepts shift involuntarily from one stimulus to the other, sometimes passing through a mixed percept known as piecemeal rivalry. It is as if the brain were wired

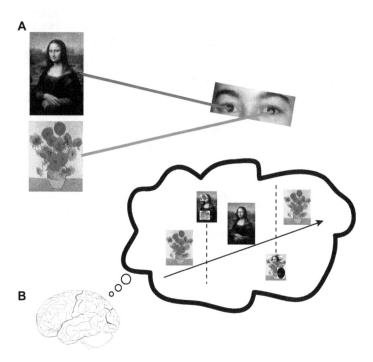

Figure 10.3 Binocular rivalry. (**A**) A stimulus (*Gioconda*) is shown to one eye, and a different stimulus (*Sunflowers*) is shown to the other eye. (**B**) Perception typically alternates between the two possible percepts, with transient periods of piecemeal rivalry where the two stimuli are merged.

to understand that there cannot be two different objects in the same location at the same time. Those two objects compete for perception; one of them wins momentarily, but the fierce competition continues, and eventually, the other object takes over. While the name and the presentation format would seem to suggest a competition between monocular channels, several pieces of evidence suggest that the competition also takes place at a higher level, between representations of the two objects: (i) it is possible to elicit *monocular* rivalry, a weaker phenomenon, where competition between two possible interpretations of the input takes place even though inputs are presented only to one eye via superposition; (ii) the stimuli can be arranged such that half of the object information is presented to one eye and half to the other eye; instead of experiencing alternations between the two half percepts, rivalry occurs between the two complete objects, which requires putting together information from the two eyes; (iii) astute experiments where the stimuli are rapidly shifted from one eye to the other further reveal that the competition can happen at the level of the object representations themselves rather than between the two eyes.

There exist several variations of binocular rivalry. *Flash suppression* refers to a situation where a stimulus – say, the *Gioconda* – is shown monocularly – say, to the right eye. Immediately following, the *Gioconda* stays on the right eye, but a new stimulus – say, *Sunflowers* – is flashed onto the other eye. Under these conditions, the new stimulus, *Sunflowers*, dominates perception, and the old stimulus, the *Gioconda*, is completely suppressed. If the two stimuli remain on the screen, one shown to each eye, eventually, binocular rivalry ensues, and perception begins to alternate between the two. An interesting variation is the phenomenon of *continuous flash suppression,* where the *Gioconda* stays on the right eye while a series of stimuli are continuously flashed to the left eye. Under these conditions, subjects perceive the continuous stream of flashed stimuli, and the *Gioconda* can remain perceptually invisible for several minutes.

As in the other examples, we expect that the activity of RGCs will be oblivious to the internal perceptual alternations in switching between one interpretation of the image and the other one during binocular rivalry. On the other hand, the NCC should directly correlate with perceptual changes.

10.5 Neurophysiological Correlates of Visual Consciousness during Binocular Rivalry

The phenomenon of binocular rivalry has been prominently studied at the neurophysiological level. Investigators search for the neuronal changes that correlate with the subjective transitions between the input to one or the other eye. An interesting property of binocular rivalry is that the phenomenon can be triggered using essentially any stimulus shape. Binocular rivalry can take place by presenting a horizontal grating to the right eye and a vertical grating to the left eye, or a picture of a face to the right eye and a picture of a grating to the left eye. Armed with the ability to interrogate neuronal responses along the ventral visual cortex (Chapters 5 and 6), we can ask whether neurons that are activated by those stimuli follow the subjective perceptual reports or not.

Nikos Logothetis and collaborators have studied this question extensively throughout the visual cortex. They employed a variety of astute strategies to train monkeys to report their percepts during the perceptual alternations. For example, periods of binocular presentation were randomly intermixed with periods of monocular presentation that can be used as controls to ensure that the monkey is reporting the percepts correctly.

The investigators recorded the activity of visually selective neurons that would respond more strongly to a given stimulus A compared to another stimulus B (similar to the examples shown in Section 6.2). Next, the investigators presented A to one eye and B to the other eye (Figure 10.4). For example, they recorded the activity of a neuron in the inferior temporal cortex that responded more strongly to a picture of an orangutan than to a picture of an abstract pattern during monocular presentation or during binocular presentation when the same stimulus was presented to both eyes. Remarkably, when the orangutan and abstract pattern were presented during a binocular rivalry experiment, the dynamic changes in the neuronal firing rate correlated strongly with the monkey's perceptual reports: if the monkey indicated perceiving the orangutan, the neuron would show a high firing rate, whereas whenever the monkey indicated perceiving the abstract pattern, the neuron would show a low firing rate. The changes in

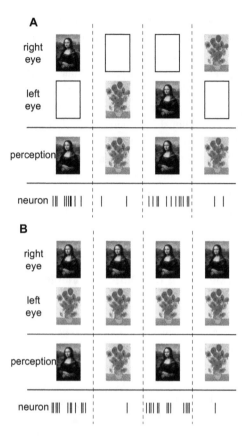

Figure 10.4 Schematic of a neuron that follows the percept during binocular rivalry. (**A**) During monocular presentation, the neuron shows a stronger response to the *Gioconda* than to the *Sunflowers*. (**B**) During binocular rivalry, the neuron shows a stronger response whenever the subject reports perceiving the *Gioconda*.

firing rate preceded the perceptual reports by a few hundred milliseconds, consistent with the idea that the neuronal responses reflect a perceptual change and that it takes time to elicit the required motor output to provide a perceptual report. The vast majority of neurons in the inferior temporal cortex showed this behavior whereby their activity correlated with the subjective perceptual reports.

The activity of neurons in the human medial temporal lobe also shows such correlations with perception. In all of these experiments both in monkeys and humans, neuronal responses may precede the behavioral report of perceptual transitions by a few hundred milliseconds. At least partly, this may indicate that we do not have very accurate ways of measuring the exact timing of the perceptual transition, and the behavioral reports may be delayed. Yet, intriguingly, human medial temporal lobe neurons may become activated well before perceptual transitions, even up to 1,000 milliseconds, and in frontal areas, some neurons were activated even earlier than that. It seems unlikely that such long delays could be ascribed purely to delayed behavioral reports. Therefore, these neurons could be involved in as yet poorly understood preconscious mechanisms that eventually culminate in perceptual transitions.

In contrast to the correlations observed for neurons in ITC and the medial temporal lobe, the activity of neurons in V1 typically did *not* follow the subjective report. Primary visual cortex neurons indicated the physical presence of their preferred stimuli, and in most cases, their activity was oblivious to the perceptual reports indicated by the monkey. Intermediate visual areas like V4 and area MT showed results that were in between those in V1 and those in the ITC. In other words, there is a progression in the proportion of neurons that correlate with the subjective report as we ascend through the visual hierarchy.

The exact proportion of neurons that correlate with perceptual transitions in a given area may depend on the experimental conditions. For example, an elegant study showed that in area MT, changing the stimulus and the context could lead to different neurons showing firing rate changes concomitant with changes in awareness. In other words, the NCC may not be static but rather may dynamically depend on the task and conditions.

One concern about these experiments is that we need to obtain a behavioral response from the subjects to figure out what the subjective percept is. Are the neuronal responses indicative of the conscious percepts, or do they reflect the decision and motor signals involved in reporting perception? Several experimental variations have been devised to address these concerns by capitalizing on ingenious ways of reading out what the percept is without a behavioral report. In these so-called no-report paradigms, either pupil size or other independent signatures of one or the other stimulus are used to deduce the perceptual transitions without an overt behavioral report. The results from the no-report paradigms appear to corroborate the results from the earlier studies, showing neuronal correlates of subjective percepts, particularly along the highest echelons of the visual cortex.

Another question that has been raised about the interpretation of studies that aim to track correlates of conscious perception is whether neuronal responses reflect changes in consciousness or changes in attention. Under most circumstances, attention and consciousness are strongly correlated, and we are conscious of whatever we are attending to. However, it is possible to design experiments where attention and consciousness are dissociated. These experiments show that subjects can consciously perceive an object or scene in the absence of top-down attentional mechanisms. Additionally, subjects can also pay attention to objects that are perceptually invisible.

10.6 Desiderata for the NCC

Experiments with bistable percepts like binocular rivalry have paved the road toward an initial understanding that changes in specific neuronal activity patterns correlate with transitions in subjective perception. At the same time, there are many other neurons in the brain that continue to fulfill their chores independently of the moment-to-moment contents of consciousness.

What would constitute evidence of finding the NCC? In parallel to the discussion of computational models in Chapters 7–9, we seek a quantitative description of subjective perception. In Chapter 8, we argued that a complete computational account of vision should be able to predict the neuronal responses to *any* arbitrary image (Section 8.14) and also predict the behavioral responses in *any* visual task in response to any image (Sections 8.12 and 13). Extending this definition to the domain of visual consciousness, four conditions should be met for a complete account of the NCC for vision:

1.   We should be able to quantitatively predict neuronal responses given a perceptual state. For example, during binocular rivalry, we should be able to predict neuronal activity for neurons in different brain areas, given the perceptual state of the subject.

2.   Conversely, we should be able to predict perceptual states from neuronal responses. By recording the activity of populations of neurons (the specific neuronal types, circuits, and areas for the NCC), we want to tell what the subject is consciously perceiving at any given time.

3.   We should be able to elicit a specific percept by activating the corresponding neuronal patterns (e.g., via electrical stimulation, Section 4.9). These neuronal patterns could be in one brain area or multiple brain areas. The resulting percept should be specific (e.g., a woman sitting in an outside park next to a tree), as opposed to merely eliciting phosphenes of light by activating clusters of neurons in the primary visual cortex at once. Furthermore, in a binocular rivalry experiment, stimulation of the NCC should be able to shift the perceptual state of the subject. This extended notion of the NCC postulates that activation of those specific neural circuits is directly and causally connected to the perceptual state. Therefore, even if the subject is asleep, activating the NCC should trigger a dream or a hallucination of that specific perceptual state.

4.   We should be able to inactivate or repress a perceptual state by modifying the neuronal activity patterns. In a binocular rivalry experiment, we could ensure that subjects do not perceive one of the stimuli by inactivating the corresponding NCC. Again, because the NCC is directly and causally responsible for perception, in principle, we could show a picture of a woman sitting in a park next to a tree, and the subject would not perceive any of that if the corresponding NCC is inactivated. This manipulation should be specific to the particular contents signaled by the NCC (e.g., closing the eyes to reduce activity in all neurons in the visual system would not constitute a test of this requirement).

Needless to say, we are still a long way from understanding the neuronal correlates of visual consciousness by meeting these four conditions. Nevertheless, these questions have become a major area of research, and we may be surprised to observe exciting progress in the field in the years to come.

10.7   Integrated Information Theory

The previous sections have focused on empirical measurements trying to elucidate which specific neuronal activity patterns correlate with subjective percepts or not. These empirical observations have given rise to accounts about the relative order in which different areas may be activated during conscious perception. The relative order of activation of different neural circuits during perceptual transitions is summarized in the idea of a global workspace that takes sensory information and spreads this information "globally," or at least to multiple other brain regions. Some investigators have proposed that the spreading to other brain regions ignites changes in subjective perception.

In parallel to the empirical observations about neural activity patterns that accompany visual consciousness, the last decade has seen the development of an elegant, ambitious, and controversial theoretical framework that deserves discussion: the integrated information theory (IIT) by Giulio Tononi. In an oversimplified form, the basic intuition behind IIT is that conscious experience represents information and that this representation is unique. This framework nicely starts with a set of five axioms (Figure 10.5) and quantitatively derives a definition of information and integration. These five axioms state that (i) consciousness exists as a unique internal experience (*intrinsic existence*), (ii) conscious experience is composed of multiple phenomenological elements (*composition*), (iii) consciousness is specific (*information*), (iv) conscious experience is unified and irreducible (*integration*), and (v) the content of consciousness is circumscribed in space and time (*exclusion*). The theory then derives postulates from these axioms to establish the necessary conditions for a system to show these aspects of experience.

According to IIT, a dynamical system of interconnected parts is characterized by a metric, denoted by Φ (phi), which has a non-zero, positive value when the system cannot be described by smaller, relatively independent, subsystems. The larger Φ, the more integrated information the system has. The theory postulates that conscious experience is proportional to Φ. The definition of Φ comprises two steps: (i) perform an imaginary partition of the system and compute ϕ, a measure of how much the two parts affect each other (i.e., how well we can predict the evolution of the system based on the conditional transition probabilities) and (ii) define Φ as the "cruelest" such partition that minimizes ϕ. Elegantly, the theory provides specific mathematical definitions to calculate these quantities, given the dynamic transitions in a system of interconnected parts like a neuronal circuit.

A major challenge in testing the IIT framework has been that, for real systems, these equations are prohibitively challenging to compute. For a given partition, the computational time grows exponentially with the size of the system. Max Tegmark and others recently developed an approximation to calculate Φ using graph theory, bringing the calculations to a polynomial dependency on the system size and making this algorithm readily applicable to the large scale of physiological recordings.

The theory is notably elegant, starting from axioms and proposing concrete quantitative definitions, which sets it apart from other discussions about consciousness, which are merely qualitative. At the same time, the theory makes many counterintuitive predictions. Any object – the cellular phone or even the chair we are sitting on – has a certain Φ value. One may expect that inanimate objects or bacteria should have $\Phi = 0$, but this is not what the theory states. Those objects may have low values of Φ, perhaps even negligibly small, but not zero. Intuitively, one would like any theory to indicate that a chair has no consciousness, not that it has a small amount of consciousness.

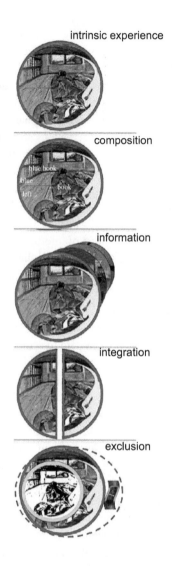

intrinsic experience

composition

information

integration

exclusion

Figure 10.5 Axioms of integrated information theory (IIT). IIT proposes **five fundamental** axioms about the nature of conscious experience: (1) intrinsic experience; (2) composition; (3) information; (4) integration; and (5) exclusion. Adapted from Tononi and Koch 2015

Perhaps this is more of a semantic concern that can be remedied by imposing a threshold on Φ.

Another bewildering aspect of IIT is that it is, in principle, possible to create relatively "simple" artificial systems with high Φ values (for the aficionados, an example is the so-called *Vandermonde* matrices). However, it seems counterintuitive that such artificial systems would show consciousness. Of course, the introspective observation that these predictions are counterintuitive does not make them wrong. There are plenty of examples in science where counterintuitive predictions have led the way to exciting new discoveries. Science should be guided by experimentally testable predictions and the empirical results, not by our taste or intuitions.

Ultimately, it will be interesting to test the integrated information theory empirically. Regardless of whether this theoretical framework is entirely right, whether it will require revisions and refinements like all other theories in science, or even if it is entirely wrong, it is the very first time that a quantitative theory has been proposed to account for one of the most elusive mysteries of human existence, consciousness.

10.8   Summary

- Consciousness has been discussed for millennia by thinkers from a wide variety of different fields, yet only recently has it become an important topic of investigation for rigorous neuroscience theorists and experimentalists.
- Experimental efforts have focused on searching for minimal and jointly sufficient neuronal correlates of consciousness, the NCC.
- Several experimental paradigms, where the input is constant yet perception changes over time, have been developed to study visual consciousness. These experiments include backward masking, attentional manipulations, visual search, and bistable percepts such as binocular rivalry.
- During binocular rivalry, neuronal responses in the highest parts of the visual cortex correlate with the dynamical changes in the contents of consciousness.
- A full description of the NCC would require a quantitative computational model that can predict neuronal responses given the perceptual state and that can also predict the perceptual state given the neuronal responses. Activating or suppressing the NCC should elicit or silence specific perceptual states.
- Integrated information theory (IIT) is the first quantitative theoretical framework that aims to explain how consciousness emerges from a dynamical system with interconnected parts.

Further Reading

See more references at http://bit.ly/2FHXycS
- Chalmers, D. (1996). *The conscious mind: in search of a fundamental theory*. New York: Oxford University Press.
- Crick, F. (1994). *The astonishing hypothesis*. New York: Simon & Schuster.
- Koch, C. (2005). *The quest for consciousness*, 1st ed. Los Angeles: Roberts & Company Publishers.
- Leopold, D. A., and Logothetis, N. K. (1999). Multistable phenomena: changing views in perception. *Trends in Cognitive Sciences* 3:254–264.
- Tononi, G. (2005). Consciousness, information integration, and the brain. *Prog Brain Res* 150:109–126.

Index

Printed in the USA
CPSIA information can be obtained
at www.ICGtesting.com
LVHW080738271023
762071LV00013B/469